ECONOMY

GASTRONOMY

ECONOMY GASTRONOMY

eat better and spend less

ALLEGRA McEVEDY
AND PAUL MERRETT

photography by georgia glynn smith

illustrations by airelle depreux

PENGUIN BOOKS

PENGUIN BOOKS

Published by the Penguin Group

Penguin Books Ltd, 80 Strand, London WC2R 0RL, England

Penguin Group (USA) Inc., 375 Hudson Street, New York,
New York 10014, USA

Penguin Group (Canada), 90 Eglinton Avenue East, Suite 700,
Toronto, Ontario, Canada M4P 2Y3 (a division of Pearson
Penguin Canada Inc.)

Penguin Ireland, 25 St Stephen's Green, Dublin 2, Ireland
(a division of Penguin Books Ltd)

Penguin Group (Australia), 250 Camberwell Road, Camberwell,
Victoria 3124, Australia (a division of Pearson Australia Group
Pty Ltd)

Penguin Books India Pvt Ltd, 11 Community Centre,
Panchsheel Park, New Delhi – 110 017, India

Penguin Group (NZ), 67 Apollo Drive, Rosedale, North Shore
0632, New Zealand (a division of Pearson New Zealand Ltd)

Penguin Books (South Africa) (Pty) Ltd, 24 Sturdee Avenue,
Rosebank, Johannesburg 2196, South Africa

Penguin Books Ltd, Registered Offices: 80 Strand, London
WC2R 0RL, England

www.penguin.com

First published by Michael Joseph 2009
Published in Penguin Books 2010
1

Copyright © Outline Productions Ltd 2009

By arrangement with the BBC.
The BBC logo is a registered trademark of the British
Broadcasting Corporation and used under licence.

BBC logo © BBC 1996

Text, recipes and preparation tips copyright
© Allegra McEvedy and Paul Merrett 2009

Photography copyright © Georgia Glynn Smith 2009

Illustrations copyright © Airelle Depreux 2009

The moral right of the author has been asserted

Set in Superclarendon, Clarendon, Cheltenham
and Akzidenz Grotesk

Printed and bound in China
Colour reproduction by Alta Image Ltd

A CIP catalogue record for this book is available from
the British Library

ISBN: 978–0–141–04550–4

CONTENTS

ECONOMY GASTRONOMY

IS ABOUT EATING BETTER AND SPENDING LESS. IT'S ABOUT CUTTING YOUR WEEKLY SHOPPING BILL WHILST MAKING THE MOST OF YOUR INGREDIENTS; IT'S ABOUT SHOWING YOU HOW TO COOK REALLY GOOD FOOD AND DISCOVERING THAT YOU'VE GOT SOME MONEY LEFT OVER AT THE END OF THE WEEK; IT HELPS YOU PLAN; AND IT PUTS EATING BACK AT THE HEART OF YOUR LIFE, WHERE IT SHOULD BE. WHAT MIGHT SURPRISE YOU IS THAT THE SECRET OF ECONOMY GASTRONOMY ISN'T CHEAPER INGREDIENTS, ECONOMY BRANDS OR BUY-ONE-GET-ONE-FREES. OUR MAGIC INGREDIENT IS JUST THAT – THE INGREDIENTS – INVESTING IN THE BEST YOU CAN AFFORD BUT MAKING THEM WORK THAT BIT HARDER FOR YOU. IN SHORT, IF YOU EMBRACE ECONOMY GASTRONOMY AS A WAY OF LIFE, YOU'LL NOT ONLY SAVE YOURSELF SOME PENNIES, BUT YOU AND YOUR FAMILY AND FRIENDS WILL FIND INSPIRATION IN THE KITCHEN, AND HOPEFULLY YOU'LL PICK UP SOME GOOD LIFE HABITS TOO.

For many of us our weekly schedule is not entirely predictable, however we can pretty much bank on being in some evenings, and wouldn't it be nice not to be scrabbling around on these occasions, but to know you have a yummy supper to look forward to? Yet most of us only think about what we want to eat five minutes beforehand. Which means nuking ready meals or ordering takeaways a bit more than is healthy. It shouldn't be like that. If you want to go on holiday, generally speaking you don't decide at the last minute or you'll end up paying through the nose for a flight. We understand this about travel arrangements but it doesn't seem to have filtered through to food. Yet thinking about what to cook and eat in a similar way – by putting some time and planning into it – dramatically cuts down on bills and waste, whilst giving your tastebuds something to get hold of.

These days there doesn't seem to be the same amount of respect for ingredients or production methods. Before factory farming, it was a big thing to buy a whole chicken and absolutely no part of it would have gone to waste. Mum or Granny would have made sure of that. Any food from any part of the world at any time, stacked up high in the supermarkets – is it any wonder we've started taking food in abundance for granted? Currently what we eat, our life force, seems to come fairly low down on the priority list. Awareness of food is increasing, but many meals being put on tables every day come from huge factories or greasy takeaways and are hardly what you can stand back and honestly call 'good food': that is to say they taste good and aren't bad for you.

This book takes us back to a time before convenience made us complacent and, let's face it, just a bit lazy. There are tips on how to plan your meals, how to shop, how to get two or three meals out of one 'bedrock recipe' and how best to use up leftovers. You'll also cut down on waste: we're all guilty of throwing far too much away, and remarkably we do it without thinking and without guilt. Economy Gastronomy makes you question the decisions we've been making that have come to be accepted as the norm: chucking something away unopened because it's out of date; watching food we've bought with our hard-earned cash shrivel and die, be it bread or grapes or, worst of all, food that had a life, such as chicken or fish. Surely that's just a bit wrong?

As a side effect of taking a bit more interest in your kitchen and your attitude to mealtimes, you'll also notice a decrease in packaging in your life, which has got to be a good sign that you're helping our planet. All of that whilst you're inadvertently saving for a holiday, or being able to pay off some bills or a loan; money you are literally throwing away at the moment.

To get the most out of this book, and to live the Economy Gastronomy life, you're going to need to find time to change your shopping and cooking habits. If you decide to do this for a week, yes, you'll be eating better and saving money, but if you continue for a year and start to plan properly whilst regaining a healthy respect for the world we live in, it's going to have a profound effect on your bank account. But in order to refocus so that food becomes more central to your life, you will probably need to invest in some equipment to help you along the way. If you're going to buy stuff when you see it cheap, to make a job lot of whatever you fancy, you won't be able to if you have only an ice compartment above your fridge. Also, investing time and money in building a larder of essential ingredients, splashing out on a really good chopping board or even putting a quality saucepan on your Christmas list might not seem the best way to start saving money, but anything you do to put the joy and fun back into making food at home will more than pay you back – in cash and in sheer pleasure.

Even if by some odd fluke none of these benefits appeal to you, don't forget the most real and the most basic upside of Economy Gastronomy: you'll be eating great, wholesome, home-made food.

To get the most out of our Economy Gastronomy system, there are some really simple steps that will make a huge difference:

- **Be aware of how much you spend on food each week. Keep an eye on your shopping bills.**
- **Plan your meals for the week ahead (p.16–18).**
- **Make a shopping list and stick to it – don't get tempted to add extra unnecessary things to your trolley (p.162).**

○ Invest in a good set of store cupboard ingredients (p.12).

○ Don't waste anything – always use bits of veggies before they go off, don't pass up an opportunity to use free stuff and don't be scared to use up things that don't look pristine (Something Out of Nothing, p.192).

However often you work late or socialize or eat out, you can pretty much commit to being at home a few nights a week so we've given over half the book to helping to sort this out for you. The Bedrock chapter is the largest part of the book as we felt it was important to show how easy it can be to cook a recipe, and then to take the leftovers in different directions, such as by freezing them or by using them up in cunning and interesting ways over the next few days. It is also the section of the book where it's definitely worth making slightly more of an effort to get hold of your main ingredient: you're going to be seeing it a few times in different guises so it's worth investing in the best quality you can afford. Bedrocks work on different levels – on one hand you've got dishes like a classic roast, and what you can do with the leftovers, and on the other there are ideas for taking a common ingredient such as mince or chickpeas and using it in three different ways, thus giving you a fine supper and also goodies for tomorrow or your freezer. It's a way of making your food work for you.

All the recipes in this book have been written so that they work for real people cooking now. They are designed to be accessible, with all ingredients easily obtained from the supermarket or your local butcher, greengrocer or deli. We chose recipes that are achievable with a minimum of ingredients, knowledge and skill, and we've also tried to be realistic, grouping the recipes into chapters that mean something to the way we lead our lives – such as Weekday Suppers, which have short prep times, or Something Out of Nothing, for when you get caught short (as we all inevitably do sometimes) and it's down to what's in the cupboard and the corner shop. There are also chapters with recipes with a bit more finesse to them for when you have friends over, and one that lifts the lid on British gastropub classics.

There are many reasons why you may feel like making a change: being bored of throwing your earnings in the bin; an awareness that you're eating too much processed food; a desire to save some money; knowing deep inside that having the Chinese on speed dial isn't great; perhaps you've started to think of cooking as a chore and you've fallen out of love with your kitchen; or maybe you just want to try something new. One or a few of these scenarios is true for most of us, and either life can go on as is, or you can let Economy Gastronomy take over for a while, and give you something to think about. Give it a go and you'll soon discover that, with this book as a guide, you really can have luxury food for less: a champagne lifestyle on a lemonade budget.

PS Each recipe title in the book is followed by an Ⓐ or a Ⓟ to show which of us wrote it.

A WORD ON KITCHEN EQUIPMENT

AS CHEFS, WE LOVE KITCHEN KIT! OFFER US A SATELLITE TELLY SUBSCRIPTION OR AN ICE-CREAM MACHINE AND IT'D BE THE LATTER EVERY TIME. HOWEVER, WE'RE AWARE THAT NOT EVERYONE HAS THE SAME AMOUNT OF KITCHEN GADGETS AND KNICK-KNACKS. THROUGHOUT THE FOLLOWING RECIPES, CERTAIN BITS OF EQUIPMENT KEEP CROPPING UP AND WE'VE TRIED TO OFFER ALTERNATIVES TO THOSE WHO MAY NOT OWN THE KIT REQUIRED.

OUR ADVICE IS TO BUILD UP A LIST OF EQUIPMENT THAT YOU FEEL WOULD BEST IMPROVE YOUR COOKERY AND THEN CUNNINGLY CIRCULATE THIS LIST AMONGST FAMILY AND FRIENDS JUST BEFORE YOUR BIRTHDAY AND CHRISTMAS!

Here are some basics that will make your time in the kitchen a whole lot easier:

- Three decent knives: one chef's knife (large-bladed); one serrated; one small veg knife
- Decent knife sharpener
- An effective peeler (speed peelers are the best)
- Wooden spoon, preferably with a family history
- Slotted spoon
- Ladle with integrity (i.e. not black plastic)
- Balloon whisk
- Pepper grinder that works
- Stick blender
- Set of digital scales – far more accurate than a dial
- Colander
- Nylon chopping board kept just for raw meat – small enough to go in a dishwasher if you have one
- Nylon chopping board kept just for raw fish (ditto)
- A couple of mixing bowls of different sizes – round, not the basin kind (stainless steel is good)
- One heavy-bottomed saucepan, about 20–25cm across, depending on the size of your family (the bigger ones tend to be two-handled, which is good)
- One frying pan, around the same size, also with a thick bottom (cast iron is ideal)
- A couple of other pans of varying sizes and lesser quality, for boiling and blanching, etc

- One large roasting tray, around 6cm deep and as big as can fit in your oven
- A casseroler – like a rock'n'roller, but slower. Essentially this is just an ovenproof dish (usually china) for lasagnes and all manner of bakes
- A baking tray that doesn't buckle in a hot oven
- A couple of serving dishes/bowls that make your food look lovely on the table

And for your Christmas list:

- A food processor is an asset
- A temperature probe – not a 'cheffy' indulgence: it's a really useful piece of equipment
- A Japanese mandolin, sometimes called a *Benriner*
- A really sharp fine grater
- A pestle and mortar
- A rolling pin is not essential (cling film and a bottle of wine will do) but does send out the right message to your pastry
- A proper pair of tongs is really helpful, as is a decent flipper (thin metal, not thick plastic)
- And you can't really do without some juju – it's important to have some things in your kitchen that, although not strictly 'kit', fill you with warmth when you glance at them and make your kitchen feel like the special place it is

BUILDING YOUR RESOURCES

I LOVE MY LARDER, EVEN THOUGH I DON'T ACTUALLY HAVE ONE. FEW PEOPLE I KNOW (EXCEPT COUNTRY-DWELLERS) HAVE SPACE FOR A DEFINED ROOM JUST OFF THE KITCHEN FOR THE PURPOSE OF CULINARY BACK-UP. BUT IT'S THE BEST WORD WE HAVE FOR THAT CRUCIAL STORE OF INGREDIENTS. (I'M NOT A FAN OF THE WORD 'PANTRY'– IT HAS US ALL IN CLOTH CAPS AND FRILLY APRONS, AND 'STORE CUPBOARD' IS SO DRY, REEKING OF RATIONING, WHICH IS EVERYTHING THAT MY METAPHORICAL LARDER ISN'T.)

It's not about the location, it's just a collection of choice ingredients, ready for when they're needed – keep them in boxes above the washing machine, for all I care. Carrying a certain amount of stock (most of which will take years, not days, to go out of date) is a commitment to both preparation and home cooking – the two best friends to those on a budget.

If you are poor in time, money or both, having good resources to draw upon can turn a simple sausage into a super supper faster than a pizza can arrive on your doorstep: cheaper, probably healthier, and, as long as you've got a basic understanding of flavours, tastier too. It works on all levels. For those who like to be organized with charts and tables (like Paul), it's just a form of preparation and shows a willingness to be ready for that situation we're all familiar with – caught short with no supper. Would you go to work without your phone? No! Would you stride off on a long country walk without wellies? No! So why be so unprepared for your own hunger?

My larder is a source of warmth, comfort and interest to me. It's like having a few meaningful cookery books sitting around – interesting things in your cupboard help to define the feel of a kitchen, as well as the attitude of the cook. But essentially what we are talking about here is a collection of ingredients I know are there to help me make a meal out of nothing: what I actually have is a lot of open shelving, with stickers written on in marker pen so that I know where everything is.

In terms of sections, there are two ways to mentally build your larder. The first is in terms of storage, because in truth any all-in-one effective larder system is not just stored at room temperature (or, as we're frequently told, preferably a cool, darkish kind of place) but expands to the fridge and the freezer, as well as the booze cupboard.

Then there is another way to look at the ingredients you choose to store. And if I have a squint around my kitchen it seems the categories can be roughly divided into Basics, Builders, Zingers and Finishers:

- **Basics:** At least two oils: one extra virgin; one plain-ish with a higher burning temperature, like sunflower; and probably a very light olive or peanut oil. You need a couple of contrasting vinegars as well – one for cooking, one for 'finishing' (which immediately and neatly demonstrates the overlap in sections and general multi-purposefulness of must-have ingredients). Salt and pepper go in there too. And onions and garlic. Eggs, too. Weirdly, frozen peas as well.

- **Builders are as they sound – good bulk:** Spuds, pasta, rice, tins of pulses. A frozen block of puff pastry. Couscous.

- **Zingers are the making of a dish:** Olives and capers. That cooking vinegar. A bit of ginger . . . Some chilli. Spices. Lime leaves in your freezer. Soy and fish sauce.

- **And Finishers take it to the bridge:** your good extra virgin, Parmesan, a squeeze of lemon (also available in Basics).

Whether you choose to look at it in a creative or functional way, having a larder is just good back-up; generally there to support today's fresh ingredients, and to turn to on days when those fresh ingredients aren't around.

Making a home for these kinds of bits and pieces provides an easy way for you to make the right choices: ready meals, eating out and takeaways all have their time and place, but so does home cooking. And having some helpful things around just makes that more likely to happen – as well as yielding a much better end result.

On the Shelves	Fridge	Freezer and Other
pasta	**some cheese**: Parmesan, goat's, Cheddar	**for the freezer**:
rice	**some dairy**: butter, Greek yoghurt and crème fraîche	**pastry**: filo and puff
pulses	**a bit of pig**: bacon, sausages, frankfurters, chorizo, ham	peas
couscous	mustards	broad beans
oils: olive and sesame	capers and olives	spinach
vinegars: light and dark	Thai curry paste	prawns
dried herbs: thyme, oregano, rosemary, bay	tahini	chicken stock (home-made)
spices		lime leaves
chilli: hot sauce, smoked paprika and sweet chilli sauce		berries
dried fruit: apricots, sultanas		
nuts: including almonds, pine nuts		**other**:
seeds: like sesame and pumpkin		eggs
honey		bread
soy sauce		**booze**: cooking wine, wine, brandy, port, sherry
coconut milk		
tinned anchovies		
tinned tomatoes		
basics for baking: flour, sugar, baking powder		

STORAGE

I SPEND MUCH OF MY PROFESSIONAL LIFE IN A 'WALK-IN' FRIDGE, ORGANIZING THE SHELVES IN A BID TO MINIMIZE ANY LOSS THROUGH WASTAGE AND OVER-ORDERING (NOW THERE'S GLAMOUR FOR YOU!). SO SURELY THERE MUST BE SOME STORAGE ADVICE I CAN GIVE THE DOMESTIC COOK.

I THINK THE EASIEST WAY TO DEAL WITH STORAGE IS TO IDENTIFY THE AREAS THAT NEED ATTENTION: THE LARDER (OR CUPBOARD, AS IT'S KNOWN IN MY HOUSE); THE FRIDGE; AND THE FREEZER.

THE FRIDGE

If left alone in someone's kitchen, I feel an almost irresistible urge to check out the fridge. As far as I know, Freud never produced any theories based on the state of a person's fridge, but frankly he should have. I am always amazed at the chaos of friends' fridges. Things left unwrapped, forgotten items in a state of decay and tins of things that have no place in a fridge at all!

Based on my perfectly organized fridge at work, I reckon my top hints and tips are as follows:

- **Keep a regular check on what's in your fridge and be prepared for an emergency 'use-up' meal if required.** It's particularly important that you know what's in the fridge prior to a shopping expedition so that you don't end up buying exactly what you already have (this is a personal note to my wife).

- **Always have a roll of cling film handy to wrap up leftovers.** Cheese prefers tin foil, by the way; and if using fresh herbs or lettuces, then wrapping them in a clean, damp cloth will prolong their quality.

- **Store new behind old.** By that I mean keeping the opened jar of mayo in front of the new one so that you use things in rotation.

- **Put a temperature gauge in your fridge.** Whilst not wishing to sound like an environmental health officer, I am certain many people never check the temperature in their fridge (we do this three times a day in the restaurant!). If your fridge is above the temperature recommended by the manufacturer, then your food will spoil very quickly. The same can also apply if it's too cold.

- **Don't put tins in the fridge.** If they're closed, they should be in the larder. Once opened, decant the contents into a jar or tub.

- **Read Meal Planning on p.16!** If you have a plan for the week's meals, then everything in the fridge should be saying 'use-me-very-soon', so nothing will ever be wasted.

THE FREEZER

Freezers are very useful in the 'bid to save a quid'. However, like our old friend the fridge they can become 'coldest-dustbin-in-the-house'. Having read this book, you will very soon be turning your back on all forms of ready meals or convenience food, although I could not honestly say that my freezer is free from such things. Right now, suspended in an icy state of preservation, is a box of fishfingers (from sustainable stock, the label assures me); two bags of frozen peas; and a family-sized chicken and mushroom pie, which was on special offer according to the sticker.

In amongst this selection of goodies are a number of freezer-bags, all with sticky labels giving the dates when I made up the contents:

- Chilli con carne x 4 portions
- Bolognese sauce x 4 portions
- Cauliflower soup x 6 portions
- Apple crumble fruit mix x 8 portions

This is what your freezer is really for. Make stuff, eat some, refrigerate some, freeze the rest.

Finally, a quick word on freezing vegetables: lots of vegetables don't like to be frozen. Defrosted lettuce, for example, would make an awful salad. On the other hand peas, beans of all types, sweetcorn and cauliflower all freeze perfectly, but it does require a little work. Cut the vegetables into small pieces and blanch them in boiling water for about 30 seconds, drain well and then spread them out on a tray and put them in the freezer. When fully frozen, bag them up, label the bag, and wedge them into the freezer between the frozen haddock portions and the empty ice-cube tray. This way, your vegetables will be individually frozen rather than in a big clump. Making cooking a lot easier.

THE LARDER

See p.12 where Allegra has written about this most useful food cupboard. I would simply suggest you locate your larder somewhere dry and not too close to a heat source such as the oven. I would also recommend occasional date-checking of all your dry goods. Use-by dates, though occasionally a little strict, are there for a reason. So every once in a while run a check on your stock of semolina, plain flour and pistachio nuts . . .

Paul

MEAL PLANNING
AND THE SHOPPING EXPEDITION

IF ECONOMY GASTRONOMY IS GOING TO WORK FOR YOU, THEN THIS IS A CRUCIAL CHAPTER. ALLEGRA AND I CAN BANG ON FOR HOURS ABOUT MAKING STOCK FROM A CHICKEN CARCASS, OR PICKING WILD BLACKBERRIES, BUT IF YOU ROUTINELY SPEND TOO MUCH ON THE WEEKLY BASICS, THE GAME'S UP!

Apparently, someone somewhere (with more time on their hands than me) has worked out that, on average, one in three bags of shopping ends up in the bin. That's an awful lot of waste, so whether your motivation is environmental or economic, read on.

I come from a long line of list-writers. This may not seem like the most staggering genetic trait to talk about, but in the circumstances it's proved rather useful. Ask me to name the five best cover versions ever recorded or Brentford's ten finest goals, and I will immediately grab the nearest scrap of paper and start scribbling.

Most people do a weekly shop, and most of them write a list before they go . . . so why all the wasted food? I reckon it's because people write down what they know they haven't got, rather than what they actually need. This is because very few people I know will sit down and plan seven days' worth of meals. Imagine if you knew precisely what you would eat over the next seven days and then you went off to a shop and bought precisely those things; then (very obviously) there would be no wasted food, and no wasted money. Well, stop imagining it and give it a go!

For a professional chef, the above idea is not really that startling. We make money by careful purchasing and good housekeeping (i.e. limited waste); and we know what we need to buy because each day we check every item that goes into a dish, ordering more if we need it and less if we don't.

Anyway, your new-found food purchasing philosophy starts here . . .

MEAL PLANNING

Identify the meal that you and your household would consider the main meal of the day. For most people who work, I expect this would be the evening meal.

Sit down with other members of the household and decide what your main meal will be each night for the next seven days. Bear in mind the aim is to save money, so if anyone requests fillet steak and foie gras, ban them from the meeting. I would suggest flicking through this book, where you will find a range of cheap options for every taste (well, obviously, I would suggest that . . .).

When choosing your main meals, spare a thought for little cost-saving tricks, for example one meal creating the leftovers for the next. By this I mean that a roast chicken on a Sunday can provide the meat for a simple, tasty yet cheap pasta dish on Monday – see our Bedrock section for a much more detailed approach.

Once your main meals are planned, decide on breakfast and lunch. Sandwiches made at home are always cheaper than those bought from a shop, and with a little invention they can taste pretty good too.

Throw in a couple of treats. You know that, come Wednesday, you will be desperate for a slice of cake or a biscuit. Don't buy these treats. Make them. Flour, eggs, sugar and butter are the basic ingredients required for a wide variety of biscuit and cake recipes, so get them in and then find time for a little home baking.

Once you've agreed on all the above points, it's time to get list writing. I do this by running through each meal and listing every ingredient and the amount required. OK, it's not a two-minute job, but it is going to save you a fortune!

When you have your complete list, walk over to the fridge, the freezer and the larder, and cross off everything that you already have.

You're now ready to shop!

SHOPPING

Where you choose to shop is up to you. As you'd expect, I suggest you scour farmers' markets, local butchers, fishmongers and delis. However, I am a realist and I understand that, to most, the supermarket is favourite when judged on convenience – so let's presume that's where you will shop.

I have a few hints and tips on how you should approach the weekly shop. Some of them might even save you money. (I shall deliver these tips in list form, as would any Merrett stretching back several generations . . .)

1. Try not to go when the shop is full of people with poor trolley-driving skills and badly written lists. They get in the way of your mission.

2. Bear in mind that early in the day the reject shelf is pretty empty, and you should always check the reject shelf. Tomorrow's use-by date can be today's dinner!

3. The supermarket manager has been trained at a secret location by the country's leading supermarket manager training team in the art of selling you something you don't want or need. He will have watched as hundreds of people have left his store with a 12kg sack of brown basmati rice free with every multipack of poppadoms. Fancy cakes, reduced family-size chocolate bars and 2 for 1 ready meals will all leap out and tempt you from your money-saving ways. Stick with it – you know what you need. Buy and leave.

4. Eat before you shop. A hungry shopper is not a thrifty shopper.

5. Buy stuff that's in season. The supermarket has done much to limit the impact of the seasons and they didn't do it to save you money. Raspberries in December will cost you a fortune, as will asparagus in September. Learn to live a little more seasonally.

With all this in mind, I would expect your grocery bills to tumble. The joy is that the wider your cooking repertoire becomes, the greater the choice of great-tasting cheap meals; which all means you have more money in your pocket and more space in your wheelie bin. Lecture over.

Oh, by the way, the five best cover versions ever are:

- *'I Fought The Law'* – The Clash
- *'Respect'* – Aretha Franklin
- *'Monkey Man'* – The Specials
- *'Raspberry Beret'* – The Hindu Love Gods
- *'One Love'* – Johnny Cash

A SAMPLE MEAL PLANNER

AS YOU MIGHT HAVE GATHERED BY NOW, THE KEY TO ECONOMY GASTRONOMY IS PLANNING, AND IN ORDER TO GET YOU STARTED ON YOUR NEW CULINARY JOURNEY WE'VE PUT TOGETHER A COUPLE OF WEEKLY MENUS FOR YOU.

WE DON'T REALLY EXPECT YOU TO BE ABLE TO COOK A LUNCH EVERY DAY AND BE AT HOME SEVEN NIGHTS A WEEK, SO USE THE PLANS AS A BASE; PICK AND CHOOSE WHAT WORKS FOR YOU. THE LUNCHES ARE PARTICULARLY UP FOR CHANGE, AS THE NATURE OF OUR LIVES ARE SUCH THAT MANY PEOPLE GO OUT TO WORK, BUT SOME ARE SUITABLE FOR A PACKED LUNCH THAT YOU MAY WANT TO KNOCK UP THE NIGHT BEFORE. OTHERS ARE JUST QUICK IDEAS FOR THOSE WHO ARE AT HOME WHEN THE MIDDAY HUNGER PANGS ROAR. THE SAME FOR PUDS AND TREATS – JUST BUILD THEM INTO YOUR WEEK AT A TIME THAT WORKS FOR YOU.

THIS IS NOT A MEAL PLANNER THAT YOU HAVE TO STICK TO RIGIDLY OR ELSE THE WHOLE SYSTEM FAILS, BUT USE IT AS A GUIDE – ESPECIALLY TO SEE HOW THE IDEA OF THE BEDROCK AND TUMBLEDOWN RECIPES CAN WORK THROUGH THE WEEK – AND THIS WAY YOU'LL NEVER BE CAUGHT SHORT. NO MORE REACHING INTO THE FREEZER FOR A READY MEAL OR PICKING UP THE PHONE FOR A TAKEAWAY.

WEEK ONE

SUNDAY
Lunch: Warm poached salmon and never-fail hollandaise (p.113)
Pudding: Treacle tart (p.297)
Dinner: Spicy black bean quesadilla (p.159)

MONDAY
Lunch: Salmon and corn chowder (p.119)
Dinner: Quick spiced chicken thighs with emergency biryani (p.187)

TUESDAY
Lunch: Chorizo frittata (p.169)
Dinner: Spaghetti bolognese (p.139)

WEDNESDAY
Lunch: A very simple pasta dish with home-made tomato sauce (p.87)
Dinner: Salmon and horseradish fishcakes with crème fraîche tartare (p.115)
Treat: Anytime cookies (fresh from the freezer) (p.307)

THURSDAY
Lunch: Home-made salmon gravadlax (p.111) and cream cheese sandwich
Dinner: Thai-spiced steamed mussels (p.241)
Pudding: Rhubarb and custard pots (p.303)

FRIDAY
Lunch: Brutus salad (p.153)
Dinner: Onion bhajis, tarka dhal and almond rice (p.197)

SATURDAY
Lunch: Freshly baked bread (and cheese) with flame-grilled tomato salsa (p.155 and p.171)
Dinner: Spicy chicken bhuna salad (p.269); Salmon en croûte (p.287)
Pudding: Lemon cream with a berry compote (p.309)

WEEK TWO

BEDROCKS

SHOULDER OF PORK

SLOW-COOKED SHOULDER OF PORK
WITH SAGE POLENTA AND RUNNERS

A SNEAKY PORK SARNIE

PORK, TALLEGIO AND BROCCOLI LASAGNE

GNOCCHI AL FORNO – THE ROMAN WAY

STICKY PORK RIBS
WITH FIRE AND VINEGAR

POACHED CHICKEN

CHICKEN PIE WITH SWEETCORN,
MUSHROOMS AND TARRAGON

CORONATION CHICKEN

HOT AND SOUR CHICKEN BROTH

LAMB MINCE

ITALIAN LAMB MEATLOAF

LI'L LAMB BURGERS

LAMB, APRICOT AND PINENUT
CABBAGE ROLLS

SMOKED HADDOCK

CREAMY SMOKED HADDOCK SOUP

SMOKED HADDOCK AND TOMATO TART

OMELETTE ARNOLD BENNETT

CHICKPEAS

OTHELLO'S CHICKPEA COMFORT PIE

ANYTIME SPICY CHICKPEA LOAF

RED PEPPER HUMMUS

BOILED HAM

BOILED HAM WITH SPINACH DUMPLINGS,
ROOT VEGETABLES AND A GRAIN
MUSTARD SAUCE

HONEY AND MAPLE GLAZED HAM
WITH CHEESY CHAMP

SPINACH, HAM AND RICOTTA GNOCCHI

BRAISED BEEF

DAUBE OF BEEF WITH GREENS AND
COLCANNON MASH

PAPPARDELLE WITH SLOW-COOKED
BEEF AND MUSHROOMS

BEEF PASTIES

BASIC TOMATO SAUCE

A VERY SIMPLE PASTA DISH
WITH HOME-MADE TOMATO SAUCE

FISH STEW WITH FENNEL, SAFFRON
AND TOMATO

ONE-POT TOMATO STEW WITH PORK
MEATBALLS, CHORIZO AND WHITE BEANS

LEG OF LAMB

ROASTED LAMB WITH CANNELLINI BEANS
AND INTERESTING TURNIPS

SLOW-COOKED MOROCCAN LAMB
WITH HERB COUSCOUS

BAKED POTATO WITH LAMB
AND LEBANESE BEANS

A WHOPPING GREAT PUMPKIN

PUMPKIN RISOTTO WITH ROASTED
WALNUTS, RED CHICORY AND GORGONZOLA

PUMPKIN CANNELLONI
WITH SAGE AND RICOTTA

SPICY PUMPKIN CHOWDER

SALMON

HOME-MADE SALMON GRAVADLAX

WARM POACHED SALMON AND NEVER-FAIL
HOLLANDAISE

SALMON AND HORSERADISH FISHCAKES
WITH CRÈME FRAÎCHE TARTARE

SALMON AND CORN CHOWDER

SHOULDER OF LAMB

SLOW-ROASTED SHOULDER OF LAMB
WITH A GRILLED VEGETABLE AND WHITE
BEAN SALAD AND SMOKY AUBERGINE

SHEPHERD'S PIE

LEFTOVER SHEPHERD'S PIE BAKED IN
A LOAF WITH PICKLED RED CABBAGE

ROAST CHICKEN

TWICE-STUFFED CHICKEN WITH CREAMED
CORN AND PARSLEY POTATOES

AN INCIDENTAL CHICKEN LIVER PÂTÉ

ARROZ CON POLLO (CHICKEN AND RICE)

BEEF MINCE

SPAGHETTI BOLOGNESE

COTTAGE PIE

CHILLI CON CARNE

THIS CHAPTER IS DESIGNED TO SAVE YOU MONEY AND TIME, MAKING YOUR CULINARY LIFE EASIER AND MORE REWARDING AS A RESULT. IT REVOLVES AROUND BUYING ONE KEY INGREDIENT, WHICH WE CALL A BEDROCK, AND THEN COOKING IT IN SUCH A WAY THAT WHAT'S LEFT OVER CAN EASILY BE TURNED INTO ANOTHER MEAL OR TWO. IT'S LIKE A CULINARY GAME OF EXTREME LEFTOVERS, WITH EACH SUB-RECIPE (THE TUMBLEDOWNS) BEING VARIED AND DIFFERENT ENOUGH FROM THE INITIAL BEDROCK THAT TASTEBUD BOREDOM IS NOT AN OPTION.

We chose fourteen bedrock ingredients, all of which are familiar and readily available from the supermarket, with the idea that there will be something included here that every family in Britain loves to eat. Paul and I encourage you to buy decent-quality bedrock ingredients as you're going to be seeing them in different forms at several meals so it's worth getting the best you can afford. This might not sound like a great way to start you on a road that promises to save you money, but we guarantee that this system works. Yes, you are going to be shelling out a bit at the beginning for a whole salmon, or a shoulder of lamb, but just look at the amount that you'll get out of them.

In essence, this chapter is all about doing a bit of pleasurable meal planning, which means you'll find yourself buying fewer ready meals and getting fewer takeaways. All of that, while eating better and healthier too. What's not to like? How can it be sensible to think about today and only deal with tomorrow when it comes – day after day after day? No day is an island, but a part of the week, and getting a couple of meals in the bag just makes sense. With some of the lead ingredients, it's not so much a succession as a group cooking session: a little bit of base work, split three ways into very different results, which still saves you time and money.

It's all about Change of State: after the initial cook is done, you will have at least two more dishes already in the pipeline. There's a world of difference between creating something new and fresh with leftovers and being presented with the drabness of yesterday's food. Don't feel you have to have that lasagne the day after the slow-cooked shoulder of pork, but take a short time to throw it together, within a day or two of cooking the pork, then chuck it in the freezer . . . I guarantee there's a place in your future where you will be so pleased you did it, and that is what this chapter, indeed half this book, is all about.

Your gran would never have only got one meal out of a chicken; with the amount of food we throw away, our nation has become a little spoiled, which in turn isn't doing the world we live in any favours. Re-introducing a touch of wartime/post-war thinking just might be the antidote to our recently rocked confidence in the world's never-ending supply of money and resources.

We all eat out, we all order in, we all cook sometimes (hopefully) and we all have nights where we can't be bothered. We all have a freezer. Balancing the times you cook and eat at home with a mixture of leftovers, a few fresh ingredients and some new choice items in a cupboard, is a system that truly delivers Economy Gastronomy.

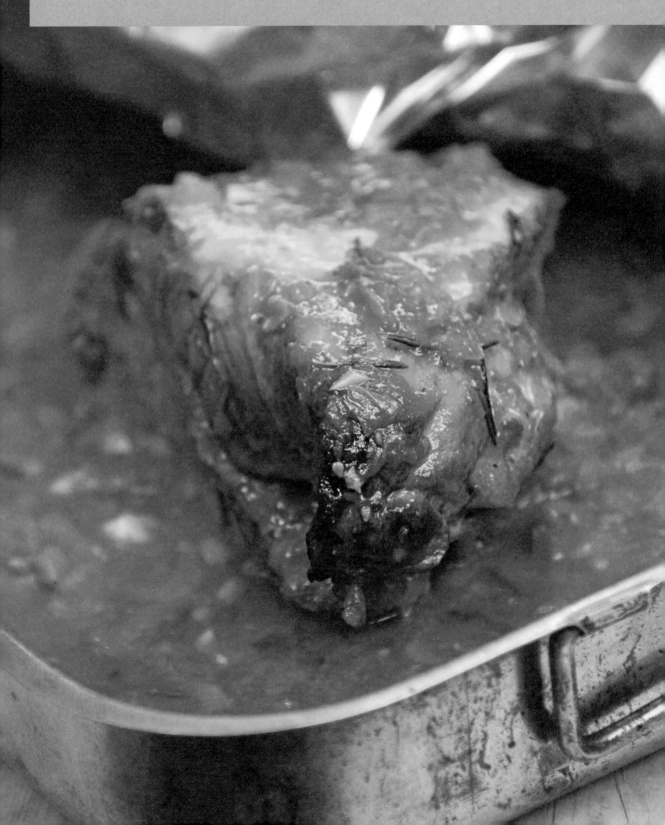

Pigs are my Number One animal, and this bedrock, plus its set of tumbledown recipes (that use the leftovers of your first recipe as the basis of the next ones) are among my favourites in this book. Minimum input from you, maximum from the pig, and you can feast on the results for days.

It's not just the pork itself, though, that leads you on to the next meal in this section – you'll also find uses for the herby tomato sauce that the meat is braised in, as well as the polenta. By thinking ahead in this way and either making a little extra of something, or keeping some to the side, you'll end up making glorious suppers galore for not much more time, money or effort.

(The ribs on p.35 will need to be finished off within a couple of days of cooking the pork shoulder – if you haven't snacked on them already . . .)

SHOULDER OF PORK
SLOW-COOKED SHOULDER OF PORK WITH SAGE POLENTA AND RUNNERS
A SNEAKY PORK SARNIE
PORK, TALLEGIO AND BROCCOLI LASAGNE
GNOCCHI AL FORNO – THE ROMAN WAY
STICKY PORK RIBS WITH FIRE AND VINEGAR

SLOW-COOKED SHOULDER OF PORK
WITH SAGE POLENTA AND RUNNERS

serves: 4   preparation time: 30 minutes   cooking time: 4½ hours

A shoulder of pork is a joint that sits between lean loin or leg and deliciously fatty belly in its structure. This means that although most commonly we Brits roast it, it actually really suits a long, gentle, slow cook, which is what we do here.

By and large, Britain has a polenta-shaped culinary blind spot. If you like creamy mashed potatoes, you'll like polenta, even more so if you enjoy a corn on the cob, as that is what polenta is: creamy corn, just made from ground instead of whole kernels.

I've used runners here, as they were in season at the time of writing, but any green veg with a bit of crunch will do.

800g pork ribs

2 onions, peeled and diced

4 branches of rosemary, stripped, stalks chucked away or kept for stock

1 teaspoon dried chilli flakes

½ teaspoon dried oregano

6 cloves of garlic, peeled and smashed with the flat of a knife

extra-virgin olive oil

salt and pepper

2.5kg pork shoulder, boned but not rolled, skin scored

5 x 400g tins of peeled plum tomatoes

5 bay leaves

60g butter

a small handful of sage leaves, chopped finely

1 litre milk

80g Parmesan, grated, plus any old pieces of rind

350g quick-cook polenta (not ready-made)

400g runner beans, cut into 3cm diamonds

Preheat the oven to 200°C/180°C fan/gas mark 6. In a deep roasting tray (mine measures 30cm x 40cm), put the pork ribs, the onion, rosemary, chilli flakes, oregano, garlic and 80ml extra-virgin olive oil and mix together. Season well with salt and pepper.

Make a hole in the middle for the pork shoulder. Nuzzle it in and rub a tablespoon of sea salt into the cuts in the skin. Once the oven is up to speed, pop the roasting tray in for half an hour.

Tip all the tomatoes into a bowl and break them up with your hands. Once the meat has been in the oven for an initial 30 minutes, add the tomatoes to the tray along with the bay leaves, giving everything a good and thorough mix and season, then stick it back in the oven for another 30 minutes.

Round about now the crackling should have crackled. If not, leave it in till it looks just about bloody perfect. Then take the tray out and turn the oven down to 160°C/140°C fan/gas mark 3, leaving the oven door open while you do the next step so it can cool down a bit.

Use a thin, sharp, long knife (and some patience) to gently ease off the whole crackling layer, and set it aside – it's ok to give in to those nibbling urges, as long as there's still some left for serving.

Spoon some tomato sauce over the naked, fatty pork top, and stir the sauce a bit. Cover with foil, and put the tray back in for an hour. Then lift the ribs out gently and put them aside for the sticky ribs recipe on p.34. Turn the shoulder over in the baking tray, shuffle the sauce again and baste the pork well with it and put back in the oven for a final hour.

When you take the shoulder out of the oven, take the foil off, flip the meat over so it's the right way up again, and baste it once more with the tomato sauce. Turn the oven off, but put the crackling back in to warm through on a tray.

While the meat is resting, put a large saucepan on a medium heat and melt the butter and a tablespoon of extra-virgin olive oil together. Fry the sage gently for a few minutes, before pouring in the milk and 500ml of water. Chuck in any bits of Parmesan rind you have too. (I like to keep the stubby bits of rind you're left with after grating a piece of Parmesan for recipes like this.)

Season well, and once everything has come up to a simmer, pour in the polenta like rain on the surface of the liquid, whisking all the time: from here it will take no more than 10 minutes to cook. Oil a baking tray lightly.

Put a second pan on with no more than 5cm of salted water for the runner beans. Cover with a lid, and once it's up to an energetic boil, drop the beans in for about 4 minutes, then drain.

Fish out the Parmesan rind now and bin it – its work is done. Finish the polenta by stirring through most of your grated Parmesan (save about a quarter to sprinkle over the dish at the end). Taste for seasoning; it will need quite a bit.

Spoon some polenta on to each warmed serving plate, then tip the rest on to the oiled tray, spreading it out with the back of a spoon to around an inch thick: once cooled, cover it with cling film and put in the fridge for when you come to make the gnocchi on p.32.

Using a good sharp knife, as this meat will now be very tender, cut four handsome slices off the pork, each around 1.5–2cm thick. Most pork shoulders have a fatter end and thinner end: start carving at the thinner end, so you'll be left with about a third of the shoulder to use as your gateway to the lasagne on p.30.

Save the rest of the tomato sauce for the lasagne as well as the gnocchi on p.32.

Arrange the soft pork and crunchy crackling on the plates, brought together by the primary colours of the tomato sauce and polenta, enhanced by some bright greenery from the runners.

A SNEAKY PORK SARNIE

Before launching yourself into the lasagne, don't miss the opportunity to cut off a couple of slices of pork for a sarnie.

Although you don't need a recipe from me for a cold pork sandwich, I've brought considerable joy to those I love with a combo of cooked, sliced beetroot, watercress and English mustard between a couple of slices of buttered white bloomer. Mayo is a personal matter.

PORK, TALLEGIO  AND BROCCOLI LASAGNE

serves: 6–8   preparation time: 10 minutes   cooking time: 55 minutes

This tumbledown recipe needs to be made within two to three days of cooking the shoulder, but once the lasagne is constructed, it can be frozen for whenever you need it.

It's rich, nap-inducing and feels just a little bit illegal, but my God, it's delicious in a roll-over-and-have-your-tummy-tickled kind of a way.

all the leftover pork from p.27 – you should have about 500g, give or take

½ the leftover tomato sauce from p.27 (about 300g)

50g butter

50g flour

500ml milk

1 teaspoon freshly grated nutmeg

salt and pepper

1 head of broccoli

12 sheets of dried lasagne

400g tallegio (a soft Italian cheese), sliced thinly

40g Parmesan, grated

Preheat the oven to 200°C/180°C fan/gas mark 6. Shred the pork with your hands into a mixing bowl, and stir through the tomato sauce.

Melt the butter in a large saucepan, then stir in the flour to make a roux. Cook this gently for a couple of minutes, before slowly adding a few tablespoons of milk. Beat fast with a wooden spoon to incorporate, then add more milk, change your tool to a whisk, and whisk away until the mixture is smooth. Keep adding milk in small amounts and whisking to make your white sauce – it should take about 10 minutes to add all the milk and bring it to a gentle simmer. Turn the heat off, and season with the nutmeg, salt, and plenty of pepper.

Chop 3–5cm off the bottom of the broccoli stalk, and trim any knobbly bits off too. Then make slices 1cm apart all the way up the trunk and through the florettes. Stack up the slices of trunk, and chop through them to make thick matchsticks. Cutting through the florettes is a slightly unruly process, but not one that needs to be done with great precision. Just ensure that you don't end up with any pieces bigger than you would want to put in your mouth. Wash the chopped broccoli well, then stir the pieces into the hot white sauce, which is now a béchamel.

Select your cooking dish: you'll need one about 30cm x 20cm, and about 6cm deep. Pour 100ml hot water into the bottom. Cover the base of your dish using four sheets of lasagne, preferably not overlapping too much – breaking them up and doing a bit of patchwork is fine.

Spread a third of the meat and tomato mixture over the pasta in the dish, then a third of the broccoli-béchamel, then a third of the tallegio. Cover with another layer of pasta and repeat the layers. Top with the final four sheets of pasta, putting the broccoli-béchamel on first then cover with the meaty tomato sauce and finish with the rest of the tallegio.

Use your fingers or the back of a spoon to push the sauce around – it's vitally important that none of the pasta, is left uncovered as it needs the wetness to cook. Sprinkle on the grated Parmesan, cover with foil and bake in the oven for 45 minutes on a tray to catch any drips, whipping off the foil after half an hour.

This lasagne is pretty rich, so serve it with a very simply dressed green salad.

GNOCCHI AL FORNO ⒶTHE ROMAN WAY

serves: 6   preparation time: 20 minutes   cooking time: 1 hour 20 minutes

It's completely up to you as to when you want to make this, but you should be aware that your leftover polenta won't look quite so alluring after sitting in the fridge for a couple of days. In the spirit of Working Smart not Hard (see p.190), and making the best use of your time, I'd be inclined to build it while the lasagne is cooking, then throw it in the freezer and eat it on a day when you'll be really pleased to see it.

The idea came, as its title suggests, from a dish I had in Rome where they often make gnocchi with polenta or semolina, as opposed to the more usual potato.

The al forno bit just means 'in the oven' (more appealing than 'baked') which, maybe wrongly, gives airs and graces to a dish that's not sophisticated at all, but just a very scrummy Italian family supper.

the other half of the leftover tomato sauce
from p.27 (300g)

250ml crème fraîche

2 tablespoons capers, rinsed and chopped

50g Parmesan, grated finely

a handful (about 25g) of basil leaves,
picked, washed and roughly chopped

all the leftover polenta (about 600g)

½ a butternut squash (around 500g),
peeled and sliced into very thin discs

300g frozen peas

Preheat the oven to 180°C/160°C fan/gas mark 4.

Mix the tomato sauce with the crème fraîche, capers, two thirds of the grated Parmesan (you'll need some to go on the top later) and the basil. Slice through the polenta about 4cm apart, then turn it through 45°, and make another series of cuts, also 4cm apart, so you have polenta diamond shapes. Choose your cooking dish: I opted for an oven-proof earthenware number but you can use what comes to hand. For this recipe it doesn't matter whether your dish is longer, flatter, smaller or higher.

Cover the bottom with a third of the butternut discs, then use about a third of the polenta to make the next layer. Pour over a third of the sauce and a third of the peas. Build three layers like this, and you're done: just scatter over the rest of the Parmesan, cover the dish loosely with foil, and bake in the oven for an hour. Take the foil off and turn up the heat to 200°C/180°C fan/gas mark 6 then put it back in the oven for 15 minutes. The dish should be nicely gratinated and bubbling gently when you serve it.

STICKY PORK RIBS [Ⓐ]
WITH FIRE AND VINEGAR

serves: 2–4 (as a snack)
preparation time: 5 minutes, plus standing time   cooking time: 15 minutes

If you followed this set of recipes from the beginning pretty much all of the work for these has already happened. All it takes now is a suitably vicious glaze, ignited in a ferociously hot oven to bring on the brimstone.*

However, if you've decided today is ribs day, and you've no time to braise them with the shoulder, you can also cook them from raw. Give them as long as you can in the marinade, then roast or barbecue for 20 minutes. Same flavours, just a bit more gnaw and chew, which in my book, is not such a bad thing.

*(*Though of course you can do it without the chilli sauce for happy kids.)*

6 tablespoons red wine vinegar
5 tablespoons runny honey
1½ tablespoons chilli sauce, more to taste if you like it hot
8–10 pork ribs

Preheat the oven to top whack – usually about 240°C/220°C fan/gas mark 9.

In a little pan, mix all the ingredients except the ribs, and simmer gently for around 10–15; minutes until it looks like a golden caramel. Take off the heat and allow to cool.

Put the ribs in a bowl and use your hands to coat them in the cooled sticky stuff. Let them soak it up for about 15–20 minutes, giving them the odd flip in the marinade during that time. For ease of washing up, I'd recommend you transfer them on to a rack over a foiled tray. Keep the marinade for basting while they cook.

Roast ferociously in the oven for 15 minutes, turning halfway through and taking the opportunity to give them a good baste. Eat as soon as they come out of the oven. A beer would be handy.

My dad is a thrifty chap who has dedicated much effort to avoid spending money unless absolutely necessary. As a child I can remember him delivering many stirring speeches on the outrageous cost of food which would often end with him stating that when he was young he only got to eat roast chicken at Christmas!

Indeed for many years a whole chicken was seen as being a bit of a luxury and, as such, every scrap of meat had to be consumed and enjoyed.

Nowadays, chicken is less a luxury and more a staple but that doesn't mean that we shouldn't still get as much from it as possible. The following meal plan takes one large chicken and delivers a whopping three meals . . . Read on, Dad!

If presented with a whole chicken, most of us would probably opt to roast it, and why not? It's a real treat. However, I think you can actually end up getting a bigger yield from boiling the bird and the flavour is every bit as good. The first step on the way is to get the bird cooked. Three delicious recipes then follow from this most basic method of cookery.

1 large chicken, 2kg, tied for roasting and giblets removed
1 carrot, unpeeled
1 leek
1 onion, unpeeled
4 cloves of garlic, unpeeled
1 sprig of thyme
10 white peppercorns (heck, use black ones if that's all you've got)

Place the chicken in a large pot. If your bird came from a reasonable butcher, you should have been given the giblets too. If so, bung them in the pot as well. Now throw in everything else mentioned and cover with cold water. Put the pot on the stove and bring to a simmer over a high heat. Then poach the chicken for an hour in the simmering stock.

The key here is to test the chicken by lifting it out of the pan and holding it up. If the juices running from the bird are clear, then it's cooked. If not, give it another 5 minutes and test again. But do be careful not to overcook the bird.

Once cooked, allow the chicken to cool in the stock, then remove it and store it in the fridge – it will keep here for a couple of days. At this point, strain the stock and discard the veg and bits. When cold, the stock can be stored in the fridge too. You should be left with around 3 litres which is the perfect amount for making both the pie and the broth on pp.38–43.

POACHED CHICKEN
CHICKEN PIE WITH SWEETCORN, MUSHROOMS AND TARRAGON
CORONATION CHICKEN
HOT AND SOUR CHICKEN BROTH

CHICKEN PIE WITH SWEETCORN, MUSHROOMS AND TARRAGON

serves: 4   preparation time: 10 minutes   cooking time: 1 hour 20 minutes (including cooling time)

Bloody hell, just writing the title makes me feel hungry! Nothing compares with home-made chicken pie. Forget all those glitzy ads trying to lure you into the supermarket to buy a pre-made pie. Honestly, it will never taste as good as this. I like a bit of sweetcorn in mine, and mushrooms and tarragon are perfect too. But please don't put them in simply on my say-so. If you prefer leeks, or bacon, or peas, just deviate from the recipe as necessary. You will need a 1 litre pie dish.

600g cooked chicken

1.5 litres chicken poaching stock (see p.37)

4 tablespoons flour and 4 tablespoons softened butter, mixed to a paste

150ml double cream

20 small button mushrooms

1 x 198g tin of sweetcorn, drained

300g pack of ready-made puff pastry

1 tablespoon coarsely chopped tarragon

1 egg, beaten

First, take your cold, boiled bird from the fridge and pick all the meat from the bones, discarding the skin. I would suggest removing the legs first and stripping them of meat, then doing the same with the wings and finally cutting the breasts away and dicing up the meat. Make sure that you strip the carcass so that no meat remains – it should look like a chicken that fell into a piranha-infested river a few minutes earlier! (Save this carcass for the Hot and Sour Chicken Broth stock on p.43.)

Mix all the white and brown meat together and then separate off 600g for the pie. Put the rest in the fridge, along with all the bones, for a later treat. Next boil the chicken stock and reduce it until about 600ml remain. Now whisk in half of the flour and butter paste gradually and reboil, whisking all the while to prevent lumps forming. Very quickly your stock should start to thicken into a glossy chicken sauce. You are looking for the consistency of, say, a creamy soup, so add a little more paste if needed. Once happy that you have a thickish sauce, pour in the cream – this will enrich everything. Now add the mushrooms and the sweetcorn, followed by the chicken. At this point the mixture should be an even balance of meat, vegetables and sauce. If yours is swimming in sauce, now would be the moment to drain a little off.

All that remains is to top it with puff pastry. However, if you do this while it's still hot, things will get messy, so pour the mixture into a pie dish and allow it to cool for 30 minutes. Meanwhile, roll out your puff pastry to cover a slightly bigger area than the top of the pie dish – it should be about 5mm thick. Now sprinkle tarragon over the top of the cooled chicken sauce and cover the top of the pie dish with pastry, having first brushed the lip of the pie dish with a little beaten egg. Trim the overhanging pastry all the way round and crimp or mark the edges with a fork.

Brush the top of the pastry with a little beaten egg too, then either refrigerate until needed or bake immediately in the oven at 180°C/160°C fan/gas mark 4. It will need about 35 minutes, by which time the puff pastry should be golden brown and totally irresistible. Serve with mash and green beans.

CORONATION CHICKEN ℗

serves: 6   preparation time: 15 minutes   cooking time: 20 minutes

If any reader has been to visit my mum on a hot summer's day, they will undoubtedly have been fed coronation chicken. It's one of her signature dishes! Apparently the dish was invented to mark the coronation of Queen Elizabeth II. My mum wasn't running the kitchens at Buckingham Palace that day, but frankly she could have been, because her version is fit for the Queen. Make this whenever you find a bit of lonely roasted or boiled leftover chicken in the fridge. Put it in sandwiches for work, serve it to friends as a dip with poppadoms or eat it as a light supper with naan bread. It's difficult to give accurate amounts without knowing how much leftover chicken you have, but the following recipe will make about enough curried mayonnaise for a whole chicken, so hopefully you can work it out from there. Any leftover curried mayonnaise will make a really funky boiled egg and mayonnaise sandwich, or try it dolloped on a baked potato.

1 tablespoon vegetable oil

1 onion, peeled and finely chopped

2 cloves of garlic, peeled and chopped

2 dessertspoons curry powder

1 teaspoon ground cumin

1 teaspoon ground coriander

1 teaspoon turmeric

250ml chicken stock

250ml coconut milk

400g mayonnaise
(home-made is definitely better, but I'm not looking!)

2 tablespoons chopped coriander

4 tablespoons desiccated coconut, toasted

cooked leftover chicken (roasted, boiled, baked)

Heat a saucepan and add a little vegetable oil. Fry the onion and garlic until golden brown, stirring frequently, then add the curry powder and spices. Just a quick word here: not all curry powder is the same, so if yours is particularly hot add a little less, or, of course, if you like things spicy then up the amount.

Once the curry powder and spices are mixed in, add the chicken stock and 200ml of the coconut milk. Boil until nearly dry. What you should have now is a pan of slightly wet curried chopped onions. Transfer to a bowl and allow to go completely cold. When cold, stir the onion mixture into the mayonnaise, then add the chopped coriander and the toasted desiccated coconut. If the curried mayo looks too thick, let it down with the remaining coconut milk.

Put your leftover cooked chicken in a bowl and spoon over enough curried mayonnaise to generously cover all the chicken. Any remaining curried mayo will keep well for several days in the fridge.

Knock up a salad of tomato, cucumber and red onion, heat up some naan bread and live like royalty!

HOT AND SOUR CHICKEN BROTH

serves: 4 as a starter, 2 as a main course
preparation time: 15 minutes   cooking time: 1¼ hours

This cleansing, healthy broth is a clever balance of hot, sweet and sour. It's staggeringly easy to make and never fails to impress the guests. In my old age I have softened my stance on the dear old stock-cube issue, but I do think that this broth has got to be made with genuine home-made chicken stock. What's more, if you have followed this recipe right from the top (i.e. the poached chicken bedrock on p.37), you now have a chicken carcass and bones in the fridge along with 1.5 litres of poaching stock – the very things you need to make this dish. However, when I simply have a chicken carcass left over from our Sunday roast, this is the perfect recipe with which to use it up, no further poaching stock required.

At first glance there may appear to be a lot of ingredients. Bear in mind, though, that lime leaves and lemon grass freeze perfectly, so they can always be on hand, while palm sugar, which you will find in your supermarket, should be one of your store-cupboard ingredients. The prawns are included because they make the whole thing that bit more glamorous, but they can be left out and this will still taste fabulous.

1 chicken carcass and bones
optional: 1.5 litres poaching stock (see p.37)
3 large red chillies
2.5cm piece of fresh ginger, peeled
6 lime leaves
2 sticks of lemon grass
50g palm sugar, grated
or about 2 teaspoons liquid palm sugar
8 raw tiger prawns, peeled
8 shiitake mushrooms, sliced
juice of 1 lime
2 tablespoons Thai fish sauce
a small bunch of coriander, leaves, stalks and all

First of all, if you have a chicken carcass or bones throw them into a pot and cover with the poaching stock for a really good strong broth. However, 1.5 litres of water poured over the chicken would work too. Simmer this for about an hour to extract as much flavour as possible. Strain and discard the bones, and pour the stock back into the pan.

Using a pestle and mortar, pound the chillies, ginger, lime leaves and lemon grass together. The idea is to break up and bruise the ingredients, not to turn them into a paste. If your mortar is a bit on the small side, you can grind each thing separately. Bring the broth back to a simmer and drop all of the bruised and broken bits in.

Next add the palm sugar. It either comes as a liquid or a solid. So whichever you have, spoon or grate it in accordingly. Simmer for 5–6 minutes and taste the broth at this stage. It should be hot because of the chillies and sweet because of the sugar, with the distinctive flavour of lime leaf, ginger and lemon grass coming through. Now throw in the prawns and mushrooms and continue to simmer for a couple of minutes.

Finish off by adding the lime juice and fish sauce, and tear in the coriander. Serve at once in bowls.

This triumvirate of 'three-ways-with-lamb-mince' is a slightly different approach to our Bedrock section. It's not a progression of dishes as seen before, just simply one cooking session which will reward you with multiple meals at the end of it. All you need to do is buy a job lot of mince (1.5kg), split it three ways, and do the base preparation for each recipe at the same time.

From there, you decide which you'd like to eat when. I'd recommend having two of the dishes the week in which you make them – they're different enough that you won't get minced out. Freeze the third, ready to be finished and cooked with a minimum of effort for a time when you're short of a meal.

LAMB MINCE
ITALIAN LAMB MEATLOAF
LI'L LAMB BURGERS
LAMB, APRICOT AND PINENUT CABBAGE ROLLS

ITALIAN LAMB MEATLOAF

serves: 4–6 (makes 8 hearty slices)   preparation time: 20 minutes   cooking time: 1 hour 10 minutes

Despite some dodgy seventies connotations, the facts of meatloaf are appealing to all: delicious, short prep time and good value. It straddles the seasons – in my mind slipping in easily with a hearty fireside winter scenario, or on a summer's picnic blanket.

4–6 slices (120g) of white bread, no crusts
5–7 tablespoons milk
1 aubergine
600g lamb mince
1 medium white onion, diced
1 teaspoon dried oregano
3 cloves of garlic, peeled and chopped
80g green olives, stoned and very roughly chopped
50g sundried tomatoes, chopped
1 handful of flat-leaf parsley (about 20g), roughly chopped
250g ricotta

Pre-heat the oven to 200°C/180°C fan/gas mark 6.

Soak the bread in the milk. Chop the top off the aubergine and cut the aubergine into slices about 1cm thick, then cut all of the slices into 1cm wide sticks. Keep the pieces with skin on them whole, and dice the rest.

In a large bowl, mix the mince, onion, oregano, garlic, olives, sundried tomatoes, parsley and diced aubergine. Add the soaked bread to the bowl only when it has absorbed all the milk. Think hard about the seasoning as you go – a generous amount of salt is the making of the dish. Once everything is well mixed, gently fold the ricotta through the mixture giving you big chunks of white going through it.

Use olive oil to lightly grease a loaf tin (mine measures about 12cm x 22cm x 6cm), and line the tin with the aubergine slices before packing the meatloaf mix into it. Give the tin a good couple of bangs on the work surface to make sure no bubbles of air are trapped. Cover the whole thing tightly with foil, put the tin on a baking tray to catch any spillages, and pop it in the oven for 35 minutes. Whip the foil off (keep it to one side) and let it roast for another 10 minutes topless.

When the loaf comes out of the oven, it's not a bad idea to press it a little by laying the foil back and then resting some weights on top for about 10 minutes. Do this in a tray as some juices will come out, making for a less nervy turn-out. Meatloaf should never be served very hot. You can enjoy this with anything from a simple salad to a pile of mash.

LI'L LAMB BURGERS [Ⓐ]

serves: 4 (makes 8 party-sized burgers, or 4 large ones)
preparation time: 15 minutes   cooking time: 12 minutes

Lamb burgers always feel much healthier and fresher than beefburgers to me – and in this instance I've made them party-sized (good for kids too) as there's something quite appealing about the snack size, rather then a massive quarter-pounder.

As a nod to the popularist, I've taken that essential burger ingredient, sesame seeds, off the buns and put them directly on to the meat. You can griddle these li'l burgers, grill them or whack 'em on the barbie.

650g lamb mince
1 teaspoon ground cumin
1 teaspoon dried mint
salt
6 tablespoons sesame seeds
4 pittas, halved
1 head of baby gem lettuce
2 vine-ripened tomatoes, sliced
8 slices of cucumber

for the yoghurt sauce
80g feta cheese, crumbled
8 tablespoons (150g) Greek yoghurt
1 handful (about 15g) of mint leaves, chopped
2 spring onions, trimmed and thinly sliced
black pepper

Make the burgers by mixing together the mince, cumin and dried mint with some salt. Divide the mix to form eight little burgers (each burger should weigh about 80g), each around 3cm tall. Tip the sesame seeds on to a small saucer.

Gently press the burgers into the sesame seeds until lightly coated all over (at this stage you can freeze them if you think you're going to be lambed-out this week).

Heat up your griddle pan, barbecue or grill (you can pan-fry them as well), but make sure that the temperature isn't at full pelt, or else the seeds will burn. Meanwhile, prepare the yoghurt sauce: mix the feta with the yoghurt, mint and spring onion. Season with pepper but no salt.

I like to cook my burgers for 6 minutes on each side (prepare yourself for a bit of an assault from the popping sesame seeds), allowing a few minutes' rest at the end. This will allow you time to give the halved pittas a quick warm through on the griddle or under the grill to make it easier to open them into pockets. Use a small, sharp knife to split one side of the bread open, then build them by stuffing with the lettuce, tomatoes and cucumber, adding the lamb burgers and dolloping over a spoonful of the special sauce. Secure with a cocktail stick.

LAMB, APRICOT AND PINENUT CABBAGE ROLLS

serves: 4 (makes 8 rolls)   preparation time: 25 minutes   cooking time: 1 hour

I don't think any single cook has influenced me more than the great Claudia Roden, and I've been making these rolls (or something a bit like them) from her seminal book *A Book of Middle Eastern Food* for years. Over in that part of the world, vegetable stuffing in various forms is a favourite pastime, and these rolls have all the joy of hidden goodies inside without any of the stress of trying to hollow out a courgette.

The recipe makes 8 rolls. I'd serve 2 for a starter, but ideally these would be eaten as part of a mezze, or, being a bit more European about it, as one of a few little sharing dishes.

90g long-grain rice
salt and pepper
1 large or 2 small heads of hispi sweetheart cabbage (the pointy cone-shaped one)
250g lamb mince
40g dried apricots, sliced
30g pinenuts, toasted
½ teaspoon ground cinnamon
8 cloves of garlic, peeled and smashed with the flat of a knife
½ x 400g tin of chopped tomatoes
1 tablespoon tomato purée
2 tablespoons extra-virgin olive oil
500ml chicken stock

Wash the rice well, and soak it in plenty of cold water for 20 minutes.

Put a heavy-bottomed saucepan filled with lightly salted water on the hob, and bring to a rolling boil. Pull off any gnarly outside leaves from the cabbage and set aside. Then choose eight handsome hero leaves – these need to be on the bigger side.

Wash all the leaves well – even the gnarly ones – and drop just the hero leaves into the boiling water for a couple of minutes to soften them up. Drain and refresh them under cold water to stop them from cooking further, but don't bother washing the pot. Use a small, sharp knife to cut out the base of the tough spines at the bottom of each leaf, and lay the leaves out on a board.

Make a mix of the mince, apricots, pinenuts, soaked and drained rice, cinnamon and some seasoning – it'll take quite a lot of mixing to incorporate all the rice. Share the mix between the leaves, making a sausage shape in the centre of each one and loosely wrapping the leaf around it, being careful to leave enough space for the rice to expand.

Line the bottom of the pot with the gnarly outside leaves. You need to have a couple of full layers, so use some central leaves if necessary too. Although the stuffed leaves are wrapped loosely, they do need to be packed quite tightly inside the saucepan. When they are neatly arranged in the pan, nestle the cloves of garlic in and around them.

Stir the tomatoes, purée, extra-virgin and some seasoning into the chicken stock and pour this on top – you want the stock mixture to just about cover the rolls, and the amount you need will vary on the size and shape of your pan, so use your judgement here. If there's not quite enough liquid to cover the rolls, top the pan up with a little hot water. If there's too much, don't use all the stock mixture.

Put a lid on, bring to a simmer then turn down to the lowest possible temperature, and allow to cook gently for an hour. Claudia says you should eat these rolls hot, but I think they're also excellent at room temperature or as a snack straight from the fridge.

Whilst many of us know that fresh fish greatly benefits our health many of us also fear that the fish we eat is endangered and should therefore be avoided. Keeping on top of all the information on fish sustainability can be quite a task and hardly something you have time to research before walking into the supermarket.

The answer is to find yourself a friendly fishmonger. By this I don't mean signing up to an online fishmongers' dating agency, I simply suggest you buy your fresh fish from a decent local fishmonger. He should be able to tell you what is fresh, what is in season and therefore good value and which fish is farmed or fished from sustainable stocks.

Now that thorny issue is out of the way you may need some inspiration – look no further! Smoking fish is something we do rather well in the UK. Whilst smoked salmon is probably seen as the premiere product I would suggest that smoked haddock is far cheaper and far more versatile.

The following three recipes are all very simple, light tasty meals. Your mission begins with a trip to the aforementioned fishmonger. Tell him you want to end up with 1kg flesh: he'll know what to give you. Ask him for natural-dyed smoked haddock. A lot of haddock these days is synthetically dyed on a mass-produced scale. Avoid this stuff at all costs. Also ask the fishmonger to skin the haddock for you and to let you have the skins. If he is a friendly chap and the queue behind you is not too long, you could ask him to remove all the pin bones that run down the centre of the fish as well. If, on the other hand, you catch him after he's lost five hundred quid on the 3.30 at Lingfield, you're just going to have to carry out this fiddly job yourself at home with a clean pair of pliers or tweezers.

So, hopefully you now have 1kg of boneless skinned smoked haddock, plus the skins (keep these for the Creamy Smoked Haddock Soup on p.55). Cut 600g from the thickest part of each fillet. This will leave you with about 400g of tail and trimmings, which should be cut into rough 2cm dice. Freeze this in two separate 200g batches for another day.

SMOKED HADDOCK
CREAMY SMOKED HADDOCK SOUP
SMOKED HADDOCK AND TOMATO TART
OMELETTE ARNOLD BENNETT

CREAMY SMOKED HADDOCK SOUP ⓟ

serves: 4   preparation time: 15 minutes   cooking time: 45 minutes

This is a meal by any definition. It's nutritionally complete and provides total satisfaction, be it for lunch or dinner. Don't be fooled by the word 'soup' in the title – this is no starter. The greens and potatoes are entirely a matter of choice and availability. I've gone for new potatoes and leeks, but your first stop should be the fridge to check what's in there.

600g raw smoked haddock, roughly chopped into 3cm dice, plus skins for stock
600ml double cream
600ml chicken stock (if you have none in the freezer, reach for a cube)
4 leeks, cut into discs about 1cm thick
16 baby new potatoes, boiled in their skins and cooled
1 generous handful (75g) of frozen peas
1 teaspoon English mustard
4 eggs

Firstly make a haddock stock. Place all the haddock skins into a pot and pour over 1.2 litres of water. Add to this a chicken stock cube. (I think the meaty chicken flavour actually works better here than fish but it's your call.) Allow the pot to boil for about 20 minutes, after which you can strain the liquid through a fine sieve and discard the cooked skin.

Put your smoked haddock stock (for that is what it now is) back on the stove and reduce it by about a quarter – this will leave you roughly 600ml of strongly flavoured stock. Pour in the cream and simmer again until it's reduced to a rich creamy haddock broth.

Drop your smoked haddock dice into the broth, along with the leeks, potatoes and peas and the English mustard. Stir everything around and simmer for about 6 minutes – which, cunningly, is the exact time it takes to soft-boil an egg.

Place the eggs in boiling water and set a timer for 6 minutes. Remove the eggs and peel while still hot. Cut each one in half (they should be soft in the centre). Top your haddock soup with the eggs, making sure you give a good portion of fish and vegetables to each person. Tear up some bread to serve with it – and enjoy.

SMOKED HADDOCK AND TOMATO TART ⓟ

serves: 4 as a lunch with salad
preparation time: 10 minutes   cooking time: 30 minutes

This is a great way of using up your leftover haddock. These tarts are simple to prepare but actually look as if you spent hours in the kitchen. This makes them ideal to serve to friends! The perfect foil for rich, creamy haddock are ripe juicy tomatoes. It's a very summery dish so don't go making it in November.

400g ready-made puff pastry, cut into 4 even blocks
300ml milk
200g smoked haddock, diced
(defrosted naturally over a couple of hours, if frozen)
8 really ripe juicy tomatoes
80g mature Cheddar, grated
4 tablespoons extra-virgin olive oil
1 tablespoon balsamic vinegar
1 tablespoon chives, finely chopped
100g watercress or rocket

Start with the pastry bases. Take a block of puff pastry and roll it out into a rough circle about 5mm thick. Put a 17cm bowl on top and cut around it to give you a raw puff-pastry disc. Fork holes right through the pastry all over. Repeat this with each block, then pop the lot in the fridge to rest for about 30 minutes.

Meanwhile, preheat the oven to 190°C/170°C fan/gas mark 5. Cover a large baking tray with a sheet of non-stick greaseproof paper, lay your discs of puff pastry on the paper and then cover them with another sheet of non-stick greaseproof paper. On top of this paper lay another baking tray and, if possible, pop a heavy ovenproof pot or dish on top to push down the top tray. This weight will guarantee that you end up with flat pastry discs (at work, we use a brick wrapped in tin foil).

I should mention that my oven at home is not big enough to cook 4 tarts at once, so I do them in a couple of hits, which really isn't that much of a hassle. Bake for 10–15 minutes (check halfway through), then carefully lift off the weight and the top tray. Peel back the paper and you should find golden-brown, crisp, round and flat puff pastry discs. They will keep happily in an airtight container for two or three days.

Next cook the haddock. Pour the milk into a small pan and throw in the fish. Bring to a simmer, then immediately remove from the heat and allow to cool. Remove the cooked haddock with a slotted spoon and discard the milk.

Cut your tomatoes into slices about 4mm thick and lay them all the way around the cooked puff pastry disc. Fill in any gaps in the middle too. Now dot the cooked haddock evenly over the top. Sprinkle with the grated Cheddar and bake at 190°C/170°C fan/gas mark 5 for 12 minutes, or until the cheese is well melted.

Make a simple dressing by mixing the olive oil, balsamic vinegar and chives. Serve the tarts with a few dressed salad leaves in the centre of each one.

OMELETTE ARNOLD BENNETT [Ⓟ]

serves: 2 generously   preparation time: 5 minutes   cooking time: 25 minutes

Arnold Bennett, the successful British novelist of the late nineteenth and early twentieth centuries, was a regular at the Savoy Hotel in London. Clearly a man of habit, he always ordered a smoked haddock omelette, and as a result the dish bears his name to this day. Personally, if I ever go to the Savoy I shall order something a little more technically challenging for the kitchen to prepare, because I know how cheap, quick and easy this omelette is to make. Stick with it and so will you.

300ml milk
200g smoked haddock, diced
(defrosted naturally over a couple of hours, if frozen)
20g flour and 20g soft butter mixed to a paste
1 tablespoon double cream, whipped
6 eggs, plus 1 yolk
a large knob of butter
50g mature Cheddar, grated

Your first job is to cook the haddock, so put the milk in a small pan and tip in the diced fish. Bring the pan to a simmer, then remove from the heat and allow to cool. Remove the fish with a slotted spoon and place to one side.

Return the milk to a simmer and then crumble in a little of the flour and butter paste (less than half to begin with). As the milk returns to a simmer once more, it should show signs of thickening. Add a little more paste if necessary – we are looking for a sauce the same consistency as, say, a thick creamy soup. Simmer for a few minutes to cook out the flour and thicken slightly more. When you are happy with the consistency, gently mix in the cooked haddock. Also gently fold in the whipped cream and the egg yolk, which are going to help give the finished omelette a golden-brown colour.

At this point, switch your grill on to its highest setting. Now you need to make the omelette, so break the 6 eggs and beat them with a fork. Heat a large non-stick pan (an ovenproof handle may prove useful here), add the knob of butter and, as it begins to foam, pour in the eggs. Stir the pan continuously until the eggs start to set on the bottom and sides – the centre should look thick and creamy. Pour your haddock mixture over the eggs, sprinkle with cheese and slide the pan under the hot grill until golden brown.

I would recommend you serve this with crusty bread and a salad, followed by a moment's reflection on how much it would have cost if you had ordered it at the Savoy!

CHICKPEAS Ⓐ

This bedrock is a little bit different, as instead of making one dish that then becomes two or three different ones, here you will find yourself making a simple base mix, which then goes in three very different directions. The main event is Othello's Chickpea Comfort Pie, but while that's cooking (half an hour or so) you'll have time to whizz up the Red Pepper Hummus and throw the Anytime Spicy Chickpea Loaf into the oven. You'll find that you'll motor through the hummus over the next couple of days, so just in case you're anxious about overdoing it on chickpeas this week, it might be an idea to throw the cooked and cooled loaf in the freezer. Pre-slice it for ease of frying, so it's there for a good munch later.

3 red peppers
3 tablespoons light olive oil
5 cloves of garlic, peeled and chopped
3 x 400g tins of chickpeas, drained
salt and pepper

Roast your peppers in whatever fashion you feel comfortable: a low open flame with frequent turning for 15–20 minutes; under the grill; or in a hot oven. It doesn't matter which way you achieve an evenly blackened skin, but when you're there, pop them in a bowl while they're still hot and cover tightly with cling film (the steam from the hot flesh will loosen the skins, making them easy to peel). Once the peppers are cool enough to handle, peel, de-seed and roughly chop them.

Heat the olive oil in a pan big enough to hold all the ingredients, and gently fry the garlic in it – you want to take it to a very light golden colour, not a toasty nut brown, as that would overpower the other flavours.

Stir in the peppers and chickpeas till well-coated, then let it all warm up a bit – this will only take a couple of minutes.

Tip it all into a food processor (or use a masher if you have strong wrists) and blitz on pulse until everything is incorporated, but in a slightly textured way – there should be no whole or even half chickpeas, but the odd discernible curve is no bad thing.

Give the mixture a generous season with salt and pepper, and take two-thirds out, splitting that into two separate bowls as you go. I'm encouraging you to leave the hummus-to-be in the food processor, as even though you're going to make the pie first, it really is only a three-minute job to finish this off, and if you put it in the fridge, it just may never happen.

CHICKPEAS
OTHELLO'S CHICKPEA COMFORT PIE
ANYTIME SPICY CHICKPEA LOAF
RED PEPPER HUMMUS

OTHELLO'S CHICKPEA COMFORT PIE

serves: 6 as a starter, 4 as a main dish   preparation time: 35 minutes   cooking time: 50 minutes

A filo pie is a thing of beauty that you don't see every day, which is a shame as it's the easiest kind of pie in the world to do: no need to make or roll pastry, and you can fill it with whatever you want. In this case, a combo of delicious Moorish flavours.

Othello, also known as the Moor of Venice, was a general in the Venetian army, and went off to fight the Turks in Cyprus. All of these places have contributed ingredients and a degree of inspiration for this pie, and, let's face it, finding out you've killed your beautiful and devoted wife because you've been stitched up by a supposed mate takes a fair bit of comforting.

This is one of those veggie dishes that goes down well with confirmed carnivores. You'll need an approximate 23cm tart ring with a loose, push-up base.

PS A roll of filo is a great thing to keep in the freezer. No need to defrost it, just pull it out and wrap it around anything, from stir-fried veg (for spring-rolls) or a spiced veggie mix (samosas) to make the kind of little parcels that everybody loves to eat. Either bake them in a hot oven (brush with butter or oil first) for about 25 minutes, or shallow fry them in about 3cm vegetable oil, turning after 4 minutes and taking out after 7-ish.

2 courgettes (around 450g)

sea salt and pepper

½ tablespoon coriander seeds

⅓ (approx. 300g) of the chickpea base mix (see p.61)

1 tablespoon fresh thyme, picked, washed and chopped

30g green or black olives, stoned weight, very roughly chopped

250g ricotta

zest of 1 lemon

100g butter, melted

around 6 sheets of filo pastry (45cm x 30cm)

Pre-heat the oven to 180°C/160°C fan/gas mark 4. Grate the courgettes coarsely, spread out on a tray or large plate, and sprinkle with around half a tablespoon of sea salt. Leave to stand for 10 minutes. In a dry pan toast the coriander seeds, shaking the pan until their scent starts to rise (about 2 minutes), then tip into the chickpea base and stir. Squeeze the water out of the courgettes over the sink, then put them in a bowl with the thyme and olives.

Split the ricotta between the bowl with the courgettes and the bowl with the chickpeas, and gently fold it into both of the mixes. Add plenty of pepper to the courgettes, along with the lemon zest.

Brush the bottom and sides of the tart ring with melted butter, and lay a sheet of filo so that half of it covers the base, the rest of the sheet draping outside it. Brush quickly with melted butter, and repeat with another three sheets of filo, rotating the tart ring through 120°, and arranging them so that half always covers the base of the ring, and half hangs outside.

Spread out the chickpea mix with the back of a spoon to form a layer at the base of the tart. Then use another three sheets of pastry as a divider between layers, arranging them in the same way as you did the sheets at the bottom of the tart, with their surplus draping over the edge and brushing each one with butter.

Cover the buttered filo with the courgette mix, then bring all the pastry sheets hanging over the lip of the tart ring up, over and around, gathering them together in a big froufrou in the middle. Brush and drizzle the top lightly and delicately with generous amounts of butter, then put on a tray and bake in the oven for 50 minutes, lifting it out of the tart ring for the last 10 minutes so that the sides turn golden-brown too.

Eat warm, to soothe the soul.

ANYTIME SPICY CHICKPEA LOAF

serves: 3–4 (makes 6 slices)   preparation time: 15 minutes   cooking time: 45 minutes

This cracking little chickpea loaf is incredibly versatile. I originally thought it was going to be the basis of a fun brunch dish (just add fried egg and a roast tomato), but when the slices came out of the frying pan, all golden and crisp, I realized that it would be a shame to limit it to one occasion. It was, quite simply, better than that.

It could be brunch, lunch or a starter, and would be yummy with anything from just a dollop of plain yoghurt and a few slices of cucumber to a full-on Greek salad. As part of a mezze or a picnic you can dress it down for family or up for guests.

Make this just once and I guarantee you'll be glad to have this recipe at your fingertips.

⅓ (approx. 300g) of the chickpea base mix (see p.61)
2 eggs, beaten
1 red chilli, finely diced, seeds left in or out
a big handful of fresh coriander (about 20g),
leaves and stalks, washed and chopped
½ teaspoon ground coriander
1 medium red onion, peeled and finely diced
salt and pepper

Preheat the oven to 160°C/140°C fan/gas mark 3. Mix everything together in a bowl, and season well. Grease a small loaf tin (10cm x 16cm x 7cm) and pour the mixture in. Bake for 35–45 minutes, turning halfway through. Check that the loaf is cooked by poking a skewer into it. The skewer should come out clean, and the top should be nicely golden.

Rest for 15 minutes, then cool before slicing into six.

Heat a healthy splash of oil in a thick-bottomed frying pan, lay as many slices as required (you may need to do this in two pans) in the hot oil and fry for just a couple of minutes on each side until golden. Serve with whatever accompaniment your taste buds and the time of day decree best.

RED PEPPER HUMMUS

makes: enough to fill 2 supermarket tubs   preparation time: 5 minutes

This costs around a quid, makes about 250g, tastes fresh and delicious and requires a full 3 minutes to make.

Or you can carry on buying it.

⅓ (approx 300g) of the chickpea base mix (see p.61)

1½ tablespoons tahini (sesame paste,
available in supermarkets and lasts for ever in the fridge)

½ teaspoon ground cumin (or more to taste)

juice of ½ a lemon (or more to taste)

salt, to taste

1–2 tablespoons extra-virgin olive oil

a pinch of cayenne or paprika

After making the chickpea base mix on p.61, carry on whizzing what's left in the food processor with the tahini, cumin and some lemon juice, adding around three tablespoons of water to help it motor round, until you've achieved a creamy consistency.

Season with salt and more lemon juice if necessary, and scoop into a pretty bowl with a healthy shot of extra-virgin olive oil and a pinch of cayenne or paprika on top.

The next day, your hummus may well have seized up a bit, but mixing in some warm water will restore the creaminess.

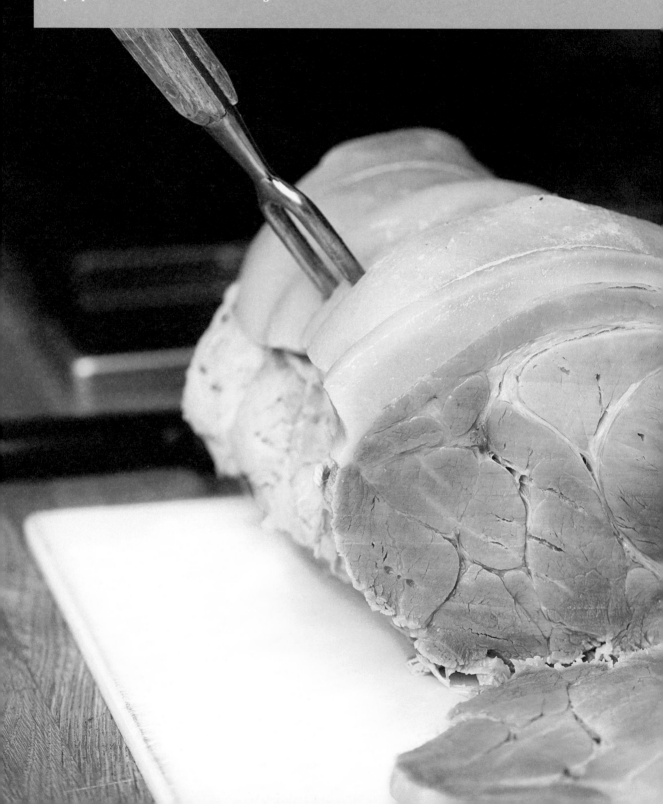

BOILED HAM [P]

preparation time: 5 minutes   cooking time: 1¾ hours

In ye olde days the definition of ham was meat from the leg of a pig which was then put through one of various types of curing processes, thus changing it from pork to ham. Nowadays ham can be taken from pretty much any part of the animal. You may think that as long as your ham started life attached to a pig you are OK, and to an extent this is true, but in generalizing the term 'ham' we have managed to lose touch with some of the traditional cuts of pork which were everyday affordable classics.

Boiled collar of ham is one such joint of meat which is far less common now than it was just after the war. In those days it would have been called boiled bacon rather than ham, because it actually comes from the shoulder of the animal. The trouble is that nowadays bacon means only one thing – grilled rashers, not a hunk of boiled meat – so the term has inevitably been dropped.

A boiled collar of ham is ideal for a meal plan because it really does provide lots of options and is very reasonably priced. What you pay for is a bone-free solid piece of meat with a covering of very tasty fat. If boiled meat is not your thing, then you could skip straight on to the honey-glazed ham recipe on p.73, but I would urge you to give the simple, traditional British boiled meat and dumplings on p.71 a go. The dumpling mix used is a very simple recipe to make – it has no suet in, so it doubles up really well as the gnocchi recipe on p.75. Whatever recipe you choose, it all starts with boiling the ham . . .

½ collar of ham, about 2.5kg (ask for it to be rolled and tied)
1 whole onion, peeled
2 whole carrots, peeled
1 whole leek
2 sticks of celery
cold chicken or ham stock – about 3–4 litres (using a stock cube is okay)
1.2 litres dry cider

When you get the collar of ham home, soak it in cold water for about two hours, changing the water a couple of times, to flush away any brine left over from the curing process. Take your largest pot and lower in the ham. Chuck in all the vegetables and cover with the cold stock and cider. Bring the pot to a boil, skim off any scum that comes to the surface and then reduce to a simmer for about 1½ hours, at which point it can be left to cool in the stock.

If you are not entirely sure that your ham is cooked after the 1½ hours, I would suggest you use a digital thermometer – a very cheap piece of kit. The ham should be 70°C in the centre. If it is, move straight to the recipe on p.70 but before slicing it, carefully cut off the skin leaving a layer of fat over the meat – leave this on as it has loads of flavour. And don't throw the glorious hammy stock away as this becomes the base of the sauce in the next recipe. However, you can discard the skin and the vegetables as they've now 'done their bit'.

BOILED HAM
BOILED HAM WITH SPINACH DUMPLINGS, ROOT VEGETABLES AND A GRAIN MUSTARD SAUCE
HONEY AND MAPLE GLAZED HAM WITH CHEESY CHAMP
SPINACH, HAM AND RICOTTA GNOCCHI

BOILED HAM ⓟ
WITH SPINACH DUMPLINGS, ROOT VEGETABLES AND A GRAIN MUSTARD SAUCE

serves: 4   preparation time: 10 minutes   cooking time: 35 minutes

Right, your ham's boiled and ready to go; either sat warm on the side or waiting in the fridge. Either way, it's ready to be used in this recipe, alongside some classic British dumplings and root veg. In the recipe I suggest making a little extra dumpling mix which can be rolled, cooked and frozen. They will go into the freezer as dumplings and emerge as bona fide Italian gnocchi, ready for the recipe on p.75. Cooking unites the world!

for the dumplings
550g fresh washed spinach
salt
250g ricotta cheese
1 egg yolk
2½ tablespoons grated Parmesan cheese
130g plain flour

600ml fresh ham stock
(from cooking the ham, see p.69)
2 carrots, peeled and cut into 2cm chunks
1 parsnip, peeled and cut into 2cm chunks
200g swede, peeled and cut into large chunks
4 generous slices of boiled ham from the cold boiled joint or cut straight after cooking (p.69)
150ml double cream
2 teaspoons grain mustard

To make the dumplings, blanch the spinach for 30 seconds in boiling salted water and then plunge it into iced water. This will both cook the spinach and guarantee a wonderful green colour. When cold, drain the spinach and squeeze out as much water as you can – a tea towel is useful for this. Now chop it as finely as you can and keep in the fridge until needed.

Put the ricotta in a bowl and mix in the egg yolk, followed by the Parmesan and the flour. Mix in your chopped cold spinach and you will end up with a soft but workable dough. Dust your hands with a little flour, pinch off lumps of dough about the size of a walnut and roll these into balls.

To cook the dumplings, drop them into a pan of simmering water and after about 4 minutes they will float to the surface, at which point they are ready. Remove them from the pan and cool in cold water. They can be refrigerated (or frozen, then defrosted) and reheated in boiling water at any time.

To cook the vegetables, put the ham stock in a saucepan and bring it up to a simmer. Drop the carrots, parsnip and swede in and simmer for about 15 minutes, until just cooked. Remove them from the stock, put them on a plate and allow them to cool.

Bring the stock to a boil and allow it to reduce to about 400ml. At this point the flavour should be fabulously meaty and slightly sweetened by the vegetables. Turn the temperature down to just simmering and drop in the slices of ham, cooked vegetables and the pre-cooked dumplings. Allow all of this to get nice and hot.

Take the hot ham out of the stock and put into your chosen serving dish. Arrange the root vegetables and the dumplings in the dish too. Keep the dish warm while you quickly turn the stock into a creamy sauce.

Reboil the stock hard for 2 minutes, then pour in the cream and boil for a further 2 minutes. At this point add the grain mustard, whisk it in and spoon over the ham in your serving dish. I would suggest a wallop of mashed potato is the best thing to serve with this dish.

HONEY AND MAPLE GLAZED HAM ⓟ
WITH CHEESY CHAMP

serves: 4   preparation time: 15 minutes   cooking time: 40 minutes

Glazed ham is a real treat hot or cold. All that bit of cold ham in your fridge needs is a sweet glaze painted on to the fat and within the hour you will have a caramelized piece of honey-roast ham. I suggest serving it with champ, which is an Irish dish traditionally made with potatoes and nettles served at Hallowe'en. Spring onions replace the nettles here and the cheese is my own customization, because I think it works really well with the ham.

a piece of cooked ham, about 1kg, with a covering of fat (see p.69)

200ml ham stock

20 cloves

1 tablespoon honey

2 tablespoons maple syrup

2 tablespoons English mustard

zest of ½ an orange

for the champ

4 servings of mashed potato

30g unsalted butter

2 bunches of spring onions, trimmed and very finely sliced at an angle

50g grated mature Cheddar cheese

Preheat the oven to 180°C/160°C fan/gas mark 4.

Remove the ham from the fridge and stand it, fat-side up, in a roasting tray. Pour the stock into the tray – this will prevent the ham drying out too much. Score the fat all over in a criss-cross pattern and stud the fat with the cloves. Mix together the honey, maple syrup, mustard and orange zest, then paint it over the ham with a pastry brush or the back of a spoon.

Place the meat in the oven and, after 15 minutes, open the door and scoop out the liquid in the roasting tray with a large spoon and pour it back over the ham. Continue to baste every 5 minutes thereafter.

A piece of ham weighing 1kg will need about 35–40 minutes in the oven. Turning the tray around in the oven during cooking can help achieve an even colour. By the time the ham is done, it will be a deep brown colour all over. Rest the meat for 15 minutes in a warm place before carving.

That gives you exactly enough time to make the champ. Get your mashed potato nice and hot – this can be done in the microwave if you have one. Transfer the potato to a pan and beat in the butter. Next add the spring onions and then the cheese. Once the cheese is melted, remove the champ from the stove and serve.

By the way, any leftover bits of ham from the meal can go straight back into the fridge, because there's another meal on the way (see p.75)!

On p.70 we made boiled ham with spinach dumplings. Well, in the tradition of Economy Gastronomy, those dumplings are about to become gnocchi!

about 20 pre-rolled and cooked gnocchi (spinach dumplings – see p.71)
½ a red pepper, cut into 1cm dice
2 tablespoons olive oil
1–2 teaspoons smoked paprika
1 x 400g tin of chopped tomatoes
150g ham, chopped
150g mushrooms, chopped
grated Parmesan cheese, to serve (approx. 30g)
1 tablespoon chopped rocket

If your gnocchi are frozen, then take them out and defrost slowly in the fridge.

To make the tomato sauce, fry the diced red pepper in a tablespoon of olive oil in a deep frying pan until they start to colour very slightly. Next add the smoked paprika and the tomatoes. Allow this to simmer and reduce until the sauce is thick and rich. Meanwhile, fry the ham bits and the mushrooms in the remaining olive oil in a separate pan and, when caramelized, drop into the tomato ragù.

Boil a kettle and pour the water into a pan over the defrosted gnocchi. Simmer them for a minute or two, then fish them out and add them to the ragù. Give it all a bit of a stir and serve sprinkled with shavings of Parmesan and the chopped rocket.

A great beef stew, or a 'daube' as the French call it, is a really pleasing affair. The main bedrock recipe, plus the tumbledowns that follow on from it, are all about saving you time, and getting a head start for this week's meals. This takes about 30 minutes to get in the oven, and a couple of hours later you have what has to be one of the most simple and comforting plates of food in the world, which can then transform into two other interesting meals for hardly any extra effort.

Smart folk will have their mushrooms on hand when making this, as you can just chuck them into the leftover meat and juices, and after half an hour of simmering, the sauce for the pappardelle recipe is done. You can then eat this pasta dish any time over the next few days, or freeze the sauce, ready to go as and when. Just remember to take out 300g of meat and a ladleful of the stock inbetween eating the daube and adding the mushrooms. This is for the unmissable Cornish pasties – keep the meat in the fridge for up to four days, and once you've built them you can also freeze them.

A note on the meat: chuck is ideal as it has a decent fat content, which you need, to stop the meat becoming dry and dull. I've done this with supermarket braising beef and proper chuck from a butcher, giving startlingly different results. For this one I'd say it's worth making a trip to the butcher's, as you're going to be seeing this meat, albeit in very different guises, at three meals, so it's worth getting the good stuff.

BRAISED BEEF
DAUBE OF BEEF WITH GREENS AND COLCANNON MASH
PAPPARDELLE WITH SLOW-COOKED BEEF AND MUSHROOMS
BEEF PASTIES

DAUBE OF BEEF [Ⓐ]
WITH GREENS AND COLCANNON MASH

serves: 4   preparation time: 15 minutes   cooking time: 4 hours

The key to this kind of cooking is made obvious by the prep time vs. cooking time. Apart from chucking some bits and bobs in a pan, all that is required of the cook is the ability to think a few hours in advance. Let the ingredients do all the work. Braised beef alongside a pile of greens and a good dollop of colcannon mash is one of my favourite things to eat as the nights get cooler.

10 shallots, peeled and left whole

3 bay leaves

350g small-cut, dry-cured bacon chunks or lardons

1 handful (about 15g) of thyme on the branch, washed and tied together tightly with string

5 cloves of garlic, peeled and chopped

3 tablespoons olive oil

1 x 750ml bottle of cheap red wine

salt and pepper

2.5kg chuck steak or braising steak, cut into 4cm dice

1 litre beef stock

2 x 415g tins of beef consommé

1kg mashing potatoes (I like King Edwards), peeled and quartered

40g butter

150ml milk

1 head (350g) of spring greens, leaves cut off and rinsed

a sprinkle of freshly grated nutmeg

4 spring onions, trimmed and sliced

30g flat-leaf parsley, chopped roughly

Preheat the oven to 170°C/150°C fan/gas mark 3, and put your biggest roasting tray (mine measures 35cm x 40cm x 6cm) on the hob over a medium heat. Tip in the shallots, bay leaves, lardons, thyme and garlic, and sweat them gently in the olive oil for 10–15 minutes until the shallots are soft and translucent, and the lardons are beginning to brown. As soon as you feel with your wooden spoon that you're getting sticky spots at the bottom of the pan, pour in the wine. Scrape at the sticky parts with your spoon and simmer and reduce for around ten minutes. If you're using a stock cube, click the kettle on now. Tip the meat into a bowl and season with three hefty pinches of salt and grind over a generous amount of black pepper.

As a nod to Elizabeth David, queen of this kind of rustic French cooking, just lay your meat on top of the onions, lardons and wine – don't mix it all in. Pour over the stock and consommé so that the meat is all well covered. Bring everything to a simmer before covering the pan tightly with foil and putting it in the oven.

From here on in, the beef will take between 2½ to 3½ hours to cook to the perfect texture and flavour. Depending on the meat you're using, and your oven, there really can be this much difference between the cooking time. After 1½ hours, fish a piece of meat out of the pan, blow on it until cool, and squeeze between your thumb and finger. If it's beginning to give a bit this means it has passed through the tough and tense stage, so take the foil off so that the sauce can reduce a bit during the last stage of cooking. If you're not convinced the meat is beginning to soften, put it back in the oven and test again in another 30 minutes. Don't worry, you simply can't overcook this dish.

Once the foil has been off for half an hour, put your potatoes into a pan of cold, salted water and bring to the boil with a lid on. Simmer till cooked – about 20 minutes. When the beef is really tender, take it out to rest, covering with the foil. Drain the potatoes, leaving them in the colander, and put the pan back on a low heat with the butter and milk in it.

Fill another pan with about 10cm of water and bring it to the boil, lid on, for the greens. I like to leave the cabbage leaves whole, and once the water is boiling add a bit of salt and drop them in. They'll only take about 5 minutes, with a stir to turn them halfway through.

When the butter has melted into the milk, add the drained potatoes and mash, seasoning to taste with salt, pepper and nutmeg. When fluffy and delicious, stir in the spring onions to turn the mash into colcannon.

Serve up immediately on warm plates – lovely tender leaves of cabbage, a pile of colcannon and a ladleful of the beef with its excellent cooking liquor, making sure that you reserve some for the next two recipes and share out the shallots and bacon. Sprinkle over the parsley to finish.

PAPPARDELLE
WITH SLOW-COOKED BEEF AND MUSHROOMS

serves: 4   preparation time: 15 minutes   cooking time: 30 minutes

From the beef stew, you are just a hop and a skip away from our pasta dish. A classic Italian combo of pappardelle and slow-cooked meat can be made with anything from oxtail to venison to hare. Letting the beef cook a little longer so that the chunks we had for our daube collapse into tender strands makes it ideal for tossing through wide-ribboned pasta.

The zingy little tomato salsa sprinkled over at the end is the making of the dish – a bit of freshness and colour to contrast with the rich and robust slow-cooked base.

about 400g leftover beef (see p.79) and around 700ml cooking liquid

300g mushrooms (oyster, button or shiitake), washed and sliced or torn

250g dried egg pappardelle (tagliatelle or fettuccini will do)

salt and pepper

1 tablespoon olive oil

1 heaped tablespoon butter, softened

40g Parmesan, finely grated

for the tomato salsa

400g vine-ripened tomatoes, cut into eighths, or cherry tomatoes, halved

a handful of basil leaves, chopped

a handful of flat-leaf parsley, chopped

1½ teaspoons red wine vinegar

Having had your fill of the beef stew on p.79, and having set aside the meat for the pasties on p.83, put all the remaining meat and juice into a wide pan on the hob. Add the mushrooms and cook over a high heat for 30 minutes, stirring regularly as the liquid bubbles down. About halfway through the cooking time, bring a large pot of water to the boil with some salt and a shot of olive oil for the pasta. Knock up the simple, fresh tomato salsa, which is the heart and soul of this dish. Mix the pieces of ripe tomato with the basil, parsley, vinegar and some seasoning to taste. Cook the pasta according to the instructions on the packet, then drain and tip it back into the pot you cooked it in.

By now, the beef and mushrooms should be looking much thicker. Use a wooden spoon to break the meat up a bit – for this dish you want to have strands of meat rather than discernible chunks. If you think your mix is still looking a bit wet, then just let it continue to simmer for a few more minutes until most of the liquid has either been absorbed or reduced away.

Gently fold the beef and mushroom mix into the pasta, stirring in the butter along with half of the Parmesan. Taste for seasoning, and serve in warm bowls, with a generous amount of the tomato salsa on top and a scattering of the remaining Parmesan.

BEEF PASTIES

serves: 4 (makes 4 pasties)   preparation time: 20 minutes   cooking time: 30 minutes

My very Cornish godmother, Jenefer (aka Jam), is eightysomething and still makes herself a pasty for lunch once a week. This recipe is not very like hers – she puts the filling in raw, which, of course, is the proper way the miners' wives used to make them. Back in those days they'd also put meat in just one half and jam in the other, so it was a main and pud all in one. However, if it hadn't been for her showing me just how easy they are, I probably wouldn't have thought of making this the final destination for our beef.

We all love a pasty from time to time, and I can't tell you how pleasing it is to have a proper home-made one, instead of something murdered in a microwave or sitting in a supermarket. Kids go nuts for them too – my nephew Alfie was beaming proud when his mates came round for tea and I'd knocked these up for them.

300g braised beef, reserved from p.79

40g butter

¼ swede (about 200g), peeled and cut into 1cm dice

2–3 carrots (200g), peeled and cut into 1cm dice

150g waxy potatoes (I like the little red-skinned Rosevals), washed and cut into 1cm dice

1 teaspoon allspice

10 sprigs of thyme, leaves picked

100g peas, defrosted or fresh

salt and pepper

flour, for dusting

500g shortcrust pastry

1 egg, beaten with 1 tablespoon water

Take the beef you set aside for this recipe out of the fridge and shred it with your fingers, chucking away any fatty bits. All the juice is good news too so stir it into the meat. Heat the oven to 200°C/180°C fan/gas mark 6, and preheat a baking tray suitable for holding four good-sized pasties on the top shelf.

Melt the butter in a wide-bottomed saucepan, and very gently fry the three kinds of diced veg with the allspice and thyme for 15 minutes, keeping a lid on and stirring regularly. Take the pan off the heat when the vegetables are cooked through but still retain some bite, and stir in the peas with plenty of salt and pepper. Add the cold meat and its liquid to the vegetable mixture, mix very thoroughly and chill in the fridge while you deal with the pastry.

Sprinkle your work surface lightly with flour, then roll the pastry out to a thickness of about 5mm, adding more flour if it looks like sticking. Use a plate or bowl about 20cm across as a template to cut out circles of pastry. In order not to waste pastry, you may find it easier to cut out three circles, then scrunch the off-cuts up and roll out again to make the fourth.

Brush around each of the circles with the beaten egg, divide your filling into four and put a pile into the middle of each pastry circle. If the meat mixture is nicely chilled, it will be stiff and easy to work with: try to make the meat in each circle a similar shape to a finished pasty, leaving a margin of about an inch around the edges. Bring the pastry up and around, using a baker's pinch to crimp the seam, securing firmly to make sure that no steam can escape through the ends. Give them another all-over, thorough egg-wash, then take the tray out of the oven, sprinkle on a little flour to prevent sticking, and gently position the pasties on it.

It'll only take about 30 minutes for these beauties to be cooked, and then they're good for 24 hours – though a pasty is at its absolute best when it's piping hot from the oven.

BASIC TOMATO SAUCE ⓟ

preparation time: 20 minutes   cooking time: 1 hour 10 minutes

This very basic tomato sauce is used in restaurants the world over. It never makes it on to a menu under the above title, but its uses are varied and essential. What the following recipe will make is basically what you should find in a tin of chopped tomatoes – a rich, fresh chopped tomato sauce – should, but never do!

The recipe I have given is for 2.5 kilos of tomatoes, which is the perfect amount for the following three recipes. I would recommend you make your tomato sauce in industrial quantities in the summer months. Scour markets for boxes of overripe tomatoes and, upon finding some, rush home and invite your friends over for a tomato-peeling party. This sauce will sit in the fridge quite happily for up to 10 days, and in the freezer for several months.

2.5kg ripe tomatoes
10 large shallots
10 cloves of garlic
a large sprig of fresh thyme
400ml olive oil

First of all, put a large pan of water on to boil with a lid on. Meanwhile, cut the eyes at the stalk end from the tomato. (The eye is the bit where the stalk connects to the fruit.) Also make a criss-cross using the tip of a knife at the base of each tomato. Now find a large bowl and fill it with cold water. If you have some ice, that would make it colder, which is even better. Have a slotted spoon handy too.

By now your pan of water should be boiling. Lower the tomatoes into the boiling water, count to ten, then lift out each tomato and drop it into the cold water. This making-cold-after-boiling process is known as 'refreshing'. I suspect it is. We have no further need for the boiling water, so you could boil your pasta for lunch in it if your green urges get the better of you! Your tomatoes should now peel very easily. Put the skins to one side then cut off the sides of each tomato so that you are left with pure tomato flesh with no skin or seeds attached. The centres of the tomato (the seedy bit) along with the skins can be frozen for use in stocks and sauces.* Now chop all the tomato flesh with a big knife until it's a pulp. Leave this to one side.

Quickly prepare the remaining ingredients for your tomato sauce: chop the shallots as finely as you can, chop the garlic to a paste and pull the leaves from the thyme.

Heat a saucepan and add half the olive oil. Allow it to get hot and then throw in the shallots, thyme leaves and garlic. Cook these for 2 minutes until softened but not coloured. Add the rest of the olive oil and the chopped tomato pulp. Mix everything around and then cover the surface of the tomato sauce with a disc of greaseproof paper.

Turn your stove as low as it can possibly go and allow the mixture to cook gently for at least an hour. If your stove is low enough, it will almost look as if the mixture is not cooking at all. This is fine: the longer it cooks the better. What you are aiming to do is gently evaporate the water contained within, leaving an intense yet fresh-tasting sauce. Remove your sauce when it has thickened slightly and is very rich and red in colour – very similar in appearance to the picture on, but not the contents of, a tin of chopped tomatoes. Allow your mixture to cool. Season as required and store in the fridge or freezer.

*(*In the restaurant, we use tomato peelings and trimmings in our 48-hour veal stock. You could too if you are the type who makes veal stock at home. Does anyone? Of course not, so freeze these tomato skins and seeds and bung them in the next soup you make.)*

BASIC TOMATO SAUCE
A VERY SIMPLE PASTA DISH WITH HOME-MADE TOMATO SAUCE
FISH STEW WITH FENNEL, SAFFRON AND TOMATO
ONE-POT TOMATO STEW WITH PORK MEATBALLS, CHORIZO AND WHITE BEANS

A VERY SIMPLE PASTA DISH [Ⓟ]
WITH HOME-MADE TOMATO SAUCE

serves: 4   preparation time: 15 minutes   cooking time: 15 minutes

My mother-in-law lives in Italy. Best place for her, you may say, but actually I'm rather fond of her and rather pleased she lives in such a gastronomic part of the world. Italian food is defined by fresh ingredients and uncomplicated recipes. I have often enjoyed freshly cooked pasta with nothing more than a great-tasting tomato sauce.

This is a dish that I do at home when time is against me. The crunchy breadcrumbs add an interesting texture, and I love wilted rocket with pasta.

500g dried pasta – farfalle or penne would be good
4 slices of white bread – a ciabatta would keep things authentic
100ml olive oil
$1/5$ quantity of tomato sauce (see p.85), warmed
a few olives
a handful of rocket leaves, roughly chopped
sea salt and black pepper
100g crumbled feta cheese

Put a pan on to boil and chuck in the pasta. It will need about 8–10 minutes to keep it al dente.

Now heat a frying pan. Whilst this gets hot, take the bread and pull it into small pieces – think of these as big breadcrumbs. Pour 75ml of the olive oil into the frying pan and fry the breadcrumbs until golden brown and crunchy. Take them out of the pan and put to one side.

Drain the pasta and return it to the pan. Pour on the warm tomato sauce, then throw in the olives and chopped rocket. Turn over the pasta a few times to mix everything up, season with black pepper and sea salt and spoon into bowls.

Sprinkle over the crunchy breadcrumbs and feta, and drizzle over the remaining olive oil.

FISH STEW [Ⓟ]
WITH FENNEL, SAFFRON AND TOMATO

serves: 4   preparation time: 20 minutes   cooking time: 15 minutes

This sort of fish stew is served all along the Mediterranean coast. Once you have a decent tomato base (and now you do), the actual cooking is quick and simple. What we have done here is customize the tomato sauce from a very acceptable yet plain tomato sauce to something positively exciting with the inclusion of the fennel, chilli, saffron and other bits. You could use this customized sauce for pasta or you could stir in some diced chicken and olives. I am merely suggesting you try a fish stew.

Allow your fishmonger to guide you in your choice of fish – huss, mullet, hake, snapper and gurnard all work well in this dish. I like to use chunks of fish on the bone for this – ask your fishmonger to chop the fish straight across, through the back bone. In the kitchen we call this cut a 'darne' of fish.

The stew can be served very simply with new potatoes and green beans, but it will be even better with a dollop of aïoli sauce, and a crusty baguette.

75ml olive oil

1 head of fennel, diced about 1cm square

½ onion, peeled and diced about 1cm square

½ red pepper, diced about 1cm square

2 sticks of celery, diced about 1cm square

2 red chillies, finely chopped

½ teaspoon saffron strands

175ml white wine

$^2/_5$ quantity of your tomato sauce (see p.85)

600g fish on the bone (400g if only using fillets)

8 king prawns – in the shell is best

20 live mussels, cleaned and prepared (see p.241 for method)

1 tablespoon chopped mixed herbs (chives, dill, tarragon and parsley are superb)

Heat a casserole pan and add the olive oil, then fry the fennel, onion, pepper and celery until softened but not coloured. Add the chopped chilli and the saffron and then pour on the white wine. Allow this to simmer gently for 5 minutes, then tip in the tomato sauce.

If making this in advance, you can now allow the sauce to tick over for a few minutes longer then cool it and store in the fridge. Alternatively, to finish the stew now, add the pieces of fish, making sure that each is covered by the sauce. I would add the prawns and mussels about 4 minutes after the fish. The stew is ready when the fish is cooked, and the fish is cooked when the flesh easily pulls away from the bone. The mussels will have opened up by now and the prawns will have gone a pinky orange.

Finally, stir in the herbs and drizzle over a little olive oil, *et voilà*! You are a culinary genius.

ONE-POT TOMATO STEW WITH PORK MEATBALLS, CHORIZO AND WHITE BEANS ⓟ

serves: 4–6   preparation time: 15 minutes   cooking time: 50 minutes

The head chefs of posh restaurants would never dream of using the phrase 'one-pot' in a menu description, because it suggests a dish of genuine simplicity. And that is the very reason that it appears in the title here – this is a genuinely simple dish.

You start with one empty pot and you keep putting in various enticing ingredients until you have a full pot. You cook it for a while, then put it on the table and within the hour it's back to being an empty pot again!

I would start by scanning the recipe and getting all the chipping-chopping nonsense out of the way first. Then you are ready to proceed to the starting line.

2 tablespoons olive oil

1 head of fennel, cut into 1cm dice

2 carrots, peeled and cut into 1cm dice

1 red pepper, cut into 1cm dice

4 cloves of garlic, peeled and chopped

1 onion, peeled and cut into 1cm dice

a pinch of dried chilli flakes

175ml red wine

2/5 quantity of your tomato sauce (see p.85)

1½ teaspoons smoked paprika

750g minced pork – ask your butcher to do this for you, using shoulder of pork

1 teaspoon crushed fennel seeds

2 teaspoons ground cumin

2 chorizo sausages

1 x 400g tin of white beans (butter beans or haricots blancs), drained

Pick your most reliable casserole pot. Heat it up and add a good glug of olive oil. Throw in the diced fennel, carrots, pepper, garlic, onion and the dried chilli. Allow this to sizzle gently and soften slightly, but don't let it colour.

Now pour 2 generous glasses of red wine. Drink one yourself (you're the cook after all!) and pour the other into the pot. It should start to simmer fairly quickly. Pour in your tomato sauce and add the smoked paprika. Let this simmer gently, covered, for about 10 minutes, while you make the meatballs.

Put the minced pork in a bowl and add the crushed fennel seeds and ground cumin. Mix together well, using your hands, then roll the mixture into balls – the size is up to you, but I would say about ping-pong ball size.

These meatballs can be thrown straight into the simmering pot, but I reckon they benefit from being rolled in a little vegetable oil in a hot frying pan to colour the outsides. This should only take 2 or 3 minutes per batch – all you want is a golden-brown surface to your raw meatballs. Now bung them in the simmering pot and mix them in so that they are submerged. Take the 2 chorizo sausages, break them into bite-sized chunks and add these to the pot.

Allow the stew to simmer away, uncovered, for around half an hour, by which time the tomato sauce will have enriched and thickened. Have a taste and if you are happy with the flavour simply mix in the drained white beans, re-simmer and serve.

There are two ways I really enjoy lamb: either roasted pink or slow-cooked until the meat is super soft and gentle. The joy of this bedrock and its subsequent tumbledown recipes is that it gives us both.

First up is the roasted leg, then once we've sliced off what we need to go with our baked spud, whatever's left on the bone goes into a big pot with some veggies and some spices. A couple of hours later it's transformed into a whole new thing of beauty.

When it comes to a leg of lamb, buy a joint that's anywhere between 2.3kg (supermarket) and 3kg (my butcher). New season's lamb, being younger, will weigh in nearer the 2.3kg end of the scale, whereas lamb that's nearly a year old (at which point it stops being called lamb and is known as hogget) is closer to 3kg. Wherever you shop, try to get the biggest leg you can find.

LEG OF LAMB
ROASTED LAMB WITH CANNELLINI BEANS AND INTERESTING TURNIPS
SLOW-COOKED MOROCCAN LAMB WITH HERB COUSCOUS
BAKED POTATO WITH LAMB AND LEBANESE BEANS

ROASTED LAMB WITH CANNELLINI BEANS AND INTERESTING TURNIPS

serves: 4–6   preparation time: 20 minutes   cooking time: 2¾ hours

At first glance, the magic of this dish is down to the well-documented love affair between the ingredients in the paste: chilli, garlic and cumin have been pulling punches from India to South America for centuries. But this is a dish of layers – physical ones, not just layers of flavour: the turnips and carrots are cooked below the lamb in a light honey stock, soaking up the juices and flavour cast-offs of the meat above it.

If you really want to get the most out of this, marinade the leg the day before.

1 leg of lamb (2.3kg to 3kg)

50g large red chillies (not the Thai bird's-eye chillies, which will be too hot)

1 whole bulb of garlic, peeled

1½ tablespoons cumin seeds

7 tablespoons light olive oil or rapeseed oil

1½ tablespoons salt, preferably flaky sea salt

8 medium carrots

600g turnips, peeled

4 tablespoons clear honey

2 tablespoons extra-virgin olive oil

for the beans

5 tablespoons extra-virgin olive oil

3 sprigs of rosemary, washed, stripped and chopped

3 x 410g tins of cannellini beans, drained (this will give you enough leftovers for the recipe on p.99)

3 bay leaves

200g baby spinach, leaves left whole; or whole-leaf spinach, chopped roughly

1 lemon

salt and pepper

First things first: if your meat has been vacuum-packed, pat it dry and give it a bit of air. Preheat the oven to 180°C/160°C fan/gas mark 4.

Using the food processor or a pestle and mortar, make a smooth paste out of the chillies, garlic, cumin, light oil and salt. This may take a bit of pushing and pulsing, but you'll get there soon enough. Use the back of a spoon to spread the paste all over the lamb, skin, meaty end bits and all. Leave for as long as you can.

Scrub the carrots, quarter the large turnips and halve any smaller ones. Measure a litre of hot water into a jug, and stir the honey and extra-virgin olive oil into it. Pour this mixture into the bottom of a large roasting tray, put the veg in it and add some salt and pepper. Rest a cooling rack over the bathing vegetables – mine tends to slip off, so I balance it on some upturned ramekins. Put the meat on the rack, and loosely drape a piece of foil over it.

Stick the joint in the oven – I like my lamb pink, so if it's nearer to 2kg I'll cook it for 1½ hours, and if it's closer to 3kg I'll give it 2½ hours. To test that it's done, stick a skewer or thin knife into the centre of it and gingerly touch it to your top lip. Don't take it off until you feel a distinct warmth, but it shouldn't be anywhere near properly hot. Add to the cooking time if you like your lamb medium.

About halfway through the cooking time, give the veg a turn, which involves lifting the leg off, of course. About 15 minutes before you reckon you're going to take it out, check the veg isn't caramelizing too much. If things look ominously dark round the edges of the pan, tip in half a mug of water.

Once you take it out, the lamb needs a good ten-minute rest with the foil still on, which gives you time to knock up the beans. Heat a heavy-bottomed pan with the oil and rosemary and fry it just for a minute or two until the rosemary starts to go golden before adding the beans and bay.

When the beans are warmed through and coated in the rosemary oil, stir the spinach into the pan, using the back of your spoon to squish the beans. Pop the lid on for a couple of minutes to let the spinach wilt, then add a generous squeeze of lemon juice, and season well.

When it comes to carving the lamb, make sure everyone has a good bit of the spicy outside bit, and save the pinker meat next to the bone for the Moroccan slow-cook on p.97. Make sure you have around a mug of beans left over to turn into Lebanese beans (see p.99). Serve with the roasted vegetables and any juices.

SLOW-COOKED MOROCCAN LAMB
WITH HERB COUSCOUS

serves: 4   preparation time: 20 minutes   cooking time: 2 hours 30 minutes

This is a big old relaxed stew, which is different enough from the roast lamb to be eaten a day or two later. It will also freeze well.

I was round at my Moroccan friend Souhail's the other night – the smell emanating from his kitchen took me right back to that most magical of countries, and a quick peek inside his pan set my mind in motion. Putting all the ingredients in one pot and letting them simmer away on the stove for a couple of hours is one of the least stressful and most pleasing ways to cook. The resulting meal is equally relaxed, in terms of the melt-in-your-mouth tenderness of the meat, and that all you need to finish it off is to knock up the couscous, which takes no more than 5 minutes.

about 1kg leftover leg of lamb,
on the bone, fat trimmed

1 x 400g tin of peeled plum or cherry tomatoes

60ml extra-virgin olive oil

1 large red onion, peeled and quartered
with the root cut out

2 carrots, scrubbed and halved lengthways

2 bay leaves

2 tablespoons tomato purée

3 cloves of garlic, peeled and sliced

1½ tablespoons harissa (spicy chilli paste)

2–3 potatoes (around 400g),
peeled and quartered

4 baby aubergines

1 large courgette, quartered,
or 2 small ones, whole or halved

150g French beans, tops trimmed

for the couscous

250g couscous

olive oil

a handful of coriander (about 30g),
washed and chopped

a handful of parsley (about 30g),
washed and chopped

juice of 1 lemon, to taste

salt and pepper

If you paid attention in *Anatomy 101*, you'll know that there's a joint halfway up the back of the leg of lamb. Bend it back, snap or cut through it and split the leg in two, so it'll be easier to fit it in a saucepan. Put the leg plus everything up to and including the harissa in a high-sided pan (mine is 25cm in diameter) and cover with water – you'll probably need 1 to 1.5 litres to cover everything nicely. Put a lid on and bring the liquid to a simmer, then turn the heat down to the lowest setting and squiff the lid slightly so that the steam can escape.

An hour after the lamb comes to a simmer, add the potatoes first, followed by the aubergines, courgette and beans. Pop the lid on and bring everything back to the boil, turn the heat right down and shift the lid again.

You don't need to stir or even look at it for the next hour and a half. When the time is up, check it's done by lifting the bone and seeing if the meat comes away easily. Turn the heat off and start working on the couscous. Boil the kettle and tip the couscous into a mixing bowl. Pour in a generous shot of olive oil, and rub the grains between your fingers for a minute so the oil coats them evenly. Pour over 300ml of nearly boiling water – enough to just cover the grains – then wrap the bowl in cling film and leave to sit for 15 minutes while you chop up the coriander and parsley and warm your bowls.

Handle your one-pot carefully: use a slotted spoon to lift out the meat on the bone and set it aside. Then transfer the veg to your serving dish. Tug the meat away from the bone in nuggets, and sit them on top of the dish. Spoon over a few ladlefuls of the rich stock – you should have about a litre left as down-payment on another meal. (Add lentils to make a soup, chuck into a casserole for added flavour, use it as gravy – whatever your need, this is instant meaty goodness. Just scrape the solidified fat off the top before using.)

Use a fork to fluff up your couscous and let some of the heat escape – don't stir the herbs in until it's stopped steaming, as the heat will darken them. Once cooled, gently mix the herbs into the couscous and season with salt, pepper and lots of lemon juice, tasting as you go to check the seasoning. Give everyone an island of couscous surrounded by chunks of meat, plenty of veg and a high tide of rich, tomatoey stock.

BAKED POTATO
WITH LAMB AND LEBANESE BEANS

serves: 2   preparation time: 20 minutes   cooking time: 40 minutes

To make this, you need a bit of cold roast lamb, sliced off the bone, and a bowlful of the cannellini beans that accompanied it on p.95.

When I think of baked potatoes, baked beans follow almost instantly in my head. I thought I'd give this British standard a little makeover to suit the ethnic flavours on the outside of the lamb, so I reworked the bean idea with the help of a spicy Lebanese walnut pesto.

What's amazing is that with such a small amount of input from the cook, a dish can be transformed into something quite so different.

around 300g leftover roast lamb, in chunks or slices

2 baking potatoes, around 300g each

Greek yoghurt, to serve

for the Lebanese walnut pesto

50g shelled walnuts

1 red pepper

1 tablespoon pomegranate molasses, or 4 tablespoons pomegranate juice

½ teaspoon ground cumin

1 shallot, peeled and grated

a small handful of flat-leaf parsley (15g), washed and chopped

salt and pepper

200–250g spinachy cannellini beans (see p.95)

2 tablespoons olive oil

Preheat the oven to 200°C/180°C fan/gas mark 6. Prick the potatoes a couple of times and whack them in the microwave on high for 15–20 minutes (or put them straight in the oven for an hour and 15 minutes, turning down to 180°C/160°C fan/gas mark 4 after half an hour). Get the lamb out of the fridge and allow it to come up to room temperature.

To make the Lebanese pesto, blitz the walnuts in a food processor until ground. Cut the pepper in half and scrape out the seeds. Grate it coarsely, chucking out any big bits of skin that fall by the wayside. Mix the ground walnuts, grated pepper, pomegranate molasses or juice, ground cumin, grated shallot, parsley and seasoning in a bowl, and set aside for the flavours to come together.

Once the spuds have been thoroughly nuked, there are a few things you can do to turn them into more traditional decent baked ones. As soon as each potato comes out of the microwave, pick it up in an oven glove and roll it around between your hands to break the insides up. Be gentle: the skin is thin and delicate when microwaved, so this has to be done carefully. Barbara Kafka, queen of microwave cookery, says that letting the potato cool for a few minutes before wetting it, sprinkling with salt and baking for 30 minutes in the oven is the best way to achieve the perfect result.

When your spuds are nearly cooked, warm the beans through in a small saucepan and stir half of the walnut pesto into it. Transfer the other half into a ramekin or a small jam jar, bang it down hard on the counter to bring any air bubbles to the top, then cover with the olive oil before sealing. This can be enjoyed as a snack on warm flatbread or with crudités later – it will keep for a month like this in the fridge.

Serve the hot spud, spicy beans and lamb with a splodge of Greek yoghurt to bring it all together.

Let's set the scene. On a trip to the market you catch sight of a pumpkin display. The impressive gourd-like vegetables look so appetizing as their burnt orange skins shine in the sun. Overcome by a sudden culinary rush to the head, you single out the most attractive specimen, pay your money, haul it home on the bus and place it on the floor in your kitchen. (You would put it on the kitchen table, but the thing is so big, you fear you won't be able to afford the osteopath's bill or indeed a carpenter to fix the table!)

This is really my problem with pumpkins – generally they are enormous; and unless you are expecting a coachload of pumpkin eaters to turn up, what are you going to do with it all? I bet the vast majority of pumpkins are only partially eaten, while the rest decay and end up on the compost heap or, worse, in the bin.

Well, fear not, because I have spent hours carefully planning a three-meal attack to deal with all your pumpkin requirements. For the sake of my recipes, I have assumed that you have purchased a pumpkin weighing at least 3kg.

Whilst the Americans are the most prolific growers of pumpkins, it's the Italians, I think, who have given the pumpkin its rightful place in the kitchen; so a risotto is the perfect way to begin your pumpkin fest. The second recipe is also Italian in spirit – stuffed cannelloni – whilst the third serving goes all exotic, with a spicy chowder.

Our first job is to get that pumpkin prepped. Take a large knife and cut it into three wedges, as evenly sized as you are able. Wrap two of the wedges in cling film and write 'cannelloni' on one and 'chowder' on the other and put them in the fridge (they will happily keep for a week or more). The third wedge is for your risotto . . .

A WHOPPING GREAT PUMPKIN
PUMPKIN RISOTTO WITH ROASTED WALNUTS, RED CHICORY AND GORGONZOLA
PUMPKIN CANNELLONI WITH SAGE AND RICOTTA
SPICY PUMPKIN CHOWDER

PUMPKIN RISOTTO WITH ROASTED WALNUTS, RED CHICORY AND GORGONZOLA ⓟ

serves: 4   preparation time: 15 minutes   cooking time: 40 minutes

While I do occasionally put a risotto on the restaurant menu, it's at home that most of my risotto production takes place. This pumpkin risotto is perfect midweek fare in my opinion – it's not expensive, yet it's nutritious and filling with no need for any side dishes.

1kg wedge of pumpkin
olive oil
½ pack of unsalted butter
2 medium onions, peeled and finely chopped
a sprig of thyme
3 cloves of garlic, peeled and finely chopped
4 handfuls of risotto rice
(about 50–60g per person)
1 tablespoon broken walnuts

up to 1 litre hot chicken stock
(it's okay to use a cube)
a little fresh marjoram, leaves picked
salt and pepper
1 tablespoon grated Parmesan
1 head of red chicory, shredded finely
200g Gorgonzola cheese,
broken into bite-size pieces

Remove the skin from the pumpkin and then cut the wedge in half. Dice both halves into rough 2cm cubes. Now put the dice from one half into a pan and cover with water. Simmer until tender, then drain off the water and purée the flesh with a liquidizer or a stick blender. This purée will be stirred into your risotto towards the end of the cooking, so put it in the fridge until required.

The second lot of dice is also going to end up in the risotto. However, it is going to be pan-fried so that the outside caramelizes. This will give the risotto a more complex flavour and is well worth the effort. Heat a frying pan and add a little olive oil. When the oil is nice and hot, add a little pumpkin and fry it until it has softened slightly and the flesh has a roasted appearance. This frying is best done in smaller batches and the pumpkin set aside to cool until needed.

Start the risotto by putting two-thirds of the butter into a heavy-based saucepan to melt. Now add the onions, thyme and garlic. Stir them into the butter and allow them to soften, but prevent them from colouring by putting a lid on the pan and turning the heat to its lowest setting. Add the rice and let it cook for a couple of minutes in the butter with the onions, thyme and garlic.

Meanwhile, heat the oven to 200°C/180°C fan/gas mark 6 and scatter the walnuts on to a baking tray. Roast the nuts for about 6 minutes, in which time the flavour will develop and the texture will become quite crunchy.

Add the stock to the rice a ladleful at a time and keep stirring as you do – this will cause the rice to release its starch, giving a good creamy consistency.

The risotto will take about 30 minutes to cook in the gently simmering stock. After about 20 minutes, add your pre-made pumpkin purée, your fresh marjoram leaves and all of your roasted diced pumpkin. Season the risotto, add a little more stock and let it cook on for another 5–10 minutes.

Test a little rice – there should be a very slight 'bite' to it. At this point your risotto needs to be served, so remove the pan from the heat and add the remaining butter. Whilst the butter melts, sprinkle in the Parmesan cheese. These last two ingredients should give your risotto a wonderfully creamy texture.

Spoon the risotto into bowls and scatter over the broken roasted walnuts, the shredded chicory and the Gorgonzola.

PUMPKIN CANNELLONI (P)
WITH SAGE AND RICOTTA

serves: 4 as a lunch with salad
preparation time: 10 minutes   cooking time: 30 minutes

You will need a baking dish large enough to hold 8 cannelloni for this recipe. Bear in mind also that the dish needs to be deep enough to hold not only the cannelloni but also some spinach under the pasta and a thick sauce on top.

I had intended to give you a recipe to make fresh pasta for this dish. However, Allegra told me she always uses shop-bought fresh egg lasagne sheets for ease. I tried it and have to admit she's right.

1kg wedge of pumpkin

olive oil

250g ricotta cheese

10 sage leaves, chopped finely

salt and pepper

6–8 fresh lasagne sheets

20 button mushrooms, sliced (about 150g)

200g raw spinach, washed

500ml milk

40g softened butter and 40g flour, mixed to a paste

175g strong Cheddar cheese

Preheat your oven to 200°C/180°C fan/gas mark 6.

Cut your wedge of pumpkin in two to give you a couple of thinner wedges. The skin can be left on. Heat a glug of olive oil in a frying pan and fry the outsides of each wedge until they are nicely browned.

Put the coloured wedges of pumpkin on a baking tray and pop them in the oven to cook – this will take about half an hour, depending on how thick the wedges are. The best way to check them is to push a knife into the flesh and if it goes in with little resistance, then your pumpkin is done. At this point remove them from the oven and allow them to cool, then remove the skin and chop the flesh into manageable chunks and put them into a large bowl.

Using a fork, very roughly mash the flesh, keeping a little texture. Add the ricotta cheese and the chopped sage and mix together. Taste for seasoning – you will probably need a little salt and a good twist of black pepper. This is the filling for your cannelloni and it can be used straight away, or you could store it in the fridge for a couple of days.

Making the actual cannelloni is very simple. Lay a sheet of fresh lasagne on a work surface, place a sausage-shaped amount of pumpkin filling down the short edge and then simply roll them up. Make sure the seal is on the bottom. Put these rolled cannelloni in the fridge until you need them.

Heat a little olive oil in a saucepan and fry the mushrooms. Turn the heat in the pan right down and then throw in the spinach. If you have just washed your spinach, there will be enough water still on the leaves to cook it through, so don't add any more. The heat of the pan will quickly wilt the spinach down, at which point tip both the spinach and the mushrooms into your chosen baking dish, discarding any liquid, and spread it out across the base. Allow it to cool slightly and then place your cannelloni on top. They should be tightly packed in, with no spinach showing. All that's required now is a decent cheese sauce.

Bring the milk to a simmer and whisk in half the flour and butter paste. Keep whisking gently as it simmers – you are aiming for a fairly thick sauce, so add a little more of the paste if necessary. Now turn off the heat and mix in the Cheddar cheese. Pour this sauce over the cannelloni and bake in the oven for 20 minutes at 180°C/160°C fan/gas mark 4 until piping hot and golden brown.

SPICY PUMPKIN CHOWDER [Ⓟ]

serves: 6 (makes 2 litres)　preparation time: 10 minutes　cooking time: 40 minutes

This is the final instalment of our pumpkin trilogy and very possibly the simplest. Pumpkin makes a fine soup but it does need to be matched with strong flavours, so the chilli and coriander work beautifully here.

1kg wedge of pumpkin /squash
50ml olive oil
1 teaspoon ground cumin
1 teaspoon ground coriander
4 red chillies, chopped   3/4 tsp crushed chillies
2 cloves of garlic, peeled and chopped
2 x 400g tins of coconut milk
1 litre vegetable stock
80g coriander, chopped   remove or finely chop stalks

Cut the skin from the pumpkin and chop the skinned wedge into large rough dice (about 2½cm cubes). Heat a large pot on the stove and add the olive oil. When the oil is nicely hot, chuck in the pumpkin and allow it to colour slightly in the heat of the pan. This can be done in several batches if need be.

Once all the pumpkin is coloured, add the spices, chilli and chopped garlic and then pour in the coconut milk and the vegetable stock. Allow this to simmer for about 20–30 minutes, until the pumpkin is soft. Finally add the coriander and then remove from the heat.

Using a stick blender or food processor, blend the soup. I like to leave a little texture to the finished soup, so don't over-blend. The soup will freeze well or serve it straight away.

SALMON Ⓐ

In terms of a set of bedrock and tumbledown recipes, what you can do with one whole fish is just amazing.

1. Take one salmon. About 2.5 to 3kg in weight. You want to buy it filleted and pin-boned, but make sure you get the head, tail and the bone that joins them as well.

2. Cut the bottom third off the tail end (the thin one) of both fillets. You're going to cure these to make the gravadlax – 5 minutes work and after 36 hours of curing, they're ready to be a nice little starter or just great sarnies. You want to do this when the fish is good and fresh.

3. Whilst making the gravadlax, put the head, bone and tail in a pot for a stock, which is the flavour-base for the salmon and corn chowder.

4. When you make the main bedrock recipe of the poached salmon, cook both fillets at the same time. That way, you've laid the foundation for your fishcakes, i.e. the poaching liquor, plus the other fillets (minus a little bit that you've nicked to flake through the chowder).

Nothing is wasted. We've used absolutely every ounce of flavour this fish had to give, which I find very, very rewarding.

SALMON
HOME-MADE SALMON GRAVADLAX
WARM POACHED SALMON AND NEVER-FAIL HOLLANDAISE
SALMON AND HORSERADISH FISHCAKES WITH CRÈME FRAÎCHE TARTARE
SALMON AND CORN CHOWDER

HOME-MADE SALMON GRAVADLAX ^A

serves: 4–6 as a starter   preparation time: 15 minutes   curing time: 36 hours

Curing salmon with salt, as opposed to more commonly with smoke, gives it a very interesting, appealing texture as well as a more delicate and less oily taste which is what defines gravadlax. Once you've seen how easy this is to make – and how cheap – smoked salmon somehow loses its allure.

Impressive and versatile in many situations, from a beautiful dinner party starter to slapping on bread with some creamed cheese for an office sarnie.

30g dill (including stalks), chopped roughly
170g golden granulated sugar
130g rock salt
½ teaspoon fennel seeds
black pepper, to taste
the tail ⅓ of both the salmon fillets

Put everything except the salmon in the food processor and spin for a couple of minutes until it looks like a bowlful of emeralds. Pull out a large square of cling film, scatter a quarter of this salt-sugar mix on it over an area the size of a salmon tail, then put one of the tails on it, skin side down.

Pack two-thirds of the remaining salt-sugar mix evenly on to the top (flesh) side, and lay the other tail fillet on top of it, flesh side down, like a fish sandwich. Finish with the last of the mix going on the top (skin) side of the upper fillet, then fold the cling film up and around it tightly. Now swathe the whole parcel again in more cling film, wrapping it as tightly as you can.

Put the salmon in a container in the fridge, as some water will be drawn out by the cure. Turn after a day, and after 36 hours it'll be ready. Don't leave it much longer than this, as it will become too salty. When you unwrap the parcel, brush off the remaining mix, run the fillets very briefly under cold water and pat dry.

Slice the gravadlax as thinly as you can using a long, sharp knife, working with the knife blade pointing toward the tail end at a 20° angle – elegant, long slices always look nicer than scraggy bits. Enjoy with thin toast or brown bread and lemon for the easiest option; however, my tip is to serve with the crème fraîche tartare sauce for the fishcakes on p.115, which takes just a couple of minutes to knock up, and goes very well with it too.

WARM POACHED SALMON
AND NEVER-FAIL HOLLANDAISE

serves: 4   preparation time: 20 minutes   cooking time: 40 minutes

Years ago, my dad (who only ever made cups of tea in the kitchen) took me by surprise one evening when he said the only recipe he wanted to learn was hollandaise sauce, as Eggs Benedict were his favourite. So together we melted butter and put on a vinegar reduction with shallots, bay and peppercorns; then, just as I was getting into the exact texture you needed your beaten egg yolks to be, I glanced across and there was Pa with a bit of a sad look in his eye. He knew he was never going to have the patience and/or necessary skill to do it on his own. All I can say is that I wish I'd known this never-fail hollandaise recipe then.

This may be the quintessential British summer Sunday lunch.

for the poaching liquor
250ml white wine
2 onions (about 400g), peeled and diced finely
3 bay leaves
500ml water (or fish stock if you have any)
salt and pepper, to taste

for the hollandaise
150g salted butter
2 egg yolks

½ tablespoon Dijon mustard
juice of ½ lemon
salt and pepper

top ⅔ of both fillets
(only one is for this dish)
700g Jersey Royals or new potatoes
a few sprigs of mint
12 spears of English asparagus,
woody ends snapped off

Put all the ingredients for the poaching liquor in a wide saucepan or roasting tray, big enough to hold the remaining two thirds of both fillets. Keep the liquor over a low heat for 20 minutes to infuse, but make sure it stays below the boil – don't let it start simmering and reduce away.

Scrub your Jerseys and put them in a pan of cold water with some salt and the mint sprigs. Bring to a simmer for 20–25 minutes.

Once the spuds are on, lay the salmon fillets in the poaching liquor, skin side down, keeping the heat very low. Season and cover with the lid or foil. After 10 minutes lay the asparagus spears in the liquid too, put the cover back on and cook for a final 5 minutes.

While the salmon is poaching, melt the butter for the hollandaise and whizz the yolks, mustard and lemon juice in the food processor for a couple of minutes until light and fluffy. Once the butter has melted, bring it to a rapid boil, then immediately drip-feed it into the whirring food processor. As soon as it's all incorporated, tip the sauce into a bowl and season with salt to taste and some freshly ground black pepper. (There's a visual argument for white pepper here, but I still don't like the flavour.)

All that remains is to gently lift the salmon on to a suitably pretty serving dish – good idea to use a couple of fish slices to lift it, and move decisively. Remember to serve only one of the pieces of fish – we have plans for the other fillet. Keep and freeze the poaching liquor as the base for your fishcakes. Don't strain it, but pick out the bay leaves. Tumble the spuds on to the plate and finish with some jaunty lemon and the finest English spears of the season.

SALMON AND HORSERADISH FISHCAKES
WITH CRÈME FRAÎCHE TARTARE

makes: 10   preparation time: 25 minutes   cooking time: 35 minutes

Fishcakes are one of the greats of our nation, and make just about the best emergency supper as they freeze well too. On my first ever kitchen job I made and rolled about fifty a day, which translated to about six months of my life with sticky fingers covered in breadcrumbs. (You'll see what I mean when you've made them.) Fresh horseradish can be kept in root form in the freezer and grated as and when from frozen. Just squeeze over a little lemon juice to revive it. This recipe makes 10 (they're pretty big, so one is enough for me, but hungry lads may eat two).

Tartare sauce should simply never be bought – it's just not worth it. This is a 3-minute knock up and substituting crème fraîche for mayo is so much lighter and even easier. The recipe will make enough to go alongside four fishcakes, as I don't usually find myself eating 10 at one sitting. If cooking more than four fishcakes, double or treble the tartare sauce recipe accordingly.

for the fishcakes

1–1.2kg mashing spuds (use more
if you have a larger amount of salmon),
peeled and halved or quartered

50g butter

100g plain flour, plus 2 handfuls

700ml reserved liquid from the salmon poaching
(top up with water as necessary)

3 eggs

400g breadcrumbs

a big handful (25g) of parsley, chopped

4 heaped tablespoons horseradish

3 tablespoons light olive oil

2/3 of the remaining poached
salmon fillet (350–400g) (see p.113)

for the crème fraîche tartare

130g crème fraîche or Greek yoghurt

2 spring onions, sliced finely

2 tablespoons capers, chopped

3 gherkins or cornichons, sliced

a handful of dill (20g), chopped

a squeeze of lemon juice

salt and pepper

to serve

200g baby spinach leaves

1 lemon, cut into wedges

First put your spuds into a pan of cold water with a large pinch of salt. Simmer for 20–25 minutes until cooked but not mushy, then drain very thoroughly so they get a chance to release some steam and dry out a bit.

While the spuds are doing their thing, melt the butter in a saucepan, then stir 100g flour into it and let it cook for a minute, stirring all the time until it starts to bubble in a frothy kind of way. Start adding the poaching liquor (complete with the diced onion) bit by bit, mixing well and thoroughly until it's all incorporated and you're left with a smooth sauce. Keep stirring over the heat for a couple of minutes to cook out the flour. This will also help thicken the sauce a bit more.

Season the sauce and let it cool, preferably in the freezer for a few minutes, which will be speedier than the fridge. Things will move faster if you spread it out on a tray to cool – the sauce needs to be cold and thick, but not frozen, to make it easier to roll the fishcakes.

While the sauce is chilling, give your spuds a mash and move them into a bowl that will fit in your fridge. Add one of the eggs, beaten, a third of the breadcrumbs (just do this by eye), the parsley, horseradish and salmon, gently flaked. Last of all, add the yummy sauce, which by now should be good and cold. Add a bit of seasoning and combine all the ingredients really well. Your hands are the best tool here.

Stick the mixture in the fridge, covered, for as long as you can. The longer you leave it, the easier it is to handle – overnight is best, but if you only have an hour I'd whack it in the freezer.

When your mixture is chilled and you're ready for the messy bit, prepare three shallow trays, plus a lightly floured one at the end to put them on: the first gets the remaining two handfuls of flour, heavily seasoned with salt and pepper; the second the two eggs, beaten with two tablespoons of water, and the breadcrumbs go in the last one.

Divide the fishcake mix into ten balls, each weighing about 200g. In batches, transfer four balls to the flour tray (don't worry about shaping them into perfect balls until you're in the breadcrumb tray). Once these are all lightly coated with flour move them to the eggy tray, which is where it starts to get messy: all of their surfaces have to be totally but lightly covered in egg for the breadcrumbs to adhere, but you don't want to leave them in the egg tray for too long or they will start going soft, making them harder to handle. Finally, they travel to the breadcrumbs, and then on to a lightly floured tray for resting until all the others are done. Shape them into your idea of a fishcake. Once you're happy with the shape, turn them over so you get a nice sharp edge. Wash your hands between batches, or you'll find you are wearing egg-and-crumb gloves. I've learnt from experience that the more of a nightmare the mix is to handle, the lighter the eat will be at the end. Now, you can either freeze the lot, or have some for supper.

To cook, preheat the oven to 180°C/160°C fan/gas mark 4. Heat a thick-bottomed, oven-proof frying pan (and I wouldn't try to cook more than four in each pan) with three tablespoons of light olive oil. When it's nice and hot, gently lay them in, fry for a couple of minutes until you can see the edges going golden, then gently turn them over and whack them in the oven for 15–20 minutes.

While the fishcakes are cooking, use the time to throw together the tartare sauce: just mix all the ingredients together in a bowl. I like to serve these with a simple spinach salad, lemon wedge and a hearty dollop of the tartare.

SALMON AND CORN CHOWDER

serves: 4   preparation time: 20 minutes   cooking time: 1 hour 15 minutes

The secret of a good chowder is a good stock, and the basis of this is already in place from our salmon bones. Simmering the shucked corn cobs gives a secondary level of stock infusion – it's amazing how much flavour they have to impart, and it makes a very compelling backdrop to all the bits of veg.

This soup proves to be a winner with all ages – colourful, too.

for the stock
bones and head of the salmon
100ml white wine
1 onion, peeled and quartered
2 sticks of celery, broken in two
1 whole chilli
3 cloves of garlic, whole and peeled
2 carrots, peeled and snapped in half
5 peppercorns
1.5 litres water

1 heaped tablespoon butter
1 large red onion, peeled and diced small
3 cloves of garlic, peeled and finely chopped
2 sticks of celery
1 red pepper
1 large potato (about 300g), peeled
salt and pepper
1 sweetcorn cob
120ml double cream
what's left of the poached salmon fillet, around 200g (see p.115)
½ cucumber
a big handful of parsley (25g)

If you haven't done so already, knock up your stock by putting all the ingredients in a pan without salt, and bringing to a gentle simmer before turning down to the point where it's just steaming. Leave on a very low heat for 45 minutes, then strain and leave to settle.

About half an hour after the stock has gone on, start to get your chowder base ready. Melt the butter in a big, wide pan on a medium-low heat, and cook the onion and garlic in it with a lid on for a few minutes without colouring.

Top, tail and wash the celery stalks well, then split each one lengthways and slice the thin sticks to make small dice. Stir the celery into the pan too, and pop the lid back on.

Use a vegetable peeler to take the skin off the pepper (very indigestible). De-seed and dice it, and add it to the pan. Grate the potato coarsely. Turn the heat up a nudge and add the potato to the pan; give it a good roll around and add a generous amount of salt and pepper.

For the couple of minutes it takes for the grated potato to warm through, stand the corn cob on its end on your chopping board and cut down it vertically in strips so that the kernels fall off. Set these aside for the time being, but cut/break the cob in two and throw this in the pot with the fish stock and double cream.

Let everything simmer away for 15 minutes, then turn the heat off. Stir in the reserved corn kernels, flake the salmon into little pieces and add it to the chowder before tasting for seasoning.

Let everything sit for a minute with a lid on while you peel and seed the cucumber, chopping it into tiny dice: this is not a camp garnish, but a part of the dish, as lightly cooked cucumber has a gorgeously delicate flavour and texture.

Take the corn-cob halves out of the chowder and stir in the parsley. Sprinkle the cucumber into individual, pre-warmed bowls and ladle over the chowder.

You would be right to suggest that one approach to Economy Gastronomy might be to buy a nice small piece of lamb just big enough for one meal – no wasted food and no wasted cash . . . However, the approach here is a little different. I am suggesting you splash out on a whole lamb shoulder and work it wisely so that you end up with three meals from it, not just one!

Sunday roast does not necessarily mean roast potatoes and gravy. Sometimes it's quite nice to strike out and do something a little different. The first recipe in my 3-day meal plan is definitely the headline act. The lamb is studded with garlic and rosemary and then cooked long and slow before being served up with grilled Mediterranean vegetables and a smoky aubergine dip.

Meal 2 is a much more British affair: shepherd's pie is often knocked up with minced lamb, however the recipe here uses the leftover roast lamb supplemented with vegetables and potatoes. The final dish is pure Economy Gastronomy – the meagre remnants of your shepherd's pie would probably be binned in any house in your street – apart from yours that is! Because you now have full access to my Leftover Shepherd's Pie Baked in a Loaf recipe on page 127.

Don't panic if the thought of lamb three days in a row seems like too much of a good thing. The shepherd's pie mix freezes perfectly, allowing you a night off cooking duties as required!

SHOULDER OF LAMB

SLOW-ROASTED SHOULDER OF LAMB WITH A GRILLED VEGETABLE
AND WHITE BEAN SALAD AND SMOKY AUBERGINE

SHEPHERD'S PIE

LEFTOVER SHEPHERD'S PIE BAKED IN A LOAF WITH PICKLED RED CABBAGE

SLOW-ROASTED SHOULDER OF LAMB ⓟ
WITH A GRILLED VEGETABLE AND
WHITE BEAN SALAD AND SMOKY AUBERGINE

serves: 4   preparation time: 30 minutes   cooking time: 3 hours

To cook the complete recipe I would actually recommend making the smoky aubergine first. This can then be kept in the fridge for at least a couple of days. On the day, I would make the salad whilst the lamb is roasting.

1 large whole lamb shoulder on the bone (about 2kg)

4 cloves of garlic, peeled and finely sliced

a few sprigs of rosemary

1 lamb stock cube, whisked into 300ml boiling water

200ml reasonably good red wine

for the smoky aubergine

2 aubergines

3 cloves of garlic, peeled and chopped

2 tablespoons Greek yoghurt

juice of ½ lemon

for the salad

olive oil

2 red peppers, deseeded and cut straight across into thick rings

2 yellow peppers, deseeded and cut straight across into thick rings

1 red onion, peeled and sliced into thick rings

3 courgettes, cut diagonally into 1cm slices

2 flat mushrooms, cut into thick slices

1 x 400g tin of butter beans, drained

20 cherry tomatoes, halved

a bunch of basil leaves, torn into large pieces

a handful of rocket leaves

100g feta cheese, crumbled

1 tablespoon balsamic vinegar

To make the smoky aubergine, puncture each aubergine all over with a skewer and finely chop 3 cloves of garlic to a paste. Place a large frying pan on the stove and allow it to get really hot, then drop the flame underneath to its lowest setting. Don't add any oil – just place the aubergines in the pan and allow the heat to char the skin and cook the insides. Turn the aubergines every 5 minutes so that each side is well cooked. If the skin is black and burned, you have done well. This is the smoky bit!

Cool the aubergines for a few minutes, then cut them open and scrape out the flesh, taking care to include all the outer flesh attached to the skin, which will taste the most smoky. Chop the flesh very finely to a purée and mix in the Greek yoghurt, lemon juice and chopped garlic. This can be done in a food processor for half the effort, and you'll get a much smoother texture. Store, covered, in the fridge.

Roasting the lamb is very simple. Preheat your oven to 200°C/180°C fan/gas mark 6. While the oven heats, take the lamb, pierce it about 5mm deep with the tip of a sharp knife and poke a sliver of garlic into the incision. Repeat this process until you have about 20 slivers of garlic dotted around the shoulder. Do exactly the same with the rosemary. Place the lamb on a roasting tray and put it into the hot oven. After about 10 minutes check that it is beginning to brown and, if so, drop the temperature to 140°C/120°C fan/gas mark 1. Pour the lamb stock and the red wine over the meat into the roasting tray. Every so often return to the oven, scoop out the stock and pour it back over the roasting joint.

Make the salad while the lamb is cooking. Heat a ribbed grill pan and wet it with a splash of olive oil. Working in batches, cook the peppers, onion, courgette and mushrooms until each is just cooked through and coloured by the ribbing in the pan. Place all the cooked vegetables in a bowl and add the tinned beans, cherry tomatoes, basil, rocket leaves and feta cheese. Then add a splash of both olive oil and balsamic vinegar. Season, toss everything together and leave to one side.

The lamb will need at least 2 hours in the oven, at which point it should be a deep brown colour and very well cooked. Obviously, if you have bought a large shoulder it may need a bit longer. You should also find that the roasting tray is full of rich lamb stock. Remove the lamb and rest it somewhere warm for up to 20 minutes before serving it. The stock in the tray should be poured into a small pan. Skim off any excess fat and add about 300ml of water. This should give you about 600ml of very rich, lamby gravy. At the table I would suggest pulling the meat off in chunks with a fork rather than carving it.

SHEPHERD'S PIE [Ⓟ]

serves: 4   preparation time: 20 minutes   cooking time: 50 minutes

Now, I love shepherd's pie made with mince, but when you use leftover roast lamb it actually tastes that bit better. This could always be because I am a penny-pinching old git who loves the taste of saving money, but I really do recommend you try it yourself. This recipe is designed to be made with a bare minimum of meat just in case, when you served your slow-roasted lamb, you were forced to watch in horror as your guests came back for more . . . and then more again. Years ago, when shepherds made pies rather than buying them, they would have supplemented the meat with seasonal vegetables, so this recipe does feel fairly genuine.

320g cold leftover roast lamb (more if you have it)
1 tablespoon vegetable oil
1 onion, peeled and finely chopped
2 cloves of garlic, peeled and finely chopped
1 teaspoon chopped rosemary and/or thyme
2 carrots, peeled and diced to 1cm cubes
½ swede, peeled and diced to 1cm cubes
1 large parsnip, peeled and diced to 1cm cubes
½ x 400g tin of chopped tomatoes
1 litre meat stock (it's fine to use a cube) – add any leftover gravy to this
150g peas (frozen are OK)
enough mashed potato to cover the top

First of all, chop all the meat into fine dice (it will never be as fine as mince, but that's OK). Then heat the oil in a wide saucepan on the stove and, when hot, add the onion, garlic and herbs and allow to colour slightly. Next add the carrots, swede and parsnip and let all this sizzle together for a couple of minutes. Tip in the chopped tomatoes and stock and bring to a simmer. Now add the chopped lamb and let the whole mixture cook down uncovered until it's thick and richly flavoured. Finally, stir in the peas and put the whole lot into an ovenproof casserole dish and allow to cool slightly.

Generously spread mash over the top and bake in the oven at 180°C/160°C fan/gas mark 4 for about 40–50 minutes, until golden brown and piping hot. Round up the sheep, sit back and enjoy your leftovers.

LEFTOVER SHEPHERD'S PIE BAKED IN A LOAF
WITH PICKLED RED CABBAGE

serves: 4   preparation time: 15 minutes   cooking time: 25 minutes

I imagine shepherds are fairly tired and hungry at the end of their day, so they probably don't leave much pie for the next day. However, if you find there is some left over I know just the thing to do. This is my own invention. Okay, I haven't discovered the genome and I didn't climb Everest in shorts and a tank top, but I have worked out a way of turning a tiny speck of leftover shepherd's pie into a meal fit for . . . well, a shepherd, I guess.

150ml malt vinegar
75g Demerara sugar
½ small red cabbage
4 crusty white rolls
at least 2 tablespoons leftover shepherd's pie per person
100g grated Lancashire cheese
sweet chilli sauce, to serve

First of all, prepare the red cabbage. This job could actually be done weeks in advance, because it keeps perfectly well in an old (sterilized) jam jar. Prepare the pickling liquor by boiling the vinegar and sugar together until the liquid is reduced by about half. Taste before cooling it – the balance of sharp and sweet should mellow the flavour but do expect it to have a kick. Meanwhile, finely slice the cabbage – and I mean finely – and put it in a bowl. When the pickling liquor is cool, pour it into the bowl and leave your cabbage to marinate for at least a couple of hours and preferably overnight.

Now you are ready to proceed. Cut the tops off the crusty rolls and pull out a little of the bread inside, though you do need to leave a decent amount intact. You should now have a roll with a cavity big enough to hold that leftover shepherd's pie. Finish the job by sprinkling the grated cheese over the visible shepherd's pie, then bake at 150°C/130°C fan/gas mark 2 for about 15 minutes, until the pie mix is hot and the cheese has melted. Don't bake it any longer, though, because the bread roll will dry out and become too crusty. Serve with the red cabbage and lashings of sweet chilli sauce.

In Britain we eat a lot of chicken, and I bet you of all the whole birds bought the vast majority of them are roasted. The sad thing is that most of the time, after everyone has enjoyed their Sunday roast, the chicken carcass is then just thrown away. Absolute madness when it has so much more to give – enough for another whole meal at least.

This bedrock and the following two tumbledown recipes all illustrate different ways to eat better and spend less. The Arroz con Pollo (chicken and rice) ensures you make the most of your chicken, and the incidental pâté ensures you make the most of your time. Just whack a few bits in a dish for the pâté, put the stuffed chicken on the shelf above them and two jobs are done at once.

ROAST CHICKEN
TWICE-STUFFED CHICKEN WITH CREAMED CORN AND PARSLEY POTATOES
AN INCIDENTAL CHICKEN LIVER PÂTÉ
ARROZ CON POLLO (CHICKEN AND RICE)

TWICE-STUFFED CHICKEN ⒶWITH CREAMED CORN
AND PARSLEY POTATOES

serves: 4   preparation time: 20 minutes   cooking time: 1 hour 40 minutes

The principal stuffing in this recipe (the one inside, not the one under the skin) is the very essence of Economy Gastronomy: it uses up old bread and gives an interesting, much lighter result than the often lead-like sage 'n' onion. It triumphs in both money and flavour, so why anyone would buy stuffing (or continue to throw away old bits of bread) in the face of such reasoning is nothing short of bonkers.

100g butter

250ml chicken stock (fresh or from a cube)

half a baguette (about 220g), preferably stale

75g smoked pancetta lardons

30g flat-leaf parsley, washed and finely chopped

2 medium shallots, peeled and thinly sliced

zest of 1 lemon

6 slices of air-cured ham
(e.g. Serrano, Parma – don't buy an expensive one)

salt and pepper

1 large chicken, the best quality you can afford
(around 2.2–2.4kg)

a few sprigs of sage, leaves picked and washed
(stalks reserved for the pâté)

1 tablespoon olive oil

around 5 spuds (about 1kg), peeled and halved

500ml chicken stock – not from a cube
in this instance

1 white onion, peeled and finely chopped

3 sweetcorn cobs

a small handful of thyme, leaves picked

50g butter

30g flat-leaf parsley, roughly chopped

Preheat the oven to 200°C/180°C fan/gas mark 6. In a saucepan, melt the butter in 250ml of stock. In a big mixing bowl, tear the bread into fingertip-sized nuggets, and mix it with the pancetta, parsley, shallots and lemon zest. Before washing the grater, pour the hot stock/melted butter combination over the grater and into the bowl to get all of the little bits of zest out. Set four slices of ham aside, then chop the rest and stir into the bread mixture, along with a little salt and a good crack of pepper. Set aside to soak for about 20 minutes, while you sort out your second stuffing.

Using your fingers, gently work your way under the skin of the breast (keeping your fingers wet will help), until you have loosened the skin of the breast from the meat on each side of the bird. Start at the open end and work right up to the wing joint at the fatter end of the breast – a butter knife or the back of a teaspoon can help if your fingers aren't long enough, but don't use anything with a point that might pierce the skin.

Get each cavity under the skin good and wet, then press two pieces of ham together and wet the outside of them too. Slide the ham slices into one cavity, making sure they get right to the end. Wet the sage leaves and slide these in on top of the ham – about 4–5 each side. Repeat with the other side.

Sit your bird in a roasting tray. Mix the bread stuffing and shove it inside the chicken – you may have some over, which you can put in a little tray and bake for 30 minutes as a cook's snack. Close up the chicken, using a wooden skewer to go through the fatter sides and parson's nose. Rub lightly all over with the olive oil, seasoning the skin too. Cook the bird breast-side down for the first hour in the middle of the oven. Turn her over for another 20 minutes so the crown browns. When cooked, drain the fat, reserving for the pâté.

The spuds go on when you turn the chicken over. Cover them with cold salted water, and simmer for 20 minutes until they are just cooked. Remove the bird from the oven and rest it, breast-side-up, on a warm platter and cover with foil.

Put the roasting tray back on the hob and simmer the fresh chicken stock in it for 5 minutes until it has reduced to the lightest of sauces. Meanwhile, stand the corn cobs on their ends on your chopping board and cut down them vertically, removing the tender kernels. Fry the onions and corn in the butter over a high heat. Stir to coat, then put a lid on for 5 minutes while you strip the thyme and stir that in too. Turn the heat off, season well and pound the kernels with the end of a rolling pin (or you can use a potato masher as a quick alternative) until you have achieved a creamy texture. Drain the spuds and toss them with pepper and parsley. Give everybody a bit of breast and leg meat and a spoonful of stuffing, saving a thigh or drumstick for your Arroz con Pollo on p.135.

AN INCIDENTAL CHICKEN LIVER PÂTÉ

serves: 8 as a starter (makes 2 or 3 jam-jars full)
preparation time: 30 minutes   cooking time: 2½ hours

Pâté lovers of the world: passing up the chance to throw this together while you're cooking your chicken would be a real missed opportunity.

Ridiculously cheap, tasty, easy and goes a long, long way.

400g chicken livers

2 small shallots, peeled and finely sliced

6–8 cloves of garlic, peeled and smashed with
the flat of a knife

a few sage stalks
(from the leaves used in the stuffing)

a few branches of thyme and rosemary,
washed and left whole

2 duck legs

250g pork belly (skin cut off but reserved)

2 tablespoons medium or dry sherry

sea salt and freshly ground black pepper

In an ovenproof ceramic tray, mix the chicken livers, shallots, garlic and herbs together. If your chicken comes with gizzards, neck and heart, clean them, then add them to the tray. Nestle the duck legs and piece of belly, plus its skin, among the rest of the ingredients in the tray, and cover with foil.

Put the tray on the oven shelf below the chicken at the same time you roast the bird, and when the chicken comes out, turn the oven down to 160°C/140°C fan/gas mark 3 and cook for another hour. When the cooking time is up, take the tray out of the oven, pull the foil off, and drain off the fat (but not the meat juices) into the bowl you poured the grease from the chicken into earlier.

Chuck out the herb stalks. When the meat is cool enough to touch, shred the duck legs and pork into a separate bowl, chucking out any huge pieces of fat, bones and belly skin, but making sure that you keep some fat with the livers. If you have a neck in there, pick the meat off that and add it to the meat from the duck and pork.

In the food processor, whizz the livers and garlic with all the juices from the bottom of the dish until totally smooth, adding a few tablespoons of the fat and the sherry. Scrape into the bowl with the shredded meat from the pork and duck, stir well and season to taste – black pepper is a must, and you'll probably need a bit of salt too.

Spoon the pâté into a large sterilized jar or a few smaller sterilized jam jars (see p.313), giving them several good, hard bangs on the table to knock the air out of them. Pour on the fat to make a sealing layer about 2cm thick – this keeps the air out of the pâté, so it will last in the jars for much longer. Keep in the fridge for a fortnight.

Keep any remaining fat in a jam jar to use for roast spuds, or instead of olive oil next time you're making roast chicken. It keeps for months in the fridge.

If paella wasn't already considered a peasant dish, I'd describe this as a poor man's paella . . . which I guess actually kind of works, given the theory behind this book.

You really don't have to have much visible meat left on your bird at all to make this Latin American standard – the main chickeny flavour comes from cooking the rice in the stock. You can also use a shorter, fatter grain, like paella or risotto rice, but I've done it here with long grain as it cooks faster.

A perfect weekday supper.

the chicken carcass, plus whatever bits of leg and breast meat you have left over, shredded

1 red onion, peeled and cut into large dice

1 teaspoon cumin seeds

2 tablespoons extra-virgin olive oil

3 cloves of garlic, peeled and sliced

1 red chilli, sliced

1 large carrot, scrubbed, halved and cut into 1cm half-moons

½ teaspoon smoked paprika

250g vine-ripened tomatoes

1 red pepper, deseeded and cut into large dice

1 x 330ml bottle of lager

400g long-grain rice

200g frozen peas, defrosted

40g coriander, washed and roughly chopped

3 limes

for the stock

1 onion, quartered

1 carrot, halved

1 celery stick

1 leek

2 cloves of garlic, peeled

2 bay leaves

a bunch of parsley stalks

and whatever else you have lurking in your fridge – see my bit about stocks on p.212

Take a good 10 minutes to really strip all the remaining meat off the carcass – even though it may look bare, it's amazing how much meat is still on there. Don't forget to flip the bird upside-down and dig around on the underside so you can get the lovely tender oysters out too.

Use your hands to break the carcass into two or three pieces, place all the bones in a close-fitting pan and cover with a litre of water with the stock vegetables. Bring to a simmer then turn down until the stock is barely steaming, pop a lid on and let it do its thing for 45 minutes. Strain it off and measure how much stock you have. There should be around 800ml. If you find you have less, just top it up with water.

In a big saucepan, fry the onion and cumin seeds in the olive oil over a high heat. After a couple of minutes add the garlic, chilli, carrots and smoked paprika, and stir the mixture well as it sizzles.

Cut the tomatoes into chunks and add them to the pot along with the pepper pieces, then turn the heat down to medium, put a lid on and let the whole concoction simmer gently for about 10 minutes.

Pour the beer in and, keeping the lid off, let the contents of the pan come to a boil, add the stock, bring back to the boil and stir in the rice. Simmer for 25–30 minutes, starting uncovered, but put the lid on when you can see the rice through the liquid and turn the heat right down low. From this point it should be done in 10 minutes.

Taste the rice to make sure it's cooked, then turn the heat off and stir the peas and the shredded chicken into the mixture. Add the chopped coriander, keeping a little back to pretty up the top of each bowl, and squeeze in the juice of around 1½ limes, tasting as you go to see if you need a little more. Cut the rest of the limes into wedges.

Check the seasoning at the end – salt is a must – before serving with the coriander on top and the lime wedges on the side.

Spag Bol

chilli con carne

cottage pie

For some reason, most of my friends assume that when I'm at home I sit down with my family to sumptuous banquets featuring the finest, most expensive ingredients imaginable. When I discussed my ideas for this book, some of them were a little surprised that minced beef was top of my list of ingredients that I thought simply must feature.

Nearly all of us have eaten minced beef at some time or another (I did yesterday, as it happens) in one of various guises. In our house, mince turns up at the dinner table at least once a week in the form of one of the recipes featured here.

I tend to cook my mince on a sort of scaled-down production-line method. I snap up a kilo or two of the stuff when I see it going cheap and then set aside a couple of hours in which that mince becomes three very different dishes. I then scoop the finished mince dishes into freezer bags and chuck them in the freezer until required. These are the ultimate home-made ready meals.

The following three recipes are presented in the above format, though of course it's entirely permissible to select your favourite and just cook that.

for the basic mince	2 teaspoons fresh rosemary, chopped
6 tablespoons vegetable oil	2kg minced beef
6 onions, peeled and chopped	2 x 400g tins of chopped tomatoes
12 cloves of garlic, peeled and chopped	2 tablespoons Worcestershire sauce
2 teaspoons fresh thyme, chopped	6 beef stock cubes

Heat a large saucepan and add half the vegetable oil, throw in the onions, garlic and herbs and allow them to sizzle away on a high heat for a few minutes – a little colour on them is no bad thing. When they are softened, turn off the heat and put the pot to one side; we'll be back to it shortly.

Next heat a large frying pan and, using a little of the remaining oil, fry the minced beef in manageable batches. Overloading the pan will not speed things up because the pan will lose heat, so take your time. The idea is to colour the mince and create a crust rather than cook it at this stage. As the meat goes a dark brown colour, so its flavour develops, giving the finished dishes a more complex taste and a better colour.

As each batch browns, tip it out of the pan and into the pot which contains your onions, garlic and herbs. Once this process is finished, put the pot back on the stove and turn up the heat. Now tip in all the tomatoes and stir it into the meat. Add the Worcestershire sauce too.

Meanwhile, boil a kettle and make up 1.5 litres of stock with the 6 stock cubes.

Pour the stock into the now-simmering beef and tomatoes and allow the whole lot to simmer for about 1½ hours, uncovered, until it has reduced slightly and started to look like a pot of braised mince should look.

At this point the meat is cooked, but it is not ready to serve. What you do now is turn this basic braised mince into the following three dishes, using a third of the braised mince above as your starting point for each. If you choose to do this later, cool your basic mince mix and store in the fridge until ready to go.

BEEF MINCE
SPAGHETTI BOLOGNESE
COTTAGE PIE
CHILLI CON CARNE

SPAGHETTI BOLOGNESE ℗

serves: 4   preparation time: 15 minutes   cooking time: 1 hour

Spaghetti bolognese originates from Bologna in Italy and is without a doubt one of the most popular dishes in the world (and rightly so).

If I were served this by a friend, I would be delighted – 'Cor, I love a plate of spag bol!' I would cry. However, if the following week I were served the same dish at a Buckingham Palace banquet, I would probably exclaim, 'Ma'am, this is a truly marvellous batch of ragù!' This is because 'ragù' is the correct term for what the rest of us know as 'spag bol'.

When required, you can simply reheat your ragù and serve it with spaghetti and lots of Parmesan cheese.

2 tablespoons olive oil
2 sticks of celery, finely diced
4 cloves of garlic, peeled and chopped
2 rashers of smoked bacon, very finely shredded
350ml red wine (2 glasses)
⅓ of your braised mince (800g)
2 x 400g tins of chopped tomatoes
1 beef stock cube, made into 250ml beef stock

to serve
350g dried spaghetti
30g Parmesan cheese, finely grated

Heat a saucepan and pour in the olive oil. When it's nice and hot, chuck in the celery, garlic and bacon and let these bits cook for a minute or two. Pour in the wine and let it boil and reduce until the pan is almost dry.

Now add the tins of chopped tomatoes. Bring these to a simmer and then pour in the braised mince that you prepared earlier. Pour in the stock too and let the contents of the pan simmer away for 45 minutes, uncovered, by which time the ragù should look very rich and sauce-like, with a good flavour.

Season the ragù as required and if storing it in the fridge or freezer spread it out thinly on a tray to quickly remove the heat before bagging it up, labelling it and putting it away.

When ready to serve, cook the spaghetti in a large pan of salted water for 9–10 minutes, until al dente. Drain well and put back in the cooking pan, pour over the bolognese sauce and mix well into the pasta. Divide between plates and hand round the Parmesan.

COTTAGE PIE [Ⓟ]

serves: 4–6   preparation time: 25 minutes   cooking time: 1 hour 40 minutes

This is mince preparation number two and frankly it may well end up as the simplest recipe in the book. I have included a good dash of Worcestershire sauce and a dash of chilli sauce because I think it is improved by having a little 'bite'. This is my own customization and one that you are allowed to kick into touch if you prefer your cottage pie in the more traditional manner.

2 tablespoons vegetable oil

2 onions, peeled and finely chopped

⅓ of your braised mince (800g)

2 large carrots, peeled and diced fairly small

2 beef stock cubes, made into 250ml strong beef stock

300g frozen peas

several dashes of Worcestershire sauce

a couple of dashes of chilli sauce

800g Maris Piper or King Edward potatoes, peeled

75ml milk

40g butter

30g mature Cheddar, grated

First of all, heat a large saucepan and add the oil. Fry the onions over a high heat until they are golden brown and then add the mince. Add the carrots and stock and let the whole thing simmer for about 45 minutes, uncovered, until the mixture is rich in flavour and fairly thick – it won't be as runny as the bolognese because it isn't going to be used as a sauce.

Towards the end of cooking, throw in the peas and the Worcestershire and chilli sauces. Taste and season as you wish and then either serve up or store for later. If storing it in the fridge or freezer, spread it out thinly on a tray to quickly remove the heat before bagging it up, labelling it and putting it away.

To serve your cottage pie, cook the potatoes in boiling salted water for 25 minutes, until tender. Drain well and mash. Add the milk and butter and mix in well. Preheat the oven to 200°C/180°C fan/gas mark 6. Spread the mince mixture into a shallow baking dish and cover the top with mashed potato. Then sprinkle over some grated mature Cheddar and bake in the oven for 30–40 minutes until it is piping hot and has a crispy brown topping.

CHILLI CON CARNE ℗

serves: 4   preparation time: 20 minutes   cooking time: 1 hour

When I was a young chef earning very little money and sharing a south London flat with friends, we used to have chilli con carne when guests or visitors came round. At all other times, we would eat tinned food and ingredients picked off the reject shelf in the local supermarket. Sad, I know, but no one had written this book back then, so how were we to know any different?

Nowadays I cook this at home and serve it as a midweek supper without the need for guests or visitors, which I guess is a mark of social success in some small way.

Everyone has a version of chilli con carne, I expect. This is mine, quick and simple, which I like to serve with rice, tortilla bread and bowls of soured cream, grated cheese and chopped avocado.

2 tablespoons vegetable oil
1 onion, peeled and finely chopped
2 cloves of garlic, peeled and finely chopped
1 teaspoon ground cumin
1 teaspoon ground coriander
1 teaspoon chilli powder
1 teaspoon smoked paprika
350ml red wine (2 glasses)
1 x 400g tin of chopped tomatoes
a splash of Worcestershire sauce
2 red chillies, finely chopped

⅓ of your braised mince (800g)
about 20 mushrooms (250g), thickly sliced
1 x 410g tin of red kidney beans, rinsed and drained
1 stock cube, made into 250ml stock

to serve
300g long-grain rice
4 warmed tortillas
142ml pot of soured cream
100g mature Cheddar, grated
1 avocado, chopped

Heat the oil in a large heavy-based saucepan and fry the onions and garlic until softened and slightly browned. Stir in all the ground spices and then pour in the red wine and let it simmer and reduce by about half.

Next add the chopped tomatoes, Worcestershire sauce and chopped red chilli and again let this simmer for a few minutes. Add your braised mince, mushrooms, kidney beans and beef stock and cook this gently, uncovered, for about 45 minutes until it's richly flavoured and thick in consistency.

If storing it in the fridge or freezer, spread it out thinly on a tray to quickly remove the heat before bagging it up, labelling it and putting it away.

When ready to serve, cook the rice according to pack instructions. Warm the tortillas in foil in the oven for 10 minutes. Put the soured cream, cheese and chopped avocado into bowls. Place the whole lot in the middle of the table and let everyone dig in.

LUNCH

**SOUPED-UP SOUP
(POTATO AND PARSLEY SOUP
WITH A POACHED EGG)**

**BUBBLE AND SQUEAK
WITH BACON AND EGG**

BRUTUS SALAD

**FRESHLY BAKED BREAD
(AND CHEESE)**

**SPICY BLACK BEAN
QUESADILLA**

**MORE THAN SIMPLY
A STEAK SANDWICH**

AS A BOY, I CAN RECALL MY DAD CYCLING BACK FROM WORK EACH DAY TO A COOKED LUNCH IN HIS HOUR OFF. IN THOSE DAYS THIS WAS FAIRLY COMMONPLACE, BUT FOR VARIOUS REASONS, BOTH SOCIAL AND ECONOMIC, THIS IS NO LONGER THE CASE. NOWADAYS, WEEKDAY LUNCH IS BOUGHT AND EATEN ON THE HOOF OR MISSED OUT ALTOGETHER.

What we are doing is slowly removing this meal from our daily routine and it's not without precedent. In years past, a cooked breakfast, afternoon tea and traditional supper were all part of the daily routine of this nation. Sadly, all three have slipped from view. Do we wish lunch to go the same way? Soon we will have nothing more than the evening meal left to look forward to.

Our friends in mainland Europe have taken a different tack. They positively love a decent lunch and think nothing of a two-hour lunch break which includes a cooked meal followed by a snooze. Surely this is preferable to a sandwich bought at the petrol station and eaten in the lift on the way to a meeting?

I have nothing against sandwiches – I love them. But if you plan on sandwiches for lunch, then at least consider making your own. A sandwich is one of the quickest things to prepare and with just a little invention (home-made coleslaw to go with some peppered salami, perhaps) they can provide a pleasing lunch.

It's on weekends that lunch comes into its own. Sunday lunch needs no explanation. A nation whose people spurn lunch all week suddenly turns into a group of frenzied lunch-eating maniacs. Roast beef, pork and lamb are consumed with passion in homes and restaurants up and down the country.

So that leaves Saturdays as the day for cooked lunches, then. Well, I for one am prepared to do my bit to preserve the classic lunch and on the following pages Allegra and I have given some cheap, simple and quick lunch options that you can enjoy any day of the week.

Paul.

SOUPED-UP SOUP ⓐ
(POTATO AND PARSLEY SOUP
WITH A POACHED EGG)

serves: 4   preparation time: 20–25 minutes   cooking time: 25 minutes

Soup is my default lunch. My screensaver, if you like. Left to my own devices, at home, I'll go for soup at lunchtime.

I don't always have home-made, the ready ones are a good enough base these days, but I can't help playing with them – mixing tomato with lentil, adding a few bits and bobs like croutons, cottage cheese, pesto and chilli (but not all together). But on cooler days, I tend to make my own much more, and this recipe takes the simple to the special with minimal effort.

1 heaped tablespoon butter
1 leek, halved lengthways, finely sliced and washed
2 cloves of garlic, peeled and roughly chopped
3 potatoes (about 600g), peeled
700ml light chicken or veg stock
salt and pepper
40g flat-leaf parsley, roughly picked and washed
4 eggs
1 smoked duck breast (or 2 thick slices smoked ham)

Put a saucepan on a high heat with the butter and when it's melted, tip in the leek and garlic. You don't want the leeks to colour, so once they're sizzling nicely, turn the heat down and put a lid on.

Cut the spuds into 2cm thick slices, stack up a few at a time, cut them into chip shapes, then line them up and chop into approximately 2cm to 3cm dice. Stir these into the pan then pour in the stock. Season with salt and pepper, turn the heat up and pop a lid on. Boil fast for 12–15 minutes until the spuds are cooked.

Ladle half of the soup into a blender and pulse until smooth. Add the parsley then pour in the rest of the soup. Blitz for a minute till the parsley is coarsely chopped – I think it looks nice if there are still visible bits of green – then pour everything back into the pan, lid on, over a medium heat.

Taste your soup – it will probably take a bit more salt and pepper at this stage. When you see it starting to steam and little bubbles just beginning to appear, crack the eggs in as far apart as you can, but not right at the edge, and put the lid back on.

Cut your duck breast in half. Slice one half, stacking the slices, and then cutting into matchsticks. Line up your matchsticks and chop again to make small dice (you can freeze the rest of the duck breast or keep it in the fridge for sandwiches/salads). Share these among four warmed soup bowls.

After your eggs have been in for 4–5 minutes, gently lift them out with a slotted spoon, taking care to release them if they're stuck to the bottom of the pan. Put one on top of the duck in each bowl and ladle the soup around.

BUBBLE AND SQUEAK
WITH BACON AND EGG

serves: 4   preparation time: 5 minutes   cooking time: 20 minutes

If one dish were to be chosen above all others to represent thrifty eating it would have to be bubble and squeak. Totally British and slightly mad, this is traditionally a mixture of potato and cabbage (or some other brassica), lightly burned in a frying pan. This burning on of a crust is very important to the flavour of the finished dish.

For some reason bubble and squeak never tastes the same when it is assembled from raw ingredients. It really does need to be made with leftovers. Cold mash and Brussels sprouts (my personal favourite) are what is needed for a decent splodge of bubble – who says the English are eccentric?

One final point: I have often been irresistibly drawn to this dish on gastro pub menus, when it's served with something delicious like wood pigeon or wild boar sausages. Lovely . . . but then I am miffed to find the bubble and squeak coming coated in breadcrumbs, done up like a fishcake. This is far too fancy . . . probably something those continental types would do! Keep it simple.

60g butter
about 20 cooked Brussels sprouts, cut in half
about 8 tablespoons cold mashed potato
4 eggs
4 rashers of bacon

Heat a frying pan and melt half the butter. Toss in the sprouts and cook them until they start to colour on the outside. Be brave at this point and allow them to go a really dark brown – the middles will remain soft and sprout-like.

Add the mash to the frying pan. I find it easiest to do this with my hands – that way you can scatter it across the whole of the pan, which makes the mixing in easier. So, mix the contents of the pan and squelch everything down so it covers the base. Now add the remaining butter by breaking off little pieces and allowing them to melt around the edges of the pan. Don't move the potato and sprout mix. Underneath it is caramelizing, even burning, which is exactly what it should be doing. After about 3 minutes scrape and mix the potato and sprouts. Try to get the burnt bits back into the centre of the mixture, so that you have a fresh surface colouring underneath. Continue to do this until your mix is well coloured and slightly crispy.

At this point fry your eggs in a separate pan and grill your bacon, because you are moments away from serving up a money-saving British classic.

BRUTUS SALAD

serves: 2   preparation time: 15–20 minutes   cooking time: 12–15 minutes

There is absolutely nothing wrong with a Caesar salad – they're just seen as being a bit boring now, and no one does them justice at home because they can't be bothered to make the dressing. Enter Brutus – punching all the flavour buttons that his old boss had before him, but to a new tune.

With the lettuce, you just want to use the crisp, inner leaves for this salad. The outer layer can be saved for Petits Pois à la Française on p.181.

Pomegranates are very Roman and the redder they are on the outside, the better the colour inside. As I'm sure you've already concluded, their seeds and juice against the creamy dressing represent blood on toga . . .

a hunk of bread (80g), whatever kind you have around, preferably white, old is good

2 cloves of garlic, finely chopped

4 tablespoons extra-virgin olive oil

salt and pepper

70g lardons

100g feta

3 tablespoons Greek yoghurt

juice of ½–1 lemon

1 pomegranate

350g cos, baby gem or romaine lettuce

Preheat your oven to 180°C/160°C fan/gas mark 4. Cut the bread into rough 2cm chunks and put them on an oven tray. In a small bowl, mix the garlic with a tablespoon of extra-virgin olive oil and some salt and pepper. Drizzle this over the bread chunks and scrunch with your hands so all the pieces are coated with garlicky oil. Stick them in the oven on a baking tray and cook for 12 minutes, shuffling halfway through.

Fry the lardons in a small frying pan over a high heat, stirring regularly so they get an even golden-brown colour. After 5 minutes they should be shrunken and crisp. Lift them out with a slotted spoon on to kitchen roll.

To make your dressing, roughly crumble up the feta into small lumps and mix with the yoghurt, the rest of the extra-virgin olive oil, the lemon juice and some pepper.

Cut the pomegranate into quarters and dig out the seeds over a bowl with your fingers. Make sure that there is no white pith because it's very bitter. Slice your lettuce into wide ribbons and give it a wash and dry.

In a large bowl, toss the lettuce with the croutons and dressing. Divide these between two plates or shallow bowls, then scatter the bacon bits and pomegranate seeds over the top.

FRESHLY BAKED BREAD [Ⓟ]
(AND CHEESE)

makes: 3 loaves   preparation time: 15 minutes, plus proving   cooking time: 40 minutes

I feel a rant coming on! Can you call yourself a cook if you can't bake bread? I don't think so. Baking bread really is one of the most basic, universal processes going. But things have changed in the last few years and nowadays most people don't even buy their bread from a baker any more, preferring to go to the supermarket.

The bread section in my local supermarket is a stunning array of loaves from around the world, all apparently 'baked on the premises'. Unfortunately, when I lurch forward uncontrollably, anxious to bag a wonderful-looking ciabatta or focaccia or farmhouse loaf, I am always rocked right back to my senses at the merest touch of this springy, airy, long-life loaf 'stone baked' right here on an industrial estate. OK, real bread lasts only a day or two before it's got toast written all over it, but that's fine. It's so good I'd be surprised if you had any left after two days.

This is my recipe for a crusty white loaf, which is a good starting point for the novice baker. As you learn the joys of bread making, you will undoubtedly ditch the recipe for a more intriguing one, and in turn you will probably start considering buying a wood-burning oven and all sorts of baker's equipment! But that's later on. Right now you simply need to get started.

A quick word about ingredients. Yeast is a living organism that is most active at around 35 degrees centigrade. It will happily live on in your fridge for about two weeks or you can freeze it. It can be obtained mail order or by begging a kindly baker (or supermarket bakery counter) to give you a little. Alternatively you can buy a packet of the dry stuff and follow the instructions.

The type of flour makes a huge difference. Strong flour has a high gluten content, which means it's ideal for bread making. However, even strong flours vary, so try a few different ones. I personally use French strong bread flour known as T55 but you can replace it with a brown or whole-grain flour if that's your thing. If you wish to increase your choice of flour beyond the supermarket selection, go online and see what you can find.

The recipe on the next page makes three loaves. They will freeze quite happily, so never make a single loaf.

1kg T55 strong white bread flour
550ml water
20g fresh yeast
15g salt
a dish of salted water
a little extra flour for dusting

If you have a food mixer with a dough hook, life is about to take a turn for the better! Bung the flour, water, yeast and salt into the bowl, attach the dough hook and switch on. If you leave the mixture turning on the slowest setting, you will quickly have a dough. Then just allow it to keep turning, as you are now 'kneading' the dough. After about 4 minutes of kneading, switch off the machine. Cover the bowl with a damp cloth or some cling film. Let this sit out at room temperature for about 1 hour, by which time the dough will have doubled in bulk. This is known as 'proving'.

For those of us without a fancy food mixer the only consolation is that we are about to burn a few calories, because bread making *à la methode traditionelle* is a fairly strenuous affair. In a large bowl mix the flour, water, yeast and salt together. The first time you will probably try using a wooden spoon. The second time you won't bother, because you will realize spoons of any sort are utterly useless – the baker is a hands-on kind of guy! Once the dough has formed a large ball, turn it out on to a floured work surface. In one motion, push the base of the palm of your hand into the dough while pushing it forward to stretch it, then lift the front edge of your dough and bring it back over to form a ball once more. Believe me, this is much easier to do than explain! Work the dough quite vigorously and quickly for at least 10 minutes. Then put it back in a large bowl and cover it with a damp cloth or some cling film. Let this sit out at room temperature for about 1 hour to double in size. While you're waiting, I'd recommend you have a cold drink and look up the price of a decent food mixer on the internet!

Next comes the 'knocking back' stage. Simply punch your aerated dough in the bowl a few times – this will knock a little air out of it, so expect it to sink back slightly. Then turn the dough back out on to a floured surface and cut it into three even-sized chunks. Shape each of them into an oval loaf by gently flattening the dough and folding the edges back underneath. The shaping of loaves takes a little practice and experience, but there is no problem with this as even the most amusing shapes can still be baked and will taste fantastic.

Place your loaves on an oiled and floured baking tray at least 20cm apart. Paint the surface of your loaves with the salted water and then dust them liberally with flour and slash them with a knife lengthways about 5mm deep. Leave them to prove once more – about 15 minutes should be fine.

Meanwhile, preheat the oven to 240°C/220°C fan/gas mark 9. Put your bread in the oven and set a timer for 8 minutes. When the timer goes off, open the oven door for 2 minutes to let the heat escape, then reduce the heat to 190°C/170°C fan/gas mark 5, close the door and cook on for 30 minutes.

Turn the baked bread out on to a cooling rack until you can't hold back any longer. Serve while still warm with unsalted butter and your favourite cheese – mine is an aged Comté, by the way.

One final thing: it's possible to save a fortune by making all your own bread, so if you intend to make it on a regular basis I would recommend a simple step that will give you a better-tasting loaf. Each time you make some dough, cut off about 10 per cent and put it in the fridge. The next dough you make should have this lump added at the initial mixing stage. Keep this system rolling over so you always have a piece of dough ready as a starter for the next session.

SPICY BLACK BEAN QUESADILLA

makes: 2 big ones, for 2 hungry people
preparation time: 15–20 minutes   cooking time: 15 minutes

Down Mexico way, one of the things that makes their food some of the most yum-a-licious on the planet is the combination of cooked and spiced versus fresh and zingy.

You may not choose to make this on your own for lunch or supper, but for a quick-and-easy mate-drops-round or family weekender, it's a bit of a winner – just maybe cut the spice down for the kids.

Freeze the tortillas and take out as you need.

1 x 400g tin black beans
½ teaspoon ground cumin
½ teaspoon dried oregano
1 teaspoon dried chilli flakes
2 spring onions, sliced
1 pepper, diced into 1cm cubes
80g Cheddar, grated
salt and pepper

4 large (25cm) flour tortillas
1 clove of garlic
2 tablespoons light oil
a handful of coriander, washed and picked
1 ripe avocado, peeled and cut into rough chunks
2 limes
2 tablespoons pumpkin seeds

In a bowl, mix the drained black beans, cumin, oregano, chilli flakes, spring onions, pepper and grated cheese. Give this a heavy season with salt and pepper, then scrunch it all together in your hands for a couple of minutes, breaking up all the beans as you go.

Lay the tortillas out on your surface, cut the clove of garlic in half and rub the cut side vigorously all over the tortillas. Halve the bean mixture between two of the tortillas and spread out to within a centimetre of the circumference. Sit the other tortillas on top (garlicky side down) and gently push down to compress.

Put a frying pan, big enough to hold a tortilla, on a low to medium heat, pour half of the oil into the frying pan and flop in one of your quesadillas. Give it 3–4 minutes on each side, pushing down from time to time with your spatula/palette knife/fish slice. Flip the tortilla over, using your hand as a guide, and cook the other side, then turn it out and do the same with the other one, pouring in the remaining oil in between.

In a small bowl, toss together the coriander, avocado, juice of one of the limes and a pinch of salt.

When you have lifted the second tortilla out of the pan, throw the pumpkin seeds into the pan and toast for 1 minute until golden, then tip them into the bowl with the coriander and avocado.

Cut your quesadillas into six and finish with a scattering of the coriander, avocado and pumpkin seeds on top. Serve with half a lime on the side. Eat hot.

MORE THAN SIMPLY A STEAK SANDWICH ⓟ

serves: 1   preparation time: 15 minutes   cooking time: 6 minutes

A few moments ago, when I met our post lady (woman, girl, person . . . I get so confused) in the street, I asked her what her favourite sandwich was. She replied that it was cheese and tomato. Actually, she only gave me this information after satisfying herself that I was not (a) insane and (b) about to ask her out for dinner. Anyway, the point is that sandwiches have been firmly on my mind. They are simply the perfect one-stop meal, especially for lunch. If you get the filling right – say, some slices of Serrano ham, rocket and a drizzle of olive oil – they are nutritiously balanced, filling and delicious.

While I probably make two or three sandwiches a week, it's a little less often that I treat myself to the unrivalled joy of a steak sandwich. Traditionally made with a flattened sirloin steak known as a minute steak, they can prove a rather expensive treat. However, this one uses a cut called bavette, a little culinary treat that the French have kept to themselves . . . up to now. A bavette will set you back a lot less than sirloin, or rib-eye for that matter, but one word of warning – don't overcook it. Medium-rare at most.

200g bavette steak
olive oil
2 slices of your favourite bread
a few slices of tomato
a few slices of red onion
some shredded lettuce
a good dollop of mayonnaise
a dollop of horseradish relish
a dollop of Dijon mustard

I definitely think that this steak is far tastier if done on a barbecue or in a ribbed grill pan, but assuming that neither is available just pick your heaviest non-stick pan. The steak requires no advance preparation at all, but if you are going to cook it rare or medium-rare, take it out of the fridge for 15 minutes prior to cooking so that it's not fridge-cold.

To cook your steak, heat the pan until it is so hot it's almost smoking, then give the steak a wipe – no more – of olive oil and cook it for about 6 minutes in total, turning it three or four times. Then rest the steak for up to 5 (unbearable) minutes while you prepare the rest of the sandwich.

The first thing to do is to toast the bread. Wipe your chosen slices with olive oil and cook them until they are crispy on the outside but still a little soft in the middle. If using the grill pan or a barbecue, they should also take on the characteristic charred markings. On one cooked slice lay your tomato and red onion topped with a generous amount of lettuce which has been mixed with mayonnaise. Now slice the steak into long slices about 2cm thick and lay them on top. Add the horseradish and mustard, or serve them on the side. Close the sandwich, cut in half, open an ice-cold bottle of beer and enjoy.

TROLLEY-BASHING

NOT HAVING ENOUGH TIME IS THE DEFINITION OF CONTEMPORARY LIVING, AND SOME CLEVER MANUFACTURERS OUT THERE HAVE WORKED OUT WAYS TO APPEAL TO THIS FACET OF OUR LIVES.

OF THE TOP CRIMES THAT YOU CAN FIND ON THE SHELVES OF YOUR SUPERMARKET, SOME ARE RELATIVELY NEW (THINK PRE-COOKED RICE, OR READY MASH) AND OTHERS ARE LEFTOVERS FROM TIMES WHEN FRESH INGREDIENTS WERE HARDER TO FIND AND STORE (LIKE PRE-SQUEEZED LEMON JUICE).

I'M ALL FOR MOVING THE PLANET FORWARD BUT THERE ARE SOME PRODUCTS AVAILABLE TO BUY NOW THAT ARE, WITHOUT DOUBT, A STEP BACK.

BEING ABLE TO KNOCK UP YOUR OWN DRESSING CANNOT BE DESCRIBED AS HARD, AND YOU CAN'T BE SO BUSY THAT YOU DON'T HAVE 15 MINUTES TO MAKE A TOMATO SAUCE. DON'T BE FORCED INTO BUYING A JAR OF PASTEURIZED RAGÚ THAT WAS COOKED MONTHS AGO, PROBABLY IN A GALAXY FAR, FAR AWAY . . . SANDWICHES ARE A CASE IN POINT.

DEEP DOWN INSIDE YOU KNOW THESE ARE NOT SENSIBLE CHOICES, SO BEFORE YOU PLEAD IGNORANCE AS TO WHAT IS AND ISN'T OK TO BUY, HERE ARE A FEW HEADLINE THOUGHTS, AND I RECKON YOU CAN WORK THE REST OUT ON YOUR OWN.

You really aren't doing yourselves any favours if you buy . . .

- Pasta sauces
- Vinaigrettes
- Ready mash
- Prepped fruit and veg, including celery/romaine hearts, peeled spuds, pre-cut fruit
- Grated cheese
- Cooked rice, polenta or couscous
- Pre-grilled burgers/pre-roasted chicken
- Breadcrumbs and croutons
- Pre-squeezed lemon juice
- Cooked cocktail sausages
- Apple/mint/tartare sauce
- 'Fresh' stock
- Cheat's pre-prepared garlic and ginger
- Prepped salads (they go off much faster)
- Marinades
- Smoothies
- Cake mix and pre-made icing
- Stuffing mix
- Some dried herbs: parsley, basil and coriander
- Instant porridge
- Ready meals (sorry)

Things it's OK to buy, though fussy foodies may tell you otherwise . . .

- Pastry

- Podded peas and broad beans, including frozen

- Ready stir-fry mix (just get more coriander, chilli and lime)

- Custard

- Tinned pulses

- Soup (sometimes)

- Curry paste

- Some dried herbs: thyme and oregano respond well

- Frozen prawns

- Chips

- Organic stock cubes for emergencies

When it comes to common sense, having a look in people's trolleys at the supermarket makes me think it's not that common after all . . .

MIDWEEK SUPPERS

CHORIZO FRITTATA
FLAME-GRILLED TOMATO SALSA

CUBAN CHICKEN
WITH RICE AND BEANS

GARGANELLI PASTA
WITH PURPLE-SPROUTING BROCCOLI

RIBS AND BEANS

ESCALOPE OF CHICKEN
WITH ROCKET, SAGE AND LEMON

FENNELLY TROUT
WITH PETITS POIS À LA FRANÇAISE

PORK AND GINGER NOODLE STIR-FRY

MACARONI CHEESE
WITH ARTICHOKE HEARTS

QUICK SPICED CHICKEN THIGHS
WITH EMERGENCY BIRYANI

PORK CHOPS WITH SWEETCORN RELISH
AND POTATO SALAD

SUPPER USED TO MEAN A LIGHT SNACK SUCH AS WELSH RAREBIT BEFORE ONE RETIRED FOR THE NIGHT. THAT IS NOT THE CASE NOWADAYS. SUPPER FOR MOST IS THE MAIN MEAL OF THE DAY.

This Midweek Suppers chapter is all about everyday food – literally. Here is a selection of meals that you can eat all week long. The ground rules for this chapter were simple: the food had to be tasty, easy to prepare, have mass appeal and not cost too much money.

Most people work all day, so the thought of coming home and starting an intricate recipe would put most of us off even opening the book. One hint I can give is to take a look at what you intend to cook before you actually start preparing it. Most recipes will have a couple of things that you can chop, mix or combine the night before, or even before you leave for work in the morning.

All in all, our supper recipes should not leave you feeling as if you have just served a state banquet at the Guildhall, so relax and give them a go.

Don't be tempted to stray from the path that is Economy Gastronomy by sneaking off to the supermarket and buying a ready meal. You will only be cheating yourself!

Paul.

CHORIZO FRITTATA

serves: 4   preparation time: 15 minutes   cooking time: 40 minutes

A frittata is an omelette with Sicilian origins, just as a tortilla is an omelette with Spanish origins. The main difference that I can see between a frittata and all the other kinds of omelette is that it is mixed, flavoured and then almost baked in the pan rather than being worked with a fork during the cooking.

This version is my own concoction. I love the way the flavours and textures complement one another. Once you have mastered the basic principle, you can have fun inventing your own version. In fact that is precisely what makes it such a good midweek supper. If you have eggs in the house and a few random bits in the fridge, you are never far from a frittata!

My Flame-grilled Tomato Salsa (see p.171) would be the perfect accompaniment.

180g chorizo sausage, peeled
up to 30ml olive oil
8 boiled, peeled, cold new potatoes, diced into 2cm cubes
8 eggs
2 teaspoons paprika
2 tablespoons soured cream
4 spring onions, sliced finely

Preheat the oven to 170°C/150°C fan/gas mark 3–4.

Choose a suitable pan for your frittata: for the above ingredients that means one at least 25cm in diameter. Unless you bought this pan last week, you may need to line the base with a snug-fitting circle of greaseproof paper to prevent the frittata from sticking. Have the paper ready, but first we are going to use the pan to fry all the bits.

Cut the chorizo into large bite-size chunks and fry in a little olive oil. When they are lightly coloured, remove and keep handy, and don't throw the chorizo-coloured oil away either.

Heat a tablespoon of your reserved chorizo oil and fry the new potatoes, again until they colour. Put these on one side with the chorizo. Now clean the pan and place your paper over the base.

Next crack the eggs into a bowl and whisk them up. Add 1 teaspoon paprika and 1 tablespoon soured cream, whisking them in too.

Tip the chorizo and potatoes into the empty pan, making sure they are spread evenly. Sprinkle over the spring onions, then pour on the egg mixture and place the pan in the oven. Bake until slightly firm to the touch and golden brown in colour. This will take about 10–15 minutes.

Serve with a dollop of the remaining soured cream, the rest of the paprika sprinkled on top and the Flame-grilled Tomato Salsa, plus a salad on the side.

FLAME-GRILLED TOMATO SALSA[℗]
WITH PEPPERS, LIME AND CORIANDER

serves: 4   preparation time: 20 minutes   cooking time: 30 minutes

My work kitchen has six chefs and right now three of them happen to be Kiwis. This means two things: first, they spend a lot of time talking about rugby, and second, at the first sight of the sun, they down tools, go home and light a barbecue. Seeing a potential problem here, I quickly installed a barbecue in our pub garden, which means they can remain at work on sunny days and stoke coals at the same time.

One of the accompaniments we often serve with grilled meats or seafood is this salsa. Don't be scared off by all the ingredients – it really is simple to put together. The best way of cooking the tomatoes and peppers is over the open flame of a barbecue, but it is possible to use a very hot ribbed grill pan. I make this at home and keep it in the fridge for emergency snacking of the healthy variety. It's really good with poppadoms!

If you're not using this as an accompaniment to the frittata on p.169, the ingredients listed here make enough to use as a dressing on four servings of grilled meat or fish, with some left over for snacking purposes.

4 beef tomatoes

1 red pepper

2 yellow peppers

1 small red onion, finely chopped

1 tablespoon sweet chilli sauce

1 teaspoon smoked paprika

the juice and zest of 2 limes

3 tablespoons chopped coriander

½ teaspoon dried chilli flakes

3 cloves of garlic, finely chopped

3 tablespoons extra virgin olive oil

Place the whole tomatoes and peppers on to the hot barbecue. Allow them to blister and colour before turning them over. They will blacken in places on the outside but this is OK – in fact, it is beneficial as it imparts a smoky quality to the finished salsa. If you're using a ribbed griddle pan, the peppers will take about 30 minutes and the tomatoes 20 minutes.

Remove the peppers and tomatoes as soon as they are blackened and blistered, before they become too soft. Allow them to cool and, using a small knife, scrape off the skins. Next cut open the peppers, discard the seeds and the stalk, then chop the flesh into rough 1cm dice. Chop the whole tomatoes into a rough dice of a similar size. Chuck all of this into a big bowl and add all the other ingredients apart from the olive oil. Stir everything together and then slowly stir in the olive oil until the mixture is loose and wet. Season the salsa and you are ready to go.

CUBAN CHICKEN
WITH RICE AND BEANS

serves: 4   preparation time: 20–25 minutes   cooking time: 1 hour

Rice and peas or rice and beans – this magical combo of white rice and black beans is known throughout Latin America as Moros y Cristianos (Moors and Christians), a cultural reference I really enjoy. Nutritionally, more of the protein in the pulses is made useful to our bodies through the presence of the rice, and in some of the poorer countries associated with these two ingredients, maximizing your protein where you can is a good idea.

Cuban food is tasty but not fancy, and as an alternative to eating in the slightly dull Communist state-run restaurants you can dine in *paladares*, literally a few tables in someone's front room (allowed as an income-booster as long as they only have a handful of customers). The *paladares* we ate in had much better food than the more formal restaurants, with a simple, home-made feel that this dish sums up.

It would be much better to buy a couple of whole chickens, take the breasts off and freeze them for later (for something like the Chicken Surprise on p.285) and make a stock out of the two carcasses. It's best if you can marinate the chicken thighs and drumsticks before cooking – the longer the better – even overnight.

2 heaped teaspoons ground cumin

2 teaspoons salt

1 tablespoon dried oregano

2 tablespoons olive oil

4 chicken legs, split into thighs and drumsticks

160g lardons (slices of streaky bacon are fine too)

2 red onions, diced

4 cloves of garlic, finely chopped

1 green pepper, cut into 1.5cm cubes

120ml red wine vinegar

300g long-grain rice

salt and pepper

1 x 400g tin black beans, drained and rinsed

750ml chicken stock

In a bowl, mix the cumin, salt and dried oregano. Add a drop of olive oil to moisten then rub it all over the chicken pieces. Mix together using your hands to make sure all the surfaces of the chicken are coated and leave for as long as you can.

Put a large, thick-bottomed metal casserole pan on a high heat. Pour a tablespoon of oil into your pan and once it is good and hot, put your chicken in skin-side down: sizzle, sizzle, sizzle. If your pan is not big enough, do this in two batches. Give these a proper 6 minutes on each side. More than just sealing them, you're getting the cooking started. You want to achieve a deep golden colour, so turn the heat down a bit if they're getting a bit dark.

Once your chicken is done lift the pieces out and put to one side. Turn the heat back up, toss the lardons, onion and garlic into the hot pan and give it a good stir. When they are nicely browned (about 5 minutes) add the pepper and vinegar. Stir well for a minute before tipping in the rice.

Give it a good bit of seasoning and mix in the black beans. Nestle all the chicken pieces into the rice, cover with chicken stock and put a lid on. Bring to a simmer then turn the heat down immediately to the lowest setting.

After 25 minutes it should all be ready (but always test the rice to make sure). Turn the heat off and let sit with the lid on for 5 minutes. Serve in a bowl with a simple salad.

GARGANELLI PASTA ℗
WITH PURPLE-SPROUTING BROCCOLI

serves: 4   preparation time: 20 minutes   cooking time: 12 minutes

When cooking pasta my natural inclination is to reach for the butter and cream when coming up with a sauce. There are two things wrong with this approach: it's far from the healthiest of options and it's not exactly cheap. Luckily, my waistline and my wallet have been spared further humiliation thanks to Chris Marriott, my number two at work, who is a bit of a master of flavour when presented with a bunch of herbs, a blender and a bowl of naked pasta. Chris doesn't usually keep a record of what he puts into a dish, which means that many of his kitchen triumphs, and there have been a fair few, cannot be replicated! However, this recipe is one that I forced him to sit down and write up immediately for the book. It's tasty, quick, cheap, healthy and any leftover dressing can be stored in the fridge for up to 10 days – in other words, ideal midweek-supper material!

Garganelli, by the way, is the more glamorous sister of penne. Rather than maintaining penne's tube shape, it softens and lies flat, making it better to eat. Of course, whatever your shop has in the way of pasta will be fine. I would say the best alternatives are penne or farfalle.

400g garganelli pasta

350g purple-sprouting or long-stemmed broccoli, leaves and all

240g peas, fresh or frozen

150g Parmesan cheese

for the dressing

a bunch (20g) of flat parsley leaves

a few sprigs (10g) of tarragon leaves

a few sprigs (10g) of mint leaves

a bunch (20g) of basil leaves

1 tablespoon drained capers, rinsed

1 clove of garlic, peeled and very finely grated

1 heaped dessertspoon grain mustard

juice and zest of 1 lemon

up to 200ml decent olive oil

1 tablespoon very finely chopped shallots

sea salt and black pepper

First of all make the dressing. It will keep in your fridge for at least a week, so I recommend making more – simply double the amounts given. Try using it as a sauce with grilled fish as well as pasta.

By far the easiest way of making the dressing is in a food processor. However, a blender or even using a knife and chopping board will do the job just as well. Put the herb leaves, capers, garlic, grain mustard and the lemon juice and zest into the food processor. Turn it on and immediately drizzle in 100ml of olive oil. After a minute or two, the jug will contain a thick, bitty, very green liquid dressing. If it is not liquid enough then add the rest of the olive oil in the same way. Pour the mixture into a bowl and add the chopped shallots, a little flaked sea salt and a twist of black pepper. Your dressing is ready.

Boil some water and cook the pasta until al dente. Drain the pasta (keeping the water) and moisten with a tiny bit of olive oil to prevent it sticking, then tip it into a bowl.

Reboil the water and drop in your broccoli. When it is just cooked but still has a bit of crunch, chuck in the peas for a quick 30-second simmer. Drain the vegetables, getting rid of all the water, then toss them into the bowl with the warm pasta. Pour over a generous splosh of your herby dressing and mix everything up. Give it a quick taste and add more dressing if needed. Before serving, use a vegetable peeler to shave the Parmesan over the top.

RIBS AND BEANS

serves: 6–8   preparation time: 25–30 minutes   cooking time: 2 hours

There's a grand misunderstanding about the difference between how long *you* have to cook for and how long *it* takes to cook. This dish takes a while from start to finish, but with little time input from the cook; it's the meat that does the work, not you. Bang-it-in-the-oven-and-walk-away cooking is the way forward for those who like flavour on a budget. It's one of my favourite ways of cooking and eating, especially as it's leaning towards finger food – it's good to get involved with your supper.

When buying the ribs, you want the little pieces for this, so either buy short ribs or ask your butcher to cut the long ones into thirds, or do it yourself at home, which is easy but requires a proper big chef's knife or cleaver.

for the marinade
2 red chillies, finely chopped
1 tablespoon oregano
5 cloves of garlic, finely chopped
½ teaspoon smoked paprika
extra-virgin olive oil

1.2kg pork ribs
600g pork belly, either one piece or 4 thick slices
1 large red onion, peeled and cut into large dice

2 carrots, peeled and cut into 1cm slices
2 x 400g tins beans
(haricot, borlotti or chickpeas)
2 peppers, ideally 1 red and 1 green, deseeded and cut into 2–3cm chunks
1 x 400g tin of chopped tomatoes
3 tablespoons red wine or sherry vinegar
500ml chicken stock
salt and pepper
extra-virgin olive oil

In a large bowl, mix the ingredients for the marinade together with a healthy sprinkling of salt and a couple of tablespoons of the extra-virgin. Coat the short rib bits in it well. Cut the pork belly into similar-sized pieces to the ribs, chuck them in and give them a good roll around, then leave to marinate for as long as possible.

Turn your oven on to 240°C/220°C fan/gas mark 9. Pack the porky bits into a roasting tray with the onion and carrots. Roast for 40 minutes, turning once, until they are nicely browned all over. Turn the oven down to 180°C/160°C fan/gas mark 4.

Drain the beans and tip them into the tray with the meat. Add all the remaining ingredients including 2 tablespoons of extra-virgin olive oil. Season with a couple of hefty grabs of salt and lots of cracked pepper.

Give it all a good stir, making sure the rib nuggets are mostly under the level of the stock, then bake in the oven for about an hour with a bit of foil tight on top. By now the meat should be pretty tender, so take the foil off and give it a last 15 minutes, just to brown the top a little. Finish with a last splosh of really good extra-virgin, serve in bowls and eat with crusty bread.

ESCALOPE OF CHICKEN [P]
WITH ROCKET, SAGE AND LEMON

serves: 4   preparation time: 25 minutes   cooking time: 20 minutes

This is a bit of a family favourite. My kids like it because they like anything in breadcrumbs, I like it because it's cheap and quick to prepare, and my wife likes it because it's light and balanced (or some such nonsense). Anyway, the point is, this is a 'please-all dish'.

4 boneless, skinless chicken breasts
10–12 sage leaves, finely chopped
12 black peppercorns, coarsely crushed
8 tablespoons plain flour
2 eggs
150ml milk
250g breadcrumbs (home-made of course!)
180g unsalted butter
juice of ½ lemon
100g wild rocket
olive oil
balsamic vinegar
80g Parmesan cheese

First of all you need to transform the chicken breasts into escalopes (originally a French term to describe meat that has been flattened before cooking). This is easily done. Just lay a piece of cling film down on your worktop, place a chicken breast on top and cover it with a second piece of cling film. Then, using a rolling pin, bat out each one until the surface area is doubled and the thickness halved – in other words, you have a bigger, thinner piece of chicken. Remove the top piece of cling film and sprinkle the escalopes with the chopped sage and the cracked pepper, pressing them lightly on to the meat so they stick.

Now the chicken needs to be coated in the breadcrumbs. The French are a truly gastronomic lot, so they also have a special word for this – *pané*. First, tip the flour into a shallow bowl. Then crack the eggs into a second bowl and whisk them together with the milk. Finally pour the breadcrumbs into a third bowl.

Take a flattened chicken breast and lay it in the flour. Turn it over a couple of times until evenly coated, then shake off the excess before dunking the chicken in the egg and milk mix. Allow the excess to drip off, then lay the chicken in the breadcrumbs. Turn it over so it is completely coated. *Voilà*, you have just prepared an *escalope du volaille pané*!

Pan-fry your escalopes in a little foaming butter for 4–6 minutes on each side until the breadcrumbs are golden and crispy and the chicken is cooked through. If, like me, you have only one decent-sized pan in the house, then pop each cooked escalope in a low oven to stay warm while you pan-fry the rest.

Before serving, melt a little extra butter in the pan and, as it turns a nut-brown colour, squeeze in the lemon juice. Pour a little of this butter over each escalope and serve with a simple salad of rocket leaves tossed in olive oil and balsamic and topped with shavings of fresh Parmesan.

FENNELLY TROUT ⒶWITH PETITS POIS À LA FRANÇAISE

serves: 6   preparation time: 45–50 minutes   cooking time: 35–40 minutes

Every now and then we find ourselves in the right place to make a down payment on a future supper, and this recipe is designed to come to mind as you're standing in the fishmonger's or, even better, when you've been fishing.

Bring the booty home, spend 10 minutes putting a bit of love into them, then wrap in foil and stick in the freezer. Cook from frozen and in the time they take to cook, knock up the very French-sounding but British-tasting accompaniment, which remains the best way I've come across to use up floppy, slightly past-it lettuce.

for the fish parcels
2 cloves of garlic, peeled
salt and pepper
75g soft butter
2 lemons
1 really big handful of flat-leaf parsley, washed, picked and finely chopped
6 whole trout (or similar fish), heads off and seasoned inside and out
1 large bulb of fennel, thinly sliced

1kg little potatoes, Charlottes are nice

for the petits pois
2 tablespoons butter
6 shallots, peeled and thinly sliced

3 cloves of garlic, peeled and roughly chopped
200ml white wine
500ml light chicken or veg stock
around 300g lettuce (baby gem, escarole or cos), roughly sliced
120g thick-cut cooked ham, Wiltshire is perfect, cut into 1cm dice (optional)
salt and pepper
250g frozen petits pois or peas
1 bunch of asparagus (about 220g), preferably British, woody ends cut off, sliced into 1-cm pieces
1 big handful of mint, picked, washed and roughly chopped
80ml double cream

Make a flavoured butter by smashing the garlic cloves with a bit of salt using the flat of your knife, then chop finely and mix this in a bowl with the soft butter, the zest of one lemon and the parsley. Season with salt and pepper. This makes about 12 tablespoons.

Tear off six pieces of foil, each big enough to wrap up a fish, and lay as many out as you can. Put a tablespoon of your flavoured butter in the middle of each and spread it out east to west about the length and breadth of your fish. Divide the fennel between the pieces of foil, laying it over butter.

Slice the other lemon and put a couple of halved slices inside each seasoned fish, then sit the fish on the fennel and dot another tablespoon of butter on top of each fish. Finish with a squeeze of the zested lemon. Bring the foil over the top of your fish and fold in the sides, so the fish are wrapped in loose, airtight packages. At this point you can start cooking or you can freeze for later. They will last for up to 3 months.

When you are ready to make your fish supper, preheat your oven to 200°C/180°C fan/gas mark 6. Put the spuds into a pan of cold salted water, bring to a simmer and cook for about 25 minutes. Once the oven is up to temperature, put the trout parcels on to two baking trays and swap their oven position round halfway through the cooking time. Fish from the fridge needs 25 minutes and fish from frozen needs 40 minutes.

Put a wide-bottomed pan on a medium heat and melt the butter in it. Chuck in the shallots and garlic, coat in the butter and stick a lid on for 5 minutes, giving it the odd stir. You don't want the shallots to get any colour, so turn down the heat if necessary. Pour in the white wine, turn the heat up and leave the lid off for about 5 minutes so the wine reduces before adding the stock. Simmer for 15 minutes.

When there's only about a centimetre or so of liquid left in the bottom, stir in the lettuce (and ham if you're using it). Season well and, a few minutes later, add the petits pois and asparagus. Put the lid on again for 5 minutes just to bring it up to temperature quickly, then stir in the mint and cream and turn the heat off. Let it sit for 5 minutes then taste for seasoning. Serve the fish out of the foil with the petits pois and potatoes.

PORK AND GINGER NOODLE STIR-FRY ⓟ

serves: 4   preparation time: 1 hour (if not using leftover pork), otherwise 25 minutes
cooking time: 1 hour 50 minutes

This simple collection of pungent flavours is a great way to use up a little leftover pork. However, it's also good enough to warrant a bespoke piece of pork belly – a cut which is not only delicious and very easy to cook but also cheap. Feel free to add to or remove from the selection of vegetables as your taste dictates.

In my opinion, many home stir-fried dishes go wrong because too much is loaded into the wok at once, meaning that the wok can never retain enough heat to quickly sear and cook its contents. Although it may seem a little fiddly, I would urge you to cook your stir-fries in smaller batches. Have a large tray ready so that you can remove the vegetables to it when cooked. Another tip is to move the vegetables around the pan with a spoon or chopstick rather than lifting the pan and tossing the ingredients. While tossing looks great, it actually means that the pan is off the heat, which kind of defeats the object.

In professional, Chinese-style kitchens stoves known as 'wok burners' are used. These have a much bigger flame than our domestic jobbies, making it possible to lift the pan and toss its contents without fear of losing heat.

600g piece of pork belly

1 star anise

1 onion, peeled and roughly chopped

vegetable or sesame oil

2 cloves of garlic, peeled and finely chopped

1 red chilli, sliced into fine rings

5cm piece of fresh ginger, peeled and finely chopped or grated

½ head of broccoli, cut into small florets

10 button mushrooms, sliced

4 spring onions, trimmed and cut finely on an angle

25 mangetouts, halved lengthways

200g dry egg noodles, cooked according to the packet instructions, then cooled in water and drained

2 tablespoons soy sauce

1 tablespoon sweet chilli sauce

1 tablespoon chopped coriander

To cook the pork belly I would suggest a gentle simmering rather than roasting. You will still end up with crispy pork when you stir-fry it, but it will be easier to cut. So, put the raw piece of belly into a large pot, cover with water, then add the star anise and onion. Simmer gently for 1½ hours, until the meat is thoroughly cooked, and leave to cool in the water. Now you can either put the pork in the fridge for later or move straight into the world of woks and chopsticks.

Cut the pork into 1cm dice and put to one side. Discard the bones. Next prep all the vegetables as described above, bearing in mind that each type of vegetable should be cut into equal-sized pieces to ensure even cooking while stir-frying. Now you can begin the fun bit.

Heat a wok on the stove until it is just beginning to smoke and pour in about a tablespoon of oil. Swill it around till the inside of the wok is covered, then pour out the excess. The pan should now be nice and hot. Chuck in the pork and sear for 5 minutes until crispy and heated through. Now stir in the garlic, chilli and ginger and stir-fry for about 1 minute. Remove all the pork and keep warm to one side.

Reheat and oil the pan, throw in the broccoli and allow it a few seconds to absorb some heat before you stir it around. It is done when it's hot and has softened very slightly. The best way of checking is to remove a piece and eat it. I definitely like some crunch left in mine. Tip out the broccoli, reheat the wok and repeat the same process with the oil before tossing in the mushrooms. When coloured and cooked do the same with the spring onions and mangetout. Each batch will cook very quickly, so be sure not to overcook them.

With all the vegetables done, add them, together with the pork and the noodles, to the wok and return the wok to the heat. Carefully toss everything together. Drizzle in soy sauce to taste and some chilli sauce for a touch of sweetness, then finally toss through the coriander. Serve in bowls immediately.

MACARONI CHEESE
WITH ARTICHOKE HEARTS

serves: 4   preparation time: 25–30 minutes   cooking time: 45–50 minutes

At our wedding we didn't have a cake, we had a cheese cake made of ten whole British cheeses, stacked up on each other in order of size, starting with a whole 20kg Montgomery's Cheddar truckle on the bottom and finishing with the tiny, pyramidal Tymsboro (a soft goat) about six feet above it. A year later we were down to the last scraps of Montgomery's, and on our first anniversary I made Susi this, her favourite supper, with the last of our wedding cheese. And who said romance was dead?

I'm assuming for this that most people have an old, hard cheese container like us – just the odd bits that are too gnarly to eat as they are, but fine to cook with. Use them up in this dish, though, of course, new cheese works too.

60g butter

300g cooked artichoke hearts
(in a jar or from the deli counter),
halved, well drained and patted dry

100g lardons or sliced streaky bacon (optional)

olive oil

350g macaroni

1 clove of garlic, peeled and smashed

50g plain flour

800ml milk

1 tablespoon grain mustard

2 pinches of ground nutmeg

160g strong hard old cheese, grated or broken up

salt and pepper

4–6 ripe tomatoes, thinly sliced

40g Parmesan, finely grated

a few pinches of dried herbs
(oregano, thyme, rosemary or a mix)

extra-virgin olive oil

Preheat your oven to 200°C/180°C fan/gas mark 6. Get a pan of water on and bring it up to the boil for the macaroni.

In a separate saucepan, melt 20g of the butter. Add the artichokes and lardons, if using, and fry until golden brown, stirring regularly for 10–12 minutes. Then scoop them out and sit them on some kitchen roll.

Once your water has come up to boil, add a splash of olive oil, chuck in your macaroni and give it all a quick, vigorous stir. Give your artichoke pan a quick wash, then put it back on the heat to dry off.

Over a low to medium heat, add the remaining lot of butter to the pan. Once it has melted, chuck in the smashed garlic clove, then a minute later stir in the flour. Keep stirring it and let it fizzle for a few minutes to cook out the taste of the flour, then add a little milk and mix together with your spoon. Once it's incorporated, pour in a bit more and then swap to a whisk so you whisk all the lumps out. Keep gradually adding milk and crank the heat up a bit. Bring the smooth sauce up to a bubble, then turn it down again and stir in the mustard and nutmeg.

Fish out the garlic clove, add the strong, hard cheese (not the Parmesan) and mix until it is all melted. Season with a few cracks of pepper and some salt.

Once your macaroni is al dente (it's important not to overcook the pasta on the first cook or else your final dish will be much heavier), drain well and add it to the cheese sauce, along with the artichokes (and lardons). Turn off the heat and transfer to an ovenproof dish. It needs to be quite wet as the macaroni will continue absorbing the sauce as it cooks. Arrange the sliced tomato on top and sprinkle over the Parmesan and herbs. Season and drizzle with extra-virgin. Put the mac 'n' cheese on a foil-lined baking tray to catch any overspills and into the middle of the oven it goes for 30–40 minutes, depending on how deep your dish is.

QUICK SPICED CHICKEN THIGHS ᵖ
WITH EMERGENCY BIRYANI

serves: 4   preparation time: 15 minutes, plus marinating time   cooking time: 35 minutes

This is a real family favourite. Cheap, quick and easy, but it also tastes really good. The marinade is really one concocted from store-cupboard ingredients, so the ethnic origins are somewhat debatable! The biryani is, of course, a bit of a super-quick bodge version of the Indian classic, but it's a great way of livening up plain rice and could actually be a meal in itself.

for the chicken/marinade

8 chicken thighs, skin on

1 dessertspoon sweet chilli sauce or mango chutney

2 teaspoons curry powder

1 teaspoon ground cumin

3 cloves of garlic, crushed

1 dessertspoon syrup from a jar of stem ginger

1 tablespoon plain yoghurt, optional

for the rice

2 tablespoons vegetable oil

½ onion, peeled and finely sliced

2 cloves of garlic, peeled and crushed

100g button mushrooms, sliced

1 teaspoon chilli flakes

1 teaspoon turmeric

500g basmati rice (a large handful per person), rinsed in cold water before cooking

100g peas

2 tomatoes, diced

First of all marinate the chicken thighs. This is best done some time before you intend to eat, but frankly, even if the chicken is only sloshed about in the marinade for 2 minutes it will taste better than nothing. For the sake of this recipe, let's imagine you choose to do this before going to work – that way the chicken will get a good flavour hit.

Slash across the chicken thighs 3 or 4 times with a sharp knife. The cuts should be about 5mm deep and their purpose is to trap extra marinade and therefore add extra flavour. Mix all the ingredients for the marinade in a large bowl, then place in the chicken thighs and give them a good rub and squeeze to thoroughly work in the marinade. Cover and leave in the fridge until ready to cook. The chicken will need about 35 minutes in a hot oven, which pleasingly gives you time to prep and cook the biryani.

Preheat the oven to 200°C/180°C fan/gas mark 6. Pick the chicken out of the marinade and place on a baking tray, leaving a little space between each thigh. Put a teaspoon of marinade on top of each thigh for luck, then bung them in the oven. The idea is that the sugars in the ginger syrup and sweet chilli sauce will caramelize in the high heat and go a very dark brown. At the same time the spices will flavour the chicken and the skin will become crispy. Check the thighs after about 15 minutes – if the colour and crispiness are right, lower the temperature to 180°C/160°C fan/gas mark 4. When done, you can rest the chicken if your rice is not quite ready.

To cook the rice, heat a large pot which has a tight-fitting lid. Add the oil, then throw in the onion and garlic and allow them to soften and colour very slightly. Now add the mushrooms and cook these for 2 minutes before adding the chilli flakes and turmeric. Carefully mix the rice into the pan. Making sure the rice is flat and level, place your index finger on the surface of the rice and add cold water until the level reaches the first joint of your finger (about 2.5cm). Bring the pan to the boil and immediately cover tightly with foil and the lid. Boil for 5 minutes and then switch off the heat and leave to stand. The steam trapped within will cook your rice perfectly.

The rice needs to stand covered for 20 minutes in total, but after 15 minutes carefully lift a small section of foil and pour in the peas and tomatoes. Cover again and leave for 5 minutes, then uncover the pan and fork the rice and vegetables together.

Serve with the chicken and a salad.

PORK CHOPS [Ⓐ]
WITH SWEETCORN RELISH
AND POTATO SALAD

serves: 2 very generously!
preparation time: 20–25 minutes   cooking time: 35–40 minutes

Veggies aside, there are few folk out there who don't enjoy a pork chop. Pigs, like chickens, are the only other animal that is reared intensively (not relevant to cows and sheep), so it's fair to hand out the same advice as with chooks: buy the best you can – it just tastes and feels better.

If this sounds like a summery supper, it is, and (apart from the pig), the star is the sunny sweetcorn relish, not gloopy and gelatinous like the bought ones, but a bright, zingy home-made version.

500g potatoes, red ones are nice for this, scrubbed
100ml white wine vinegar
1½ tablespoons golden granulated sugar
1 medium red pepper, halved, deseeded and chopped into 1cm dice
2 ears of sweetcorn
a small handful of French beans, topped, tailed and chopped into 1cm pieces
salt and pepper
2 pork chops, thicker is better
4 tablespoons mayonnaise
2 spring onions, sliced
2 big dill pickles or 4 gherkins, sliced
a squeeze of lemon juice

Cut your potatoes into small chunks (or if they're the little ones, just cut them in half), put them in a pan with salted cold water and bring up to the boil. Once soft, drain and leave them to cool.

For the relish, put a small pan over a medium heat. Pour in the vinegar and dissolve the sugar in it as it comes up to a simmer. Add the diced red pepper.

Shuck both ears of corn by standing them on one end and cutting down the side so that the kernels fall off (keep the cobs for making stock). Stir the kernels into the pan and continue simmering. When you have almost no liquid left stir in the French beans with a pinch of salt and turn the heat off.

Heat a griddle/grill/pan for the chops until smoking hot. Season your chops well on both sides and lay them on/under/in (you'll need a splash of oil if you're doing it in a pan). Turn after 6 minutes if 2cm thick – less if on the thinner side – and cook for the same amount of time.

Put the potatoes in a bowl with the mayo, spring onions, gherkins, a squeeze of lemon and quite a lot of salt and pepper. Taste and correct the seasoning.

Once your chops have finished cooking, leave them on a plate to rest for a couple of minutes before serving with your potato salad and relish, and as if by magic you have a starter pack over for tomorrow's lunch.

WORKING SMART, NOT HARD

AS REGARDS COOKING, THE WORLD IS SPLIT INTO THREE TYPES OF PEOPLE: THOSE FOR WHOM IT'S A JOY, THOSE WHO THINK OF IT AS WORK, AND A FEW, LIKE PAUL AND ME, TO WHOM IT IS BOTH. WHEN I WAS A COMMIS MY HEAD CHEF USED TO SAY TO US 'WORK SMART, NOT HARD'. MANY YEARS DOWN THE LINE I THINK IT'S ONE OF A FEW BITS OF CHEFFY KITCHEN LINGO THAT IT'S WORTH THE DOMESTIC COOK TAKING ON BOARD TOO.

THE IRONY IS THAT YOU HAVE TO HAVE A CERTAIN AMOUNT OF KNOWLEDGE AND EXPERIENCE UNDER YOUR BELT TO KNOW HOW TO MAKE THAT TIME/LABOUR/MONEY-SAVING CALL, BUT MY AIM HERE IS TO OPEN A DOOR THAT GETS YOU THINKING IN A MORE EFFICIENT KIND OF WAY.

WORKING SMART, NOT HARD, CAN TAKE ON DIFFERENT FORMS:

1. While you're there . . .

- If you're cooking, you might as well use the time and energy (both yours and the cooker's) to best advantage. A couple of quick ones to illustrate the point: whenever I roast meat, I always put some veg (any of onions, spuds, carrots, swede, shallots, garlic cloves) around or, if I'm cooking on a rack, below the meat. It just makes sense to knock out one of your accompanying veg at the same time, then you've only got to think about a few greens at the end. Same applies to any big slow-cooks.

- Or if you're making something like cookies or muffins, do a double batch and freeze half.

- You can add spinach, or Savoy, or peas, or any green veg, to a pan of simmering pasta a couple of minutes before it's done, and when you drain it all, you're well on the way to a finished dish.

- Using telly or chatting to get through the more tedious but regular kitchen jobs (such as picking herbs – thyme's the worst – or peeling roots and alliums, shelling peas, or grating Parmesan) is an effective way of making your prep time pass quickly.

- Planning and shopping more than one meal in advance is a really good timesaver. It's boring to have to run out to the shops all the time.

It's about using what's already going on, either in minutes or joules.

2. Play the long game

- Unless you know something that we don't, we all plan to be here for supper tonight, and tomorrow, and next week. You'll find your culinary life much easier, and more rewarding, if you don't see it as a succession of one-night-stand suppers, and view it instead as rolling hills of meals all the way as far as the eye can see, i.e. until next week. Stocks are a great example of this. Throwing a stock on so you have it ready for a starter pack whenever you might need it is just a great idea (see p.213).

- Or take five minutes to knock up a compound butter (like in my trout recipe, p.180): whizz a pat in the food processor with lemon zest, garlic, parsley, chilli flakes and seasoning, then wrap in cling film like a sausage and freeze. Now all you have to do is slice a fat disc off to finish anything from steaks to prawns to bruschetta.

- Also, having a few things in the store cupboard saves you running out just when you need something (see p.12).

3. Put the love where it's going to be felt

- Twenty-five years ago, Shirley Conran said: 'Life is too short to stuff a mushroom', and it still holds true. Sometimes, there are great shortcuts to the finishing line, in the form of a supper that fills you with happiness.

- Take some of the stresses out of what you're cooking (e.g. sometimes buy pastry, don't always peel the spuds), but the flip side of that is there are also products on shelves that are a step too far – with too much convenience, flavour is lost (see Trolley Bashing p.162).

- Most importantly of all, buy the best ingredients you can afford and don't be over-ambitious with what you do with them.

4. Use the food wisely, Luke

- Just like the young Jedi, you too must make the right decisions about your leftovers and freezer-lurkers. These are all down-payments on another supper – your work is already in the bag, and by choosing and combining your resources well, with maybe a thoughtful and loving makeover, these flavour-packs can form the basis to your next meal (see Bedrocks).

- Who needs smoke and mirrors (pasta sauces, bought stock, ready meals) to deflect your tastebuds' attention when you can cut to the culinary core with your ingredients?

Once you're aware of it, there are many instances where these simple words of wisdom apply, because as much as cooking can be a joy, an easy life isn't such a bad thing either.

SOMETHING OUT OF NOTHING

**ONION BHAJIS, TARKA DHAL
AND ALMOND RICE**

**BARLEY AND BITS SALAD
WITH HONEY'D GOAT'S CHEESE TOAST**

SPINACH TORTILLA

NORWEGIAN FISH PIE

HOT DOG HOTPOT

PASTA E FAGIOLI

BAKEWELL IN A BAG

ICED COFFEE THREE WAYS

IN MY LATE TEENS THE JOB OF SUPPER-MAKER UNEXPECTEDLY LANDED ON MY LAP, AND LIKE MOST TEENAGERS I HAD NO INTEREST IN, OR CONCEPT OF, PLANNING. THE SATURDAY SHOP MADE SENSE AS FAR AS SUNDAY LUNCH, BUT INVARIABLY BY TUESDAY EVENING, MY DAD AND I WERE SITTING DOWN TO A MEAL OF THINGS I'D THROWN TOGETHER – AND BELIEVE ME, IT WASN'T ALWAYS THAT PRETTY.

Apart from an innate love of the kitchen, the other thing I inherited from my mum – crucial to making something out of nothing – was a good larder, quite literally. Like any good home-maker (and I'd like to be clear that you don't need to have kids to be a good home-maker), she had accumulated a store cupboard full of pulses, pastas, biscuits, baking goods, tinned veggies and the like. So before you read on and think that there are recipes in this chapter where you can make a three-course dinner out of a packet of frozen peas and a couple of gnarly cheese slices, turn to p.12 where you must first learn the art of a good larder.

Now, with at least the bare necessities of a larder in place, we are ready to proceed: this chapter is dedicated to all of those who meant to get to the shops today but didn't quite make it, whether you were too busy brokering power-deals or just got stuck in your pyjamas. These recipes are for big-hearted folk whose friends drop round early evening, are still there at suppertime and there's now't about. Or for the home-worker, when no sandwich delivery company has turned up. Or the kids are suddenly starving . . . as are their four unexpected playmates – and you've just got back from holiday.

There are many occasions where even the best menu planner gets caught with their trousers down, and being ready for them, in terms of having both a recipe or two to draw upon and a few handy ingredients in the house, just makes your life that bit easier. It saves you bucks by not ordering expensive takeaways and, bearing in mind we're not going for Michelin stars here, these are all useful and scrummy recipes to be able to rustle up.

If there's one area where now, twenty years on, I'm still Throwing Stuff Together, it's puddings: not being one of the world's great pudding eaters, I just forget that for some, dinner isn't dinner without a bit of sweetness – it's amazing how the right flourishes can pass off a few sliced oranges and a drop of rosewater as a gourmet Middle Eastern dessert.

My aim with this chapter is to give you an injection of ideas and then adapt them depending on what you have around – because that's the reality of how life works. Even when you're planning for the unplanned, you still need to have a Plan C, and that is called your imagination. Ideally you will always have some semblance of freshness in your house – an ageing courgette, a slightly shrinking bulb of fennel, a few onions, spuds and garlic at the very least. Cabbage takes a decade to die. Some kind of herb effort is easily achieved – thyme and rosemary last for ages stored correctly in the fridge – but most universal of all is flat-leaf parsley.

Between your larder, the odd bit of fresh and the corner shop all the recipes in this chapter are within reach. So you can create something out of nothing, pull supper out of thin air and make a miracle out of loaves and fishes.

ONION BHAJIS, TARKA DHAL AND ALMOND RICE

serves: 4   preparation time: 45 minutes   cooking time: 1 hour

Considering this chapter is supposed to be about relying solely on your store cupboard and a little bit of fresh in the fridge, there are quite a few ingredients in this. However, there's nothing here that I wouldn't expect an interested cook to have knocking around or that a trip to the corner shop couldn't sort out.

This is the best kind of vegetarian meal where you honestly and truly just don't miss the meat. We should all be eating a bit less meat, and for those who are phobic about not having their carnivorous fix twice a day, this isn't a bad place to start for supper. Once you've made your own bhajis, you'll never enjoy another deep-fried stodgy brown greaseball again . . . which may be a bit of a double-edged sword.

for the bhajis
150ml Greek yoghurt
75g gram or plain flour, plus 2 tablespoons
½ teaspoon ground cumin
½ teaspoon garam masala
a pinch of salt
1–2 red or green chillies, finely sliced
1 large white onion, peeled and sliced
(or 4 spring onions and ½ white onion)
30g coriander, washed and chopped,
a couple of sprigs reserved
juice of 1 lime
¾ teaspoon turmeric
1 litre light oil (like sunflower, re-usable after)

for the dhal
5 cloves of garlic, peeled and sliced
1 teaspoon spices (use seeds like mustard, cumin, coriander and cardamom)
3 tablespoons groundnut or vegetable oil
250g dried split peas, yellow or green

for the rice
2 tablespoons butter
80g flaked almonds
350g basmati rice

to serve
plain or Greek yoghurt
mango chutney

To make the bhajis, in a big mixing bowl, stir together the yoghurt, 75g flour, cumin, garam masala and salt, plus 3 tablespoons of water, to make a smooth batter and set aside somewhere warm.

Jumping to the dhal, in a heavy-bottomed, medium-sized saucepan, fry the garlic and spices in the oil slowly and gently for 5 minutes over a low to medium heat until an all-over deep golden brown. Pour in the split peas and give them a good roll around in the garlicky oil, then pour in 750ml of cold water and turn the heat up high. Bring to the boil, then skim off the scum. Turn the heat down, cover and simmer steadily for 35–45 minutes, stirring occasionally until the peas are soft and there's no water left.

Combine the rest of the bhaji ingredients, except the oil, and stir into the base batter. Again, leave somewhere warm for 15 minutes. Choose a pan to cook the rice in and melt the butter in it over a low heat. Add the almonds and let them fry gently for the few minutes it takes them to go a glorious golden colour. Stir in the rice and cover with 500ml water. Put the lid on, bring to a simmer and turn the heat down for 10 minutes, then turn it off, but leave the lid on so it steams for 5 minutes. Turn the oven on to a low warming temperature and stick your plates in.

Heat up the oil for the bhajis in a big pan – you need it to be at least 5cm deep. See if the oil is hot enough by dropping a strand of onion in – it needs to fizzle and float, not drop to the bottom. Use a dessertspoon to take blobs of the mixture and drop them into the oil. Do four at a time – you're aiming to make 12. Give them 3–4 minutes each side, then keep them warm in the oven.

The dhal should be there by now – mushy peas and no more liquid – so turn it off before it starts to catch. Once you've finished cooking, mash the peas up a bit with the back of a spoon. Taste for seasoning. If it goes a bit thick and dry as it cools, stir in some warm water to restore it to a creamy consistency. All that's left to do now is to serve everything up with yoghurt, mango chutney (essential), the sprigs of coriander and a bit more lime if you have it knocking around.

BARLEY AND BITS SALAD
WITH HONEY'D GOAT'S CHEESE TOAST

serves: 4 as a starter or 2 as a main course
preparation time: 15–20 minutes   cooking time: 30–35 minutes

The joy of this is that it's a proper veg-box clear-out of all the quick-cook stuff, as opposed to the roots. We all end up with half a bag of mangetouts or sugar snaps, a quarter of a cabbage, an ear of corn and a stray courgette in our fridge, and the beauty of this filling salad is that it uses any stray odds and ends without looking like it. French beans, fennel, asparagus, peas and cucumber all work fine too, but leave asparagus tips whole.

I'm relying on you having a few soft fresh herbs around too. Wilting parsley, dodgy dill – doesn't matter (although coriander doesn't work so well), this dish indiscriminately uses whatever you have, bound with barley and lifted by the scrummy toasts that are the real superstar.

100g pearl barley or pearled spelt

500ml vegetable or light chicken stock
(make it half strength if using a cube)

2 cloves of garlic, finely chopped
with salt to make a paste

salt and pepper

400g any quick-cook veg, cut into small pieces

100g goat's cheese

4 slices bread

2 teaspoons honey

1 lemon

50ml extra-virgin olive oil

25g soft herbs (parsley, basil, chives, mint or dill)

Preheat the oven to 180°C/160°C fan/gas mark 4.

Starting from cold, bring the barley and stock up to the boil, then simmer gently for about half an hour. When you can see the barley through the liquid, put a lid on it and turn the heat right down: the idea is that the barley absorbs all the flavour of the stock, rather than having it thrown down the drain. If the barley is cooked but there is still some liquid left, boil it hard for a few minutes until it's all gone, taking care not to let it catch on the bottom.

Once the barley is cooked, stir in half of the garlic paste, then season well and spread out on a plate to cool.

Rinse the pan out, fill it with salted water and bring to a rolling boil. Drop all of your vegetables into it, stick a lid on and prepare a bowl of very cold water, preferably iced. As soon as the veg pan comes back to the boil (2–3 minutes), strain and tip the blanched vegetables into the cold water (this keeps them green and stops them cooking, which is essential for this super-fresh and crunchy salad). Once the veg is cool, drain it.

Split the goat's cheese among the four pieces of bread, then drizzle with honey – about half a teaspoon on each. Put a piece of foil on a baking tray and bake them in the oven for about 12–15 minutes. You will smell it when they are ready: the cheese will have melted and the honey caramelized.

Rustle up the dressing with the juice of half the lemon. Whisk in the extra-virgin olive oil, stir in the remaining garlic and finish with the chopped herbs.

In a big bowl, mix together the barley and veg bits with the dressing and some seasoning, then taste. You want this one to be dressed pretty sharply to play with the honey. Serve with lemon wedges and the scrummy toasts.

SPINACH TORTILLA [Ⓐ]

serves: 4–6   preparation time: 20–25 minutes   cooking time: 20–30 minutes

This tortilla is Iranian, known as kuku in its native country, and it typifies the Middle East to me. While a Spanish tortilla is a wonderful thing, it's quite heavy, and this takes the same basis of spuds and eggs, but turns it into a much lighter, greener eat.

Once you've tried it, you'll understand why it is traditionally eaten as part of the big New Year celebrations, which fall on the first day of spring in the Iranian calendar. It just feels like a real bite of freshness and contains the prize-winning combination of all the best recipes: delicious, quick, cheap and easy.

1 large King Edward potato

2–3 cloves of garlic, peeled and roughly chopped

100g fresh spinach, washed and chopped
(or 200g frozen spinach, defrosted, squeezed and chopped)

salt and pepper

60g fresh herbs, ideally parsley and coriander or dill and mint too (but only as part of a mix), washed and roughly chopped

4 spring onions or ½ regular onion, peeled and finely chopped

6 free-range eggs, beaten

4 cardamom pods, bashed and seeds removed

30g butter

things to serve with it

a bit of salty cheese like feta

a bunch of radishes

some yoghurt

First, make your mash in the time-honoured way: peel, dice large, cold water to cover, pinch of salt, simmer, drain and mash. Preheat your oven to 180°C/160°C fan/gas mark 4.

If you're using frozen spinach, heat a tablespoon of olive oil and fry one clove of chopped garlic, then a minute later, add the spinach, give it a quick toss and warm through. Season with salt, pepper and a squeeze of lemon. Now chop all of the greenery and onions, including the fresh and raw or frozen and sautéed spinach, and mix into a bowl with the beaten eggs. Whisk in the garlic, cardamom seeds, seasoning (needs quite a bit) and once the spud is mashed, stir that in too.

I cook mine in a 25cm frying pan, but my Iranian friend Goli, who taught me this, says she does hers in a Pyrex dish. Any which way, melt a little butter and let it run all round the inside of the pan or dish. Pour in the egg mix and bake in the oven until the middle is just set, probably about 20–30 minutes, depending on the depth of your vessel.

Let sit for at least 10 minutes before serving with any of the suggestions above, or just enjoy it on its own.

NORWEGIAN FISH PIE

serves: 4   preparation time: 20 minutes   cooking time: 40–45 minutes

Earlier this year, we went on one of our madder trips on a Norwegian car ferry up to the Arctic Circle to try and see the Northern Lights. Switching from plane to boat in Tromsø, we had a white-knuckle landing through a 10-mile blizzard on to a runway thick with ice and, rather shakily (fear and frost), headed into town very glad to be alive. Whilst doing some fast-freeze acclimatizing, we arrived in thick snow at the poetically named Emma's Dream Kitchen, where this dish (or something pretty like it) hit the spot with a bull's-eye to the tummy and all was right with the world again.

In a light less Northern, we might confuse this with a tuna pasta bake.

30g unsalted butter
½ teaspoon caraway seeds
30g plain flour
500ml whole milk
160g pasta (macaroni, penne or fusilli)
100g cream cheese

salt and pepper
½ onion, finely chopped
1 x 130g tin of sustainable, dolphin-friendly tuna, drained
60–80g breadcrumbs
6–8 fat anchovy fillets, halved lengthways

Preheat the oven to 200°C/180°C fan/gas mark 6 and put a pan of salted water with a lid on to boil for the pasta.

In a separate pan, melt the butter and fry the caraway seeds in it gently for a couple of minutes before mixing in the flour. Continue to stir this over a low heat for a few minutes before adding about a quarter of the milk. Beat this in to make a smooth paste, then add another quarter and use a whisk to incorporate it. Add the remaining milk in two batches, making sure it's got no lumps before adding the next.

When your water is up to a fast boil, drop the pasta in and cook it al dente. Drain well in a colander. Bring the white sauce to a simmer and immediately turn it off, then mix in the cream cheese. Season it with salt and pepper.

Add the onion, tuna and pasta to the white sauce then tip the lot into a baking dish. Taste and season again, then cover with breadcrumbs and use the anchovy fillets to make the shape of the Norwegian flag on the top (or not, if you're feeling more sensible).

Bake in the oven for half an hour, by which time the top should be nice and golden and it should all be bubbling invitingly round the edge.

HOT DOG HOTPOT [Ⓐ]

serves: 4   preparation time: 20 minutes   cooking time: 20–25 minutes

Without meaning to put you off, frankfurters are the new Spam: meat that lasts. You know how to put it in a bun and have it as a snack, but this recipe takes the joy of a hot dog and makes it into a whole supper.

Hot dogs always remind me of my time in New York: at the end of every hectic Friday night shift we would go and buy ourselves a couple of 79¢ dogs, and this dish recreates the soothing effect our late-night snack had on our service-battered souls.

2 tablespoons butter
2 tablespoons light olive oil
2 medium onions (about 500g), peeled and sliced
2 cloves of garlic, peeled and chopped
8 frankfurters, cut into 2cm chunks
salt and pepper
450g vine-ripened tomatoes
400g wedge of white cabbage

2 tablespoons mustard (ideally 1 Dijon and 1 wholegrain, or whatever you've got)
4 tablespoons red wine vinegar
400g fresh egg noodles or 200g dried egg noodles, rehydrated according to the instructions on the packet
500ml chicken stock

Put a thick-bottomed pan on a high heat with the butter and oil. Once hot, chuck in your onions followed by the garlic and frankfurters. Cook and stir for 5 minutes until lightly browned. Drop the heat down to medium, add a hefty pinch of salt and put a lid on for 5 minutes.

Get a small pan of water on to boil. Wash your tomatoes, cut out the cores and cross the bottoms. Drop the tomatoes into your pan of boiling water and prepare a bowl of iced water. After 1 minute, use a slotted spoon to lift the tomatoes out, drop them into the iced water and leave to cool for a minute or two until you can peel them easily.

Slice the core out of the cabbage wedge, cut the wedge into three or four pieces, then break the leaves up in a colander and give them a quick rinse.

Don't forget to keep stirring your onion pan – the onions should be starting to caramelize and smelling like hot dog onions. Once they're well and truly there, stir the mustards in well, followed by the vinegar, and bring the heat back up to full pelt so the vinegar reduces away – just a couple of minutes.

Drop the cabbage in, give it a mix and put the lid back on. After a couple of minutes, add the noodles and give them a good roll around. Pour in the chicken stock. Bring this up to a simmer, season, make sure that everything is under the surface, then leave to simmer for a last 5 minutes.

Cut your blanched, peeled tomatoes in half, use your fingers to dig the seeds out, which you chuck, and then roughly chop the flesh. Mix these into your hotpot. There should be quite a lot of liquid remaining – it's supposed to be soupy.

When serving, aim for the noodles first, then top the bowls up with the other bits and pieces. Good doggie.

PASTA E FAGIOLI

serves: 4 generously
preparation time: 20–25 minutes   cooking time: 35–40 minutes

Fagioli means beans, the ones of the pulse rather than green variety, and this is my all-time favourite default supper. A beautiful, thick, flavour-laden soup, just like the Italians do best. The basis for it is a home-made stock – there's no getting around that – but by this stage in the book, I'm confident you'll have some in your fridge and/or freezer.

From there it's a walk in the park: a tin of beans (really any will do), a couple of handfuls of any kind of pasta, have a rootle around in your fridge for veg – anything from potatoes to peas, it really doesn't matter. What does matter is Parmesan and extra-virgin. And the stock. And that's it.

I usually make a double batch while I'm there because the flavour tends to be better the next day, which makes it ideal for freezing.

1 onion, peeled and diced

2 cloves of garlic, peeled and chopped

½ teaspoon dried chilli flakes

extra-virgin olive oil

600g mixed veg (courgette, fennel, swede, spuds, sweet potatoes, leek, celery, carrots, peas), diced into 1cm squares, apart from the peas

salt and pepper

a few pinches of dried herbs
(rosemary, oregano and thyme are best)

1 litre chicken or veg stock

80g pasta, any kind,
broken into 3cm pieces if necessary

1 x 400g tin of beans, drained
(cannellini, borlotti, haricot or chickpeas)

2 bay leaves

50g chunk Parmesan,
plus any old rind, finely grated

1 large or 2 small very ripe tomatoes,
finely chopped

In a heavy-bottomed pan, fry the onion, garlic and chilli in 4 tablespoons of the extra-virgin for a few minutes. Add all the chopped veg (except the peas – they come later), some salt and pepper and the dried herbs and fry on a high heat for a couple of minutes until it's all glossy. Turn the heat down to medium high, put a lid on and keep frying the veg, stirring it every so often, for about 10 to 15 minutes – you want it to look like it's lightly cooked before you add the stock.

Pour in the stock and stir in the pasta, beans and bay leaves – peas here too if you fancy. Add a bit more salt. Bring to the boil, then turn down and simmer gently for about 25 minutes. Mix together the Parmesan and tomato in a little bowl with 2 tablespoons of extra-virgin olive oil.

If you're not about to keel over with hunger, let it sit for 10 minutes before ladling into bowls with a spoonful of the cheesy-tomato mix on top, a few cracks of black pepper and a generous flourish of extra-virgin.

BAKEWELL IN A BAG [Ⓐ]

makes: about 12 slices
preparation time: 15 minutes   cooking time: 30–40 minutes

We owe the lovely bit of the 'bag' (as opposed to fiddling around with tart cases) to the great Nigel Slater, who makes one with fruit in the middle. He, in turn, credits the Americans for this rougher, more farmhouse style of tart/pie.

Made 100% from ingredients anyone with an interest in cookery would have around. It's very easy, and looks exceedingly friendly on your kitchen table – doesn't last long there though . . .

130g ground almonds (whizzed up flaked or whole will work too, but save a handful for the top)

100g butter, soft

100g caster sugar

1 egg, beaten

a few drops of vanilla extract

1 x 500g packet of shortcrust pastry

5 tablespoons jam (I like raspberry best, but any will do – doesn't even have to be red)

2 tablespoons milk

Preheat the oven to 200°C/180°C fan/gas mark 6. In a mixing bowl, use a wooden spoon to blend the ground almonds with the butter and sugar. Mix in the egg white (but save the yolk) and vanilla and put in the fridge for a minute to firm up. Flour your surface and roll the pastry out to roughly 30cm x 30cm.

Lightly flour a baking tray or shallow roasting tray with a bit of a lip – the one I used was about 25cm square, but the size doesn't really matter – you just need the lip to support the pastry. Roll out the pastry to a thickness of about 5mm, then gather it up around your rolling pin and gently lay it down so it falls over the edges of your tray.

Splodge the jam in the middle and use the back of the spoon to roughly spread it out over a circle of around 20cm. Gently dollop the almond mix on top of the jam to cover it – you don't have to be too precise because it will sort itself out in the oven, but try not to spread the jam out too much.

Now – and this sounds a lot scarier than it actually is – bring the pastry up and around on all sides so that you have an open-tart-sack-bag-thing, where you can see the almond mix inside the crater.

Brush the pastry all over with the milk mixed with the egg yolk and sprinkle with a touch of caster sugar.

If you have any, scatter over a few flaked or whole almonds and bake in the oven for around 25 minutes. Turn the oven down to 160°C/140°C fan/gas mark 3, open the door and flap it a few times to cool it down. Cook for 10 minutes more until it looks luscious – it also suits a dusting of icing sugar once it's cooled down.

I object to waste and I make coffee in one of those multi-sided Italian coffee makers that you put on the hob. Because they're a bit of a faff (but undeniably produce the best coffee domestically), sometimes when there's a bunch of people around, you over-provide and the leftover fabulous coffee is distinctly sink-bound. Having been to coffee plantations and seen the effort involved in picking those beans, this is the kind of waste that particularly upsets me.

This page has got it all: long drink, boozy shot, emergency pudding and worldwide beneficiary points too. You need to have reasonably strong coffee to make the basic freeze recipe – thin, weak stuff won't pack a punch at the finishing line.

THE BASIC FREEZE

makes: 16 ice cubes (multiply as necessary)   preparation time: 5 minutes, plus freezing time

220ml strong coffee
2 tablespoons golden granulated sugar (it's a ratio and taste thing,
but start with this as a guideline and then let your tastebuds take it from there)

Stir the sugar into the coffee and pour it into ice-cube trays.

COFFEE GRANITA CRUNCH

makes: 2 puddings   preparation time: 2 minutes

10 ice cubes
6 cubes of frozen coffee
a shot and a bit of coffee, almond or hazelnut flavoured liqueur (optional)

Put the glasses in the freezer an hour ahead. Whizz the ice cubes on their own until they look like crushed ice, then add the coffee cubes and booze and blend for a further 5 seconds. Pour immediately into the iced glasses – the texture should be more slush puppy than granita – wetter and more intense.

ICED BOOZY SHOTS

makes: 4 shots   preparation time: 2 minutes

3 cubes of frozen coffee
1 shot of coffee liqueur
1 shot of water

Blend, pour into shot glasses and wait for the liquids to just begin separating before you serve.

FRAPPUCCINO

makes: 1 very cool, very long drink or 2 small ones   preparation time: 2 minutes

6 cubes of frozen coffee
200ml milk
a small handful of ice

Chuck it all in the blender and serve in a tall glass with more ice and compulsory straws.

PUT A STOCK IN IT

IT'S PROBABLY THE SINGLE BEST INVESTMENT OF TIME AND MONEY ON THE PLANET AND YOU NEED HARDLY ANY OF EITHER TO KNOCK ONE UP. THIS SIMPLE ACT OF SANITY CAN TRANSFORM MANY A MEAL FROM DULL TO DELICIOUS. THROWING AWAY A CHICKEN CARCASS (RAW OR COOKED) OR SOME MANKY PIECES OF VEG, WITHOUT OFFERING THEM THE OPPORTUNITY TO GIVE WHAT'S LEFT OF THEMSELVES, IS NOT ONLY A WASTE OF A TREMENDOUS TASTE-RESOURCE, IT'S ALSO PLAIN RUDE TO OUR PLANET.

Both food waste and food costs are at an all-time high. In our 'civilized' country, many of us are so short of time that we can't see the wood for the trees and are guilty of food choices that would make our grandparents turn in their graves. Sure, you can buy stock in various forms, but fresh doesn't taste of much and costs over £1 for half a litre; and the flavour of the cubes isn't that great, they're quite salty and really only there as a last resort. Alternatively, you can take literally three minutes and chuck one on the stove yourself. Less than an hour later it's done, and is ready for straining and saving for when you need it. Any regular stock-maker can attest to that and, aside from that, if you've never made a stock in your life you have no idea of the simple pleasure you're denying yourself.

I love the smell of a simmering stock, and actually chose an apartment in Manhattan just because my Jewish neighbours always made the corridor smell of chicken soup. It's a relaxing smell to match the relaxing simmer and, as the old saying goes, is good for the soul.

Please don't think I'm encouraging you to launch yourself into the Michelin world of blonde veal stocks and shiny demi-glaces . . . Just a few bits of veg (carrots, onion and a stick of celery if you have it); some aromatics (peppercorns, bay, thyme, rosemary); some protein (chicken or fish); and a bit of anything else you fancy (the brown leaves on a bulb of fennel, some dried chilli if you're fond of fire and, personally, I haven't thrown away parsley stalks for years). Unashamedly, keep any nearly dead veg in the fridge until your next stock session – there's just so much flavour left in them to give.

Stocks take ingredients on their last legs that are heading for the bin and give them one last chance to make culinary gold. And though this may be the stuff of alchemy, it's not magic. Anyone can chuck some bits in a pan, cover them with water (you never add salt to a stock till you use it in its final destination), simmer for 45 minutes . . . and that's it.

Ask your fishmonger for the fish bones (free), or buy a whole chicken rather than portioned limbs in order to get yourself the carcass (free), or use up random bits of veg like munched-on corn cobs, the hearts of which still have so much flavour. Because that is the bottom line. These things may not be the prettiest you've ever seen, but if we go through life only going for the pretty and perfect, wouldn't that just about ruin our planet? These uglies have great flavour, and to throw them out while they still have so much taste locked inside them is just plain nuts.

At the risk of giving you a bit of fighting talk (designed to spur you into action rather than give you the fear), I'd go as far as to say that if you can't get your head around shoving a stock on the stove, you're never going to get the thought behind Economy Gastronomy. And that means you might as well resign yourself to a life where eating at home is dominated by ready meals and takeaways . . . And what kind of home is that?

HOME-MADE TAKEAWAYS

PEPPERONI PORKY PIZZA

CHINESE-STYLE CRISPY DUCK

THAI PRAWN CURRY

COLONEL MERRETT'S
BUCKET OF CHICKEN

SPICY LAMB SHISH KEBAB

CURRIED MUTTON
WITH GREEN CHILLI AND ALMONDS

NEVER-FAILED-YET BASMATI RICE

ALONG WITH CHEAP AIR TRAVEL AND THE WORLD-WIDE WEB, BEING ABLE TO GET A TAKEAWAY – EVEN BETTER IF IT'S DELIVERED TO YOUR HOUSE – IS ONE OF SOCIETY'S GREATEST POST-WAR PROGRESSIONS.

Indian, fish and chips, Turkish, Chinese, pizza, Thai, Lebanese, diner, modern British, sushi . . . or whoever else happens to have settled near you and set up a kitchen. As a Londoner, I adore having all of this at the end of the phone and, though I hate to admit it, take it for granted.

And that really is the point about takeaways in the here and now. Too many of us have lost the sense of it being 'occasion' food. Somebody cooks exactly what you ask them to cook right there and then – surely that's a king's privilege?

This Pandora's box has been flung open for a long time: when I worked in New York more than ten years ago, I was so (naïvely) impressed when my flatmate got breakfast delivered from the corner deli at the weekend: that was the ultimate, and the ultimate in stupid. Some foods are just not designed to travel, and scrambled eggs, hash browns and toast are a few of them.

Like most things that seem glamorous, there's a downside to them too. In the world of takeaways the image of the sad fatty in front of the telly is enough to stop most people overindulging. But if you do find yourself taking too much interest in the menus that flop through your letterbox (and vanity isn't proving a deal breaker), then try these on for size: money, taste, health and freshness.

If it looks like I'm trying to position your local kebab shop on the axis of evil, that is not my intention, particularly if your local takeaways are small, independent businesses making nice food. I'm all for giving them your trade, but, and it's a big one, takeaways are addictive . . . or, at the very least, habit-forming.

Back in the seventies, walking up to the Turkish kebab shop on Shepherd's Bush Road with my dad was a big treat. Remembering that feeling and comparing it with when we order in these days, I feel as if I've spoiled the treat. Because takeaways have become a bit of an abused privilege.

Weirdly, it wasn't till Paul and I came up with the recipes for this chapter that I properly went head to head with some of my favourite takeaways. And without sounding disrespectful to the people who've fed me for years, I was amazed how much yummier the home-made versions were.

But don't take my word for it: gather your ingredients, make your favourite takeaway and taste the difference.

Consider the gauntlet thrown.

PEPPERONI PORKY PIZZA

serves: 4   preparation time: 20–25 minutes, plus at least 1 hour 20 minutes proving
cooking time: 12–15 minutes

Given that we all know how to make a tomato sauce, the stumbling block to having home-made pizza more often must be the dough, or, more specifically, the idea of preparing ahead. Knocking up the dough actually takes fewer than 10 minutes (less when you've done it once or twice) and proving it takes about an hour. You can even do it in the morning before you go to work, chuck it in the airing cupboard or near a radiator (any warm place will do) and no harm will come to it. This sauce recipe makes enough for two lots of pizza. You might as well do double and keep it in the fridge/freezer for next time – it makes a nice pasta sauce, too. I do my pizza on one big square tray, making the most of the shape of my oven.

for the dough
260g strong white flour
¾ teaspoon yeast
(try to get the one that doesn't have to be dissolved first, so it can go straight into the flour)
¾ teaspoon sugar
1 teaspoon salt
140ml warm water
olive oil

for the sauce
1 large red onion, peeled and diced
2 cloves of garlic, peeled and roughly chopped
3 tablespoons olive oil

½ teaspoon dried oregano
½ teaspoon dried chilli flakes
150g lardons
250g beef mince
2 x 400g tins of plum tomatoes
(chopped or broken up by hand)
salt and pepper

for the topping
80g mushrooms, washed, trimmed and sliced thickly
1 green pepper, deseeded and sliced
80g block of mozzarella, for grating
12 slices of pepperoni

To make the dough, put all the dry ingredients into a big bowl and make a well in the centre. Gradually add the water, and as the dough starts to bind together splosh in just under 2 tablespoons of olive oil. Keep mixing and gradually adding water until the dough comes away from the sides. Do the last bit by hand. If it gets sticky, add a touch more flour. Once you have a smooth ball of dough, knead it on a flat, lightly floured surface for 5 minutes. Use the ball of your hand to push the dough away from you, then fold it back over towards you using your fingertips. Keep repeating this action. To test if your dough is ready to prove, poke it and, if it bounces back and pretty much fills up the hole, it has been worked sufficiently. Use both hands to briefly shape the dough into a ball. Wash and dry your bowl, put a healthy splash of oil into the bottom and use your fingers to spread the oil up the sides. Put the dough ball in the bowl and roll it around to lightly cover with oil. Cover the bowl with a clean tea towel and put it in a warm place to prove for an hour or more.

Now for the sauce. Over a medium heat in a thick-bottomed pan, gently fry the onion and garlic in the oil for a few minutes. Add your oregano, chilli flakes and lardons, give it a stir, then pop a lid on and leave on the heat for 15 minutes, stirring regularly to make sure it's not catching. Once everything in the pan is looking and smelling good, tip in the mince and turn the heat to high. Break it up and stir well. When the mince starts to brown, add the tomatoes, turn down to a medium heat and leave it to simmer with the lid off for 20 to 25 minutes. Again, stir regularly to stop it sticking. Preheat your oven to the highest it will go.

Roll out the pizza dough on a floured surface until it is around 2mm thick, using the edge of your rolling pin to keep the sides straight and the whole thing square-ish. Flour your chosen tray (mine's about 30cm square). Roll the dough a bit bigger than your tray, then flip it up around your rolling pin and flop it over the tray. Ideally it will fall over the sides a bit. Leave it to firm up and have a mini prove for 15–20 minutes.

Your sauce should now have reached a thick consistency. Taste, season and leave to cool whilst you prepare the toppings. Ladle half the sauce over the pizza base and spread it out evenly, leaving a couple of centimetres around the edge (the rest goes in the fridge/freezer for later). Scatter on the toppings, finishing with the pepperoni. When the oven is hot, put the pizza on the bottom of the oven rather than on a shelf and cook for 12–15 minutes until it looks even better than any takeaway pizza, because you made it all yourself.

CHINESE-STYLE CRISPY DUCK [Ⓟ]

serves: 4 as a starter
preparation time: 15 minutes, plus marinating time   cooking time: 2 hours 40 minutes

In our house on your birthday you are allowed to choose what everyone eats that evening. This quaint tradition is one put in place by my mum when I was young. Every year I chose macaroni cheese. Mum must have chuckled all the way to the supermarket, knowing that once again her son had picked practically the cheapest meal ever invented. She would skip down the aisles past the foie gras, truffles and lobster, stopping briefly in the dairy section for a pound of Cheddar, then it was over to dry goods for a packet of macaroni.

When I had children this rule was introduced into our house, but unfortunately my children are not quite as economy-conscious as the young Paul Merrett was. Every year they both demand that we phone the local Chinese restaurant and order crispy duck with all the trimmings. Upon arrival, they then insist that it must be eaten on our knees in front of the telly (a big no-no under normal circumstances).

Realizing that I could not withdraw the 'choice of birthday food' rule but fearing eventual bankruptcy, I decided to look into producing my own crispy duck. I was horrified to find that it's a lengthy process and one quite unsuitable for the home cook. I needed an easy (yet cheap) alternative and the following recipe is, I believe, just that. Some planning ahead is needed as the duck legs need marinating a couple of days before.

4 large duck legs (look for the farmed variety)
1 tablespoon light soy sauce
5cm piece of fresh ginger, finely grated
2 cloves of garlic, peeled and chopped
1kg duck fat

8 spring onions
1 cucumber
Chinese pancakes
150ml hoisin sauce

To marinate the duck, put the legs in a shallow dish or sealable bag and pour over the soy sauce. Add the ginger and garlic and rub the marinade all over the legs, then cover and keep in the fridge.

You can cook the duck legs well before you want to eat them – in fact, I recommend you do this the day before. First, preheat the oven to 150°C/130°C fan/gas mark 2. Take the duck legs from the fridge and place them in an ovenproof dish with the bits of ginger and garlic and the soy sauce. Then melt the duck fat slowly in a saucepan on the stove. When it's simmering, pour it over the legs, making sure they are submerged in the fat. Cover the dish with tin foil and pop it in the oven.

The duck legs will take at least 1½ hours to cook, but check them every 45 minutes or so to make sure the duck is still submerged. The fat should be simmering gently and the duck skin should be fairly white or translucent-looking. After 1½–2 hours the meat should be soft. Check this by poking in the tip of a knife. Cook for a little longer if there's any resistance, then remove the legs from the fat (this can be strained and kept in the fridge – great for roasting potatoes) and let them cool on a plate. They can then be transferred to the fridge until the meal is required.

About 45 minutes before you wish to eat, heat the oven to 180°C/160°C fan/gas mark 4. Place the duck legs on a wire rack over a roasting tray to catch any drips. Then pop the tray in the oven and cook until the legs are hot right through and the skin is really (I mean really) crisp. This takes about 40 minutes.

Meanwhile, shred the spring onions, cut the cucumber into thin strips and pour the hoisin sauce into a dish. Put these on the table. Next, wrap the pancakes in a clean, damp tea towel and give them 5 minutes in the oven to warm through before putting them on the table too. Finally, take the duck from the oven and, using a fork, shred all the meat from the bone on to a large plate. And that's it!

THAI PRAWN CURRY

serves: 4   preparation time: 25–30 minutes   cooking time: 40–45 minutes

Having stormed our pubs and high streets in the eighties, Thai food was the first real challenger for the Favourite Asian Takeaway Cup that had been held by China for so long – and the green curry was their team captain.

This recipe uses a base paste that you can get from most supermarkets. It is not the same as a jar of green curry sauce, because this way you still do the cooking and control the flavours whilst having a hefty chunk of the basic work done for you. Lime leaves live in the freezer and, although not readily available, it's well worth nipping into an Asian shop once in a blue moon to stock up – there's nothing that adds the right smell to a green curry more than lime leaves. I'm assuming you'll want jasmine rice, but I've also assumed you can follow the directions on the packet. I like mine pretty wet, but isn't that the best bit of a green curry?

jasmine or basmati rice

600g (around 6 each) tiger prawns, heads and shell on

3 tablespoons light groundnut or sunflower oil

4 cloves of garlic, 2 whole and smashed, 2 peeled and roughly chopped

2 green chillies, 1 whole and 1 chopped

2 sticks of lemongrass

lime leaves (optional)

a big clutch (70g) of bean sprouts

a big handful (30g) of coriander, roughly chopped including stalks, except for a few pretty sprigs

2 spring onions, thinly sliced on a long diagonal

2 limes (1 for the curry, 1 to finish)

50g ginger, trimmed, washed, sliced and diced small

2–4 tablespoons Thai green curry paste (depending on strength)

1 x 400ml tin of coconut milk

2 peppers (preferably yellow and green), deseeded and cut into chunks

120g closed cap or button mushrooms, washed, tips trimmed and thickly sliced

a big handful of sugar snap peas

4–6 heads (300g) of bok choy, halved through the root

fish sauce

Peel the prawns, keeping the end of the tail on (just looks nicer, I think) and put the heads and shells in a smallish saucepan. Measure half the oil into the saucepan with the shells and chuck in the whole smashed cloves of garlic, the whole chilli and 1 stick of lemongrass. Fry on a high heat for a few minutes until the shells change colour. If you have a spare couple of lime leaves chuck them in too. Pour in 500ml of water and bring it up to a fierce simmer for 15–20 minutes: instant prawn stock.

In a bowl, mix the bean sprouts with the sprigs of coriander and the sliced spring onions. Dress with the juice of half a lime and set aside.

Meanwhile, heat the rest of the oil in a wide, heavy-bottomed pan and gently fry the ginger, shortly followed by the chopped garlic and chopped chilli, if you fancy. Take off a couple of the outer leaves of the lemongrass, then very thinly slice the fat bottom quarter and add this in, saving the tops for later. Once this is all smelling good and strong – just a minute or two – stir the paste in well.

Strain the stock through a sieve into a measuring jug, making sure you turn over and push down the shells to get out every last drop. About ten pushes should give you around 300ml. Add the stock to the pan and simmer hard for 5 minutes, then pour in the coconut milk. Any lime leaves and lemongrass tops, tied together with string, can also go in now. Turn the heat right up. After a few minutes, stir in the peppers and mushrooms. Simmer hard with the lid off for just a couple of minutes, then add the sugar snaps and prawns, stir and sit the bok choy on top.

Four minutes later, turn the heat off. Stir in the chopped coriander and season with a hefty dash of fish sauce, lime juice and a pinch of salt, if necessary. The other lime can be cut into wedges for serving alongside the curry with your rice and a handful of the crunchy bean sprouts and coriander to top it off.

COLONEL MERRETT'S BUCKET OF CHICKEN ⓟ

serves: 4   preparation time: 20 minutes, plus marinating time
cooking time: 50 minutes

If anyone chances upon my MP3 player they will find, among the obscure early Clash recordings, the vast selection of rare Northern Soul and the entire Paul Weller back catalogue, a number of not quite so cool ditties that I listen to when no one is around. This is known as a guilty pleasure, apparently.

My guilty food pleasure is crispy chicken purchased from a well-known high-street chain (where the mixture of herbs and spices allegedly remains a closely guarded secret). For many years I would occasionally sneak off into town with my children and pick up a few portions of this delicacy said to originate from the southern states of the USA.

Then, a few years ago, I made a television programme, after which covert crispy chicken purchasing became off limits. Each time I entered the shop someone would rumble me and shout something offensive about TV chefs buying takeaways. There was only one thing for it – I would have to send my wife in instead. Unfortunately, she refused, telling me that it was far too expensive for a bit of old chicken and that she hated the soggy chips. 'Cook it yourself,' she helpfully suggested, adding, 'You are a chef, after all. Their spicy secret can't be that hard to work out.' Well, here it is – my guilt-free version of the high-street classic.

4 chicken thighs

4 chicken drumsticks

1 whole head of garlic
(optional, if you want to make stock)

sprigs of thyme
(optional, if you want to make stock)

100g flour

1 teaspoon ground cumin

1 teaspoon cayenne pepper

1 teaspoon celery salt

½ teaspoon English mustard powder

½ teaspoon salt

300ml milk

1 litre vegetable oil

4 baked potatoes,
left to go cold in the fridge overnight

½ head of Savoy cabbage, finely shredded

1 large gherkin, grated

2 carrots, grated

1 red onion, peeled, halved and finely sliced

100g mayonnaise (home-made is always best,
but if no one is looking . . .)

To cook the chicken, place the thighs and drumsticks in a pot and cover with water. (If you add a head of garlic and some thyme, you will have a chicken stock left by the time the chicken is cooked – perfect for keeping in the fridge for another day.) Simmer for about 30 minutes, or until the chicken is cooked through. Allow the chicken pieces to cool in the stock, then remove them and store in the fridge until required.

Mix the flour with the cumin, cayenne, celery salt, mustard powder and salt in a large bowl. Toss the chicken in the seasoned flour. I leave the skin on, but it can be removed. Once thoroughly floured, dip the chicken pieces in the milk and then back in the flour. This double-coating means they will be extra crispy.

Pour the oil into a large pan. It needs to be at least 10cm deep and, very importantly, not be too near the top. Heat it to 170°C before any frying takes place (use a digital cooking probe; see p.10). To test it, drop in a cube of white bread. When it quickly goes gold brown, then you're about there. Finally, once you start to heat the oil, don't wander off and get distracted as it can easily overheat and explode. Fry the chicken pieces in batches. Carefully lower them into the oil with a slotted spoon and remove when crispy, golden and cooked right through. This takes about 4–5 minutes.

Keep the chicken in a warm oven whilst you knock out the potato wedges. Cut the cold baked potatoes into wedges and cook exactly as you did the chicken, in batches in the hot oil, for approximately 2 minutes. Meanwhile, put all the vegetables and mayonnaise in a bowl and mix everything together to make creamy coleslaw. Enjoy your guilty pleasure, perhaps with 'Silver Lady' by David Soul playing in the background!

SPICY LAMB SHISH KEBAB

makes: 4   preparation time: 20 minutes, plus marinating   cooking time: 20–30 minutes

If there's one smell that defines the Middle East, an area of the world I adore and felt instantly at home in, it's that of grilling meat over hot coals.

Translating hot coals over here is obviously a BBQ at first glance, but as we mostly eat indoors, the authentic taste can be pretty readily achieved with a griddle pan. Though not an essential bit of kit (and not very cheap either, being made of cast iron), there is no doubt in my mind that they are absolutely worth it. They make your meat, veggies and fish taste like your holidays and it's a healthy way of cooking too. If you do choose to buy one, go for one with ribs that are about a centimetre thick. Thick lines have meaningful contact with the meat/fish/veg, thus giving them a touch of the right flavour and letting any fat (like with lamb and pork) run away into the gullies. This recipe would work well with chicken too – use breast cut to the same size and cook it for a minute less each side.

If you thought the best kebab you ever had was the one you stumbled into at the end of a drunken evening, I beg to differ.

for the lamb
2 cloves of garlic, peeled and finely chopped
¾ teaspoon ground cumin
600g lamb (preferably leg), diced into 3cm cubes
salt
light olive oil, if using a pan

for the yoghurt sauce
150g Greek yoghurt
1 tablespoon tahini (not essential,
but good and it lasts for ever in the fridge)
a handful of mint, picked and chopped
2 tablespoons extra-virgin olive oil
2 cloves of garlic, peeled and finely chopped
a touch of salt

to build the kebab
4 x 20cm flatbreads
200g red or white cabbage, thinly shredded
chilli sauce
2 tomatoes, sliced
½ red onion, peeled and thinly sliced
4 dill pickles, thickly sliced
pickled chillies (I like 2 or 3 on my kebab)
a squeeze of lemon juice

Mix together the chopped garlic with the cumin, then roll and coat the lamb cubes in it well. You can cook this straight away, but more of the flavours will be absorbed by the meat if you leave it out at room temperature for a few hours, or overnight in the fridge. When you're ready to eat, put your griddle/pan on a high heat and get it smoking hot.

If you have a griddle, you won't need any oil. If you're doing it in a pan, you may need a tiny splash. Quickly place each lamb cube on the griddle (i.e. don't just tip in the bowl of meat) and leave to sizzle. This makes a bit of yummy-smelling smoke, so get the extraction on/windows open. Season with salt whilst on the griddle.

After 3–4 minutes, turn the meat, and use this time to mix the yoghurt sauce ingredients together in a little bowl.

After a further 3–4 minutes, take the lamb from the griddle/pan, put in a bowl, turn the heat down and let it sit for a few minutes. Lay each flatbread in turn on the griddle/in the pan to soften them up a bit, or you can warm all of them at once in a preheated oven (150°C/130°C fan/gas mark 2) for a couple of minutes.

Now build your kebabs. Put a healthy splodge of yoghurt sauce on each flatbread, then pile on the cabbage, chilli sauce, tomato, onion, dill pickle and top it off with the lamb, a bit more yoghurt sauce, some pickled chillies and a squeeze of lemon juice. Roll it up, pick it up and munch on down. Winner.

CURRIED MUTTON ⓟ
WITH GREEN CHILLI AND ALMONDS

serves: 4   preparation time: 30 minutes   cooking time: 2 hours 15 minutes

I love a good curry. No, actually it goes beyond love! Every so often I yearn for spicy food. Luckily this country boasts many fine Indian restaurants, but eating out is a relatively expensive business, so most of my curries are home-made. The temptation is to pick up the phone and order a takeaway, but that still costs money. The answer, of course, is to cook your own.

This is a simple, tasty beginner's curry, with relatively few ingredients – all of them easily obtainable. I have chosen to use mutton because it's a meat often used in Asian restaurants. Mutton is lamb that is older than a year. Because it's slightly older, it is a little tougher and, therefore, requires slightly longer cooking. The payoff is in the flavour.

1 tablespoon vegetable oil
½ onion, peeled and chopped
2 cloves of garlic, peeled and chopped
2.5cm piece of fresh ginger, peeled and grated
6 cloves
6 cardamom pods
2 or 3 green chillies, very finely sliced
5cm piece of cinnamon stick
500g shoulder of mutton, cut into 5cm cubes
180g natural yoghurt
½ lime
3 tablespoons coconut milk

for the spice and almond mix
1 tablespoon ground coriander
1 dessertspoon ground almonds
1 teaspoon turmeric
1 teaspoon ground cumin
½ teaspoon chilli powder
a pinch of black pepper

You will need a pot with a lid for this recipe, as the idea is to trap the steam and moisture created by the ingredients instead of adding lots of liquid. So, heat the pot up on the stove and add vegetable oil. Fry the onion, garlic and grated ginger for about 5 minutes, until they soften and colour very slightly.

Put the ingredients for the spice and almond mix in a bowl. Add the cloves, cardamoms, green chillies and cinnamon to the onions and allow to fry for a few seconds. Next add the spice and almond mix and stir in. Add the meat and mix it in well.

Pour in the yoghurt and, over a low heat, gently bring the curry to a simmer. At this point the pot's contents will look quite dry, but steam will soon be created as it simmers with a lid on. If at all worried, now would be a good moment to add a little water – say, 3 tablespoons. Cook the curry slowly for about 1–2 hours, or until the mutton is really tender. Once it's cooked, check for seasoning and finish the dish by adding a squeeze of lime juice and the coconut milk. Serve with my Never-failed-yet Basmati Rice (see p.231).

NEVER-FAILED-YET BASMATI RICE ^P

serves: 4   preparation time: 5 minutes   cooking time: 20 minutes

I am including this recipe because nothing ruins curry quicker than a dodgy bowl of rice. This method of cooking basmati rice was taught to me by an Indian kitchen porter at the Ritz, where I did my training. He didn't speak a word of English and I speak even less Urdu, but by watching him I picked up a few simple tips which have never failed to produce great steamed rice.

vegetable oil
400g basmati rice
optional: 1 onion, peeled and finely sliced
optional: 2 cloves of garlic, peeled and finely chopped
optional: any or all of the following spices: 1 teaspoon turmeric,
½ teaspoon chilli flakes, 2 inch cinnamon stick,
1 teaspoon cumin, 1 teaspoon fennel seeds

Heat a little oil in a pot with a tight-fitting lid (this is crucial). Meanwhile, wash your rice gently. The more you mix it around, the more you will scratch the grains, which means more starch will be released and your rice will become gluey . . . which is not good. Now drain the rice.

At this point you could add any or all of your optional ingredients to the pot. Alternatively, you can just go for the plain variety. Either way, add your rice to the hot oil and shake the pan a little to get everything sizzling. At the final shake ensure your rice is lying flat and level across the pan. Now pour in cold water. Place the tip of your finger on the top of the rice. The water should come up to the first joint of your finger.

Bring the water to the boil, then cover the pan with the tight-fitting lid and boil it hard for 5 minutes. Switch it off and leave it to stand, covered, for 20 minutes. DON'T BE TEMPTED TO LIFT THE LID! The steam trapped inside is busy cooking the rice. After 20 minutes, lift the lid, fork the rice through and serve immediately.

WASTE AND THE ISSUE OF OFFNESS

IT'S HARD NOT TO GET REALLY UPSET ABOUT WASTE, KNOWING THAT WE LIVE IN A COUNTRY WHERE WE THROW AWAY A THIRD OF THE FOOD WE BUY. AND YET WE ALL DO IT.
BEFORE WE GO ANY FURTHER, READ THIS:

Every DAY we throw away:

- 7 million slices of bread (worth £140 million a year)
- 1 million slices of ham (worth £30 million a year)
- 4.4 million whole apples (worth £300 million a year)
- 440,000 ready-made meals
- 5.1 million whole potatoes (worth £140 million a year)
- 660,000 eggs (worth £50 million a year)
- 260,000 unopened packs of cheese (worth £40 million a year)
- 2.8 million tomatoes (worth £80 million a year)
- 1 million plums (worth £70 million a year)
- 1.2 million whole sausages (worth £60 million a year)
- 550,000 rashers of bacon (worth £50 million a year)
- 330,000 chicken portions (worth £70 million a year)
- 82,000 whole dessert cakes and gateaux (worth £20 million a year)
- 300,000 unopened packets of crisps (worth £20 million a year)
- 700,000 unopened packets of chocolate and sweets (worth £40 million a year)
- 2,900 unopened cans or bottles of lager (worth just under £10 million a year)

Source: WRAP Food Waste Report – 'The Food We Waste' (April 2008)

Last year in the UK, nearly 1 million tonnes of food that hadn't even been touched was thrown away. Interesting behaviour. Of course, the big questions are 'why is this happening?' and 'what can we do to make it less shameful?'

Much of it is a sad by-product of progress: many people are now spending less time in the kitchen, and paying for other people to do it for us (ready meals, prepped veg, etc.). This has created a bit of distance between us and the things in our fridge or cupboard, as we don't have the same understanding of them. We've lost confidence in knowing when food's still OK, meaning how long it's really going to last, and when, exactly, it's beyond recovery.

Hating to sound like an old bat, common sense isn't what it used to be. Nowadays we watch anything from a bag of spinach to a loaf of bread – even chicken, food that had a life – slowly dying over days, and instead of taking a small amount of action to save it, we just ignore it and walk on by.

We can now get beautiful-looking ingredients from anywhere in the world, any time. Whatever you want, whenever you want, stacked in abundance on the shelves. That's just asking for a throw-away culture.

And just to round off the rant, we've become a little bit disrespectful of the time it takes to grow beans, rear a pig, make cheese. A lot of labour went into that thing you've just chucked, and that, to be honest, is just plain thoughtless.

But somewhere inside, we know that our disposable culture is not a sustainable one. What kind of people throw away 20,000 tonnes of breakfast cereal every year because they are too busy to finish it? (I know I've been part of that statistic.) We have become complacent about the world's resources, and I'm not even going to mention the millions of people all over the world who would be very grateful for that half-bowl of muesli every morning.

In this bountiful modern world we live in, waste represents the ugly underside. It's going on in every home in the nation, yet we've been sluggish in taking personal responsibility . . . and action.

First and foremost, become a Fridge Prefect. Know what's there, roughly how long you've got, and, most importantly, if it's right on the edge, do something about it there and then. Wilted, browning basil makes pesto in 5 minutes; squishy fruit becomes a smoothie in seconds. If they're on the use-by date* and you haven't time to cook them, chicken and fish can both go a couple more days with a wash under cold water, a pat dry, a squeeze of lemon and a bit of a marinade in extra-virgin olive oil and some herbs.

Just like us, fruit and veg does not always grow picture-perfectly. Walking down those aisles can be reminiscent of *The Stepford Wives* (see Sad Fruit Made Happy p.311). The truth is, it's the not-advert-perfect fruit and veg that generally have the best flavour; it's the real-looking ones, the honest ones.

And then there's the planning thing: for most of us, life isn't like how it was for our parents, and certainly not how it was for their parents. But equally, is that a reason to toss out half of the salad we buy?

As a starter pack of thoughts, there are a few suggestions of how to use up the top ten ingredients that Britain throws out, as compiled by WRAP (Waste & Resources Action Programme) on p.254 and have a look at www.lovefoodhatewaste.com as well. But back to the common-sense thing. You really do know it already: buy only what you're going to eat, and don't let food fester in the fridge.

That bit is just logic, but what I really want to know is, what loonies are throwing out all that beer and chocolate?

GASTRO-PUBONOMY

CREAMY GARLIC RABBIT CASSEROLE

THAI-SPICED STEAMED MUSSELS

CREAMY HAM HOCK CASSEROLE
WITH GOAT'S CHEESE CROSTINI

NAVARIN OF LAMB

VEAL RATATOUILLE

PROVENÇAL FISH SOUP

PAN-FRIED LAMB'S KIDNEYS ON TOAST

SEARED SQUID WITH CHORIZO

THIS CHAPTER SUGGESTS THAT YOU SAVE MONEY BY COOKING GASTRO-PUB-STYLE FOOD FOR WHICH YOU'D HAPPILY PAY GOOD MONEY ON A SATURDAY NIGHT. SURELY THIS IS A CONTRADICTION IN TERMS? AM I OFF MY ROCKER? WELL, YES, POSSIBLY, BUT THAT'S NOT THE POINT. THE POINT IS THAT CHEFS NEED TO MAKE A LIVING FROM THE CRAFT OF COOKING, SO WE BECOME VERY GOOD AT THRIFTY SHOPPING – USING LESS FASHIONABLE CUTS OF MEAT AND FISH AND COOKING ONLY SEASONAL FRUIT AND VEGETABLES.

My journey in food has taken me all the way from the poshest Michelin-starred food to the very real world of the gastro pub. I can't put fillet steak, loin of lamb or turbot on my menus (as much as I love them all) as they're all very expensive, so my solution is to be a little more inventive with cheaper ingredients.

As you turn the following pages, you will see pictures of veal shins, lamb's kidneys, fish heads and rabbit, all of which sell very well. People often comment on how much they have enjoyed these things but then add that they would never cook them at home. Well, that's all about to change: here are the recipes and all the ingredients are sitting waiting for you in your butcher's, grocer's and fishmonger's, so you really have no excuse.

OK, you might not rush out and braise veal shins on a Wednesday night after work, but why not give them a go at the weekend?

Incidentally, while many of these dishes have been hijacked by us chefs, most of them have their origins in traditional peasant cookery. Take the Navarin of Lamb, for instance; it uses neck of lamb, which is considerably cheaper than loin of lamb. The neck is a tough piece of meat and almost inedible if not cooked properly, yet if cooked slowly over an hour or so the result is meat that simply melts in the mouth. All the cunning gastro chef has done is reinvent these classics and hope you don't discover that you can cook them yourself at home. Oops!

Where there is a bit of messy preparation, I have suggested asking the fishmonger or butcher to do the prep for you, but why not give it a go? Unprepped meat is cheaper than prepped, obviously, so it is worth trying your hand; and nothing will impress bystanders in your kitchen more than you pulling out a whole, skinned rabbit and deftly dissecting it for the pot!

Paul.

CREAMY GARLIC RABBIT CASSEROLE Ⓟ

serves: 4   preparation time: 20 minutes   cooking time: 1 hour

My daughter would shoot me if she knew this was going in the book because in her world rabbits are fluffy things with big eyes and floppy ears. Oh well . . . Of course, if we go back a couple of generations, rabbit was a national staple, probably purchased off the local poacher. Nowadays it seems to exist only on restaurant menus, though in France and Spain it's still a very popular meat. I would urge you to give it a go. The farmed stuff is fairly mild in flavour and very tender. This casserole is an ideal starting-point.

Check with your butcher about rabbits. Mine has them in stock most days, but it may be worth putting in a call. Ask for a large farmed rabbit cut as follows: 2 shoulders; 2 hind legs; 2 hind thighs; 4 bits from the back of the animal (the saddle).

If the liver and kidneys are available, take them too, then fry in garlic butter and have them on toast as a snack for lunch. This is a bonus meal for the cook!

1 tablespoon vegetable oil

1 large farmed rabbit, cut as described

1 dessertspoon flour

½ leek, cleaned and chopped into rough 2cm dice

1 onion, peeled and roughly chopped

1 stick of celery, chopped into rough 2cm dice

a few white peppercorns

2 whole heads of garlic

6 fresh sage leaves

a decent sprig of fresh thyme

300ml white wine – nothing too dry

1 litre chicken stock

600ml double cream

200g mushrooms – I would go for oyster and shiitake, but button are cheaper

a good knob of butter

1 tablespoon chopped chives

Start by heating a little vegetable oil in a casserole pot. Meanwhile, toss the rabbit pieces in the flour – this will help thicken the sauce later. Now, in manageable batches, add them to the hot pot and allow them to slowly caramelize. Don't rush this process – remember, caramelize not burn! When all the rabbit is done, leave it to one side.

Throw the leek, onion, celery, peppercorns, one head of garlic (cut in half horizontally), the sage and thyme into the pot and soften them for about 5 minutes. Add the wine and allow it to boil, then reduce by half. Next, add the stock and the caramelized rabbit. The stock should just cover the rabbit and needs only to simmer very gently. After about 1 hour the rabbit will be cooked, at which point remove the pieces and leave them, covered, in a warm spot.

Turn up the heat and let the stock boil rapidly for 5 minutes, then add the double cream and simmer for around 10–12 minutes. In this time the creamy sauce should reduce and thicken slightly. Pass the sauce through a fine strainer and pour into a clean pot (you should have about 1 litre). Put the rabbit pieces back in the sauce and bring to a simmer for up to 10 minutes.

Meanwhile, peel and crush some cloves from the remaining head of garlic to a fine paste and start by adding about a teaspoon (or as much as you like) to the sauce to give it a sweet garlicky kick.

Finally, tear the oyster mushrooms in strips and thickly slice the shiitake, then fry in butter for 5 minutes until caramelized. Scatter them over the casserole together with the chopped chives, and serve.

PS I must say to my rabbit-loving daughter that Allegra forced me to cook rabbit! I didn't want to, honest.

THAI-SPICED STEAMED MUSSELS

serves: 4   preparation time: 20 minutes   cooking time: 7 minutes

This is a quick, cheap, simple lunch dish. It involves very little work save for a short expedition to the fishmonger's to collect the mussels. Don't be scared of cooking mussels at home – just make sure they are fresh and that each shell is closed before you cook them and open after they are cooked. The coconut milk and spices go very well with the mussels – so well, in fact, that you should pick up a French stick of bread for 'mopping-up' duties.

The best bit about this dish is that it allows you to demonstrate your cooking skills in public. It needs to be cooked at the last minute, so make sure everyone is close by as you start emptying all the mussels into a pot – they will be impressed, I promise.

2kg mussels
1 x 400ml tin of unsweetened coconut milk
1 dessertspoon red curry paste
300ml chicken stock
1 red chilli, sliced into fine rings
2 cloves of garlic, crushed
2 spring onions, finely sliced on an angle
2 tablespoons very coarsely chopped coriander

Clean your mussels well and debeard them by pulling away any stringy bits. If any are open, give them a sharp tap and discard any that don't close. Pour the coconut milk into a bowl and whisk in the curry paste and the chicken stock. Then place a pot big enough to hold about twice the amount of mussels you have ready on a high heat. When it is good and hot, tip the mussels straight in – they should sizzle and hiss a little, at which time you can add the coconut milk mixture. The liquid won't quite cover the mussels but that's OK. Bring to the boil, then put a lid on the pot and keep things boiling for a couple of minutes.

Remove the lid and chuck in the chilli and garlic. Give the mussels a good stir and boil again for a minute or so, by which time they should all have opened. Taste the spicy liquid and if you're happy – you will be! – sprinkle over the spring onions and the coriander. Then just put the pot in the middle of the table and let everyone dive in.

CREAMY HAM HOCK CASSEROLE ⓟ
WITH GOAT'S CHEESE CROSTINI

serves: 4   preparation time: 20 minutes   cooking time: 2 hours 50 minutes

Ham and cheese – thrifty grub dressed to impress. Believe me, this dish will do it for everyone . . . Ham hocks are taken from the end of the leg – basically it's the ankle of the animal and should be bought from your butcher. A good tip when buying a ham hock is to soak it in water for at least half an hour, to remove the salty brine.

Both the cooking of the ham hocks and the making of the sauce can be done the day before and they can be kept in the fridge. Planning is key!

2 x 1.5kg unsmoked ham hocks (or use smoked if you prefer)

1 carrot, unpeeled and left whole

1 onion, peeled and left whole

2 star anise

a few sprigs of fresh thyme

2 chicken stock cubes

12 fresh English asparagus spears, woody stalks snapped off, cut into 3cm pieces

a handful of fresh or frozen peas

chopped fresh parsley and tarragon

for the sauce

150g butter

120g plain flour

1.2 litres ham stock (from cooking the ham hocks)

125ml double cream

125ml milk

for the crostini

a French stick, cut into 8 long diagonal slices and lightly toasted

150g crumbled goat's cheese (or any leftover cheese will work)

Put the ham hocks, carrot, onion, star anise, thyme sprigs and stock cubes into a large pot and pour in enough cold water to cover everything. Add another 2.5 litres of water and slowly bring to a simmer (this can take about 30 minutes), skimming off any frothy stuff from the top as this can make the stock bitter.

Let the hocks simmer away for about 2 hours, checking every so often that it doesn't need topping up with water. Turn off the heat and allow the hocks to cool to room temperature in what is now a hammy-flavoured stock.

Take the hocks out of the stock and remove and discard the fat and skin that surrounds the meat. Pick off all the pink meat – it will come away fairly naturally in bite-sized pieces, which is good as we don't want it too straggly. Put the meat in a dish, covered, in the fridge until later. Pour the stock through a strainer so you are left with clear liquid. (Rather than throwing them away, the carrot and onion could now be blended with any leftover stock to make a broth – who says there's no such thing as a free lunch?)

To make the sauce, melt the butter in a saucepan and then throw in the flour. Stir this mixture about for a minute or so, then add a ladleful of the ham stock. The mixture will sizzle and seethe, but be brave and give it a stir. Immediately add a second ladleful and again stir it into the butter and flour mixture. Keep doing this until you have added the required amount of ham stock, allowing the sauce to return to the boil every so often.

By now you will have a thick sauce. Bring it to the boil, then stir in the cream and the milk. Reboil once more before removing from the heat. The sauce will be the consistency of thick double cream.

Cook the asparagus in boiling water for 1 minute then add the peas and cook for another minute. Drain and rinse in cold water to cool. Just before serving, reheat the sauce, add the flaked ham hock and stir in well. Add the asparagus and the peas, then stir in the chopped herbs. Transfer to a serving dish and keep warm.

Meanwhile, divide the crumbled goat's cheese between the French stick slices and place them under a hot grill. When the cheese has melted, lay the crostini on top of the ham hock casserole and serve with new potatoes.

NAVARIN OF LAMB [Ⓟ]

serves: 4   preparation time: 20 minutes   cooking time: 2¼ hours

Ah-ha! My computer's spellchecker did not know what a navarin was – but then again neither does my neighbour nor my best friend. The navarin is fairly unknown in this country. It is a hearty French stew made with neck of lamb and very often it is served with baby turnips (*navets* in French, hence 'navarin' – they're a clever lot, the French). So, with very simple ingredients and next to no hassle – it just simmers for a couple of hours – this is truly one of the best recipes I know.

A quick word on neck fillet of lamb: don't confuse this with loin of lamb, which does look very similar. Neck fillet is a much tougher piece of meat, requiring a long, gentle cooking. It is also much cheaper than loin of lamb, however one can't be swapped for the other.

Before serving up in a big casserole dish, the navarin is scattered with crunchy spring vegetables. These can all be pre-boiled and reheated in a little foaming butter when you are ready. The choice is yours, but a good mix would include baby turnips, carrots, peas, sugarsnap peas, broccoli florets, cauliflower, button onions and green beans.

1.2kg neck fillet of lamb, cut into 7.5cm cubes

1½ tablespoons flour

1–2 tablespoons vegetable oil

1 onion, peeled and chopped

1 whole head of garlic, cut in half horizontally

350ml white wine

300g chopped tomatoes (or some tomato ragù that you made in the summer!)

sprigs of thyme and rosemary

500ml lamb or chicken stock (use a cube or, preferably, your homemade version)

400–500g selection of spring vegetables (see above), peeled and chopped, or left whole if using baby turnips, for example

Dust the chunks of lamb with the flour – this will help thicken the sauce later. Now, in your most reliable casserole pot, heat some of the vegetable oil. Put a few chunks of lamb in and colour them until golden-brown on all sides. The caramelization process is best done a bit at a time, so don't overload the pot. This is an important stage because it not only gives the finished sauce a wonderful rich sandy-brown colour but also adds to the flavour. As each batch of lamb is coloured, remove it and set aside, add a little more oil to the pot and do the next batch of lamb. The browning takes about 20 minutes. When you've finished, don't clean the pot as it is now full of flavour.

You might need a little more oil here. Throw the onion and garlic into the pot and allow to caramelize slightly too. Then pour in the wine, which will sizzle and boil almost immediately. Allow the wine to reduce by half before adding the chopped tomatoes and the herbs. Again, boil until reduced by half, then pour in the cold stock and add the meat. It should be just covered by the stock.

Very slowly return the contents of the pot to a simmer. Now put a lid on the pot and simmer gently for 1 hour. During this time get your vegetables ready.

Check the navarin after an hour. Give it a stir and have a taste. All being well, it should require about another 30 minutes, at which point the sauce will be thick and rich and the lamb will be beautifully soft and tender. Either serve up now, topped with the vegetables, or allow to cool and reheat today, tomorrow or the next day. Lovely served with some crusty bread and a little mash too, but I shall leave that up to you.

VEAL RATATOUILLE [Ⓟ]

serves: 4   preparation time: 20 minutes   cooking time: 2 hours 20 minutes

Put bluntly, a shin of veal steak is a sawn section of veal shin cut straight through the bone. The bone marrow is often left in the bone, which adds a wonderful richness to the dish.

Your butcher will undoubtedly be impressed when you stroll in and nonchalantly ask for a few shin of veal steaks – all his other customers will have been in buying sausages and chicken breasts, so he will be pleased to have the chance to speak to such an obviously knowledgeable customer. If he is a man of the world, he may enquire whether you intend to make the classic Italian dish of braised veal shin with wine, lemon rind and tomato called Osso bucco. Tell him you are preparing a very similar dish requiring the same cut of veal.

Once back home, the preparation is fairly straightforward. However, the result will be truly impressive.

vegetable oil

4 x 300g veal shins on the bone
(ask your butcher for an osso bucco cut)

1 tablespoon plain flour

4 shallots, peeled and roughly chopped

2 cloves of garlic, peeled and chopped

3 tomatoes, cut into rough dice

a sprig of thyme

1 star anise

10 black peppercorns

375ml full-bodied red wine

1.5 litres of beef stock
(home-made or bought from your butcher)

1 aubergine, cut into 2cm cubes

1 red pepper, diced into 2cm squares

1 yellow pepper, diced into 2cm squares

1 green pepper, diced into 2cm squares

12 cherry tomatoes, halved

2 courgettes, cut into 2cm cubes

12 small button mushrooms, halved

2 tablespoons basil leaves, roughly diced

First of all, select a good thick-based casserole pan and put it on the heat with a glug of vegetable oil. Meanwhile dust your veal shins with flour, then place in the pan and allow them to colour all over – this will take about 5 minutes – then put them to one side.

Now throw the shallots and garlic into the pan and when they are golden-brown add the tomatoes, thyme, star anise and peppercorns. Turn the heat down low and allow the tomatoes to cook for a few minutes. Now add the red wine and bring it to a simmer. You want to reduce the wine to ¼ of its original volume. Pour in the cold beef stock and return the browned veal to the pan.

Very slowly, bring the stew back to a simmer. This slow reheating allows the meat to retain its juices – it can take about 20 minutes. When the stew has reached a simmer, cook it for 1 hour. At this point the veal shins should be lovely and tender – if they still feel a little tough, then cook on for a further 15 minutes. Remove the veal from the pan and keep covered to one side.

Next, pass all the contents of the pan through a strainer and discard all of the bits so that only the cooking liquid remains. This liquid will be the consistency of single cream. Put the liquid back in the pan and bring to the boil. Reduce it by about a half, allowing the liquid to thicken to the consistency of double cream. This is the finished sauce for the dish – put the veal back in this sauce and either cool, refrigerate and reheat later or serve straight away.

To finish the dish, gently reheat the veal in the sauce.

In a small glug of olive oil, separately pan-fry the aubergine until it softens and colours slightly, then add to the veal shins. Sauté the peppers in another small glug of olive oil until they soften and add these to the veal as well with the tomatoes, courgettes and mushrooms. Simmer for 6 minutes and finally sprinkle over the basil and serve with lots of mashed potatoes.

PROVENÇAL FISH SOUP Ⓟ

serves: 4 as a main course   preparation time: 40 minutes   cooking time: 1½ hours

Pick a restaurant, any restaurant, by the sea in the South of France and I bet they will have a version of Provençal fish soup on the menu. Some will call it bouillabaisse and serve it over two courses – first the soup, followed by the fish which kindly donated their bones to the soup – others will just sell you the soup, but either way it will be served with crusty French bread and rouille (which will keep for a few days in the fridge and is lovely as a dip with bread).

There is a tremendous amount of flavour in a fish head and a good wallop in the bones, so if you are a regular fish eater it is well worth asking your fishmonger to give you the head and bones from any fish you want him to fillet. You will build up a small pile of bones and heads in your freezer which can be made into this culinary classic for no extra cost. Now that truly is Economy Gastronomy! Prawn heads and tails are fabulous for this, too, so if you scoff a pint of prawns don't throw them away. The best fish for the job are hake, mullet (red and grey), bass, bream, gurnard, monkfish and snapper.

2 tablespoons olive oil

1.5kg fish bones and heads, washed and drained, no need to chop if whole

a handful of prawn shells

1 onion, peeled and roughly chopped

4 cloves of garlic, peeled and roughly crushed

1 head of fennel, roughly diced

½ red pepper, roughly diced

½ teaspoon fennel seeds

1 star anise

2 tablespoons brandy (optional)

6 large ripe tomatoes, each cut in 6 wedges

1 tablespoon tomato purée

a couple of pinches of saffron
(don't save money by leaving it out)

1 litre fish stock
(a couple of fish stock cubes would be fine)

40g white rice

for the rouille

1 medium potato, peeled and diced

1 fish stock cube, made into 300ml stock

3 cloves of garlic, peeled

½ red pepper, diced

a pinch of saffron

1 egg yolk

60ml extra-virgin olive oil

Heat the olive oil in your biggest pot – you do need a fairly wide-bottomed deep pot. Empty in the fish bones and prawn shells and fry hard for 2–3 minutes, allowing them to catch very slightly.

Add the onion, garlic and fennel and let them sizzle for 2 minutes, before adding the pepper, fennel seeds and star anise. Cook for another 2 minutes, then pour in the brandy. If you wish you can strike a match and flambé it, which will impress bystanders, but it's not too important. Next, add the tomatoes and saffron. Allow the mixture to bubble a bit, then pour in the fish stock. Bring to a simmer and add the rice, which is going to act as a thickening agent for the soup.

Simmer the soup very gently for about 45 minutes – by now there will be a glorious aroma filling your kitchen. (Shut your eyes and you would swear you were in St Tropez.) By this time, the contents of the pan will be cooked through and the soup is ready to be blended. Remove the fish heads and bones and discard them. A small domestic stick blender may struggle to cope with this amount of fish soup, so if you have a jug blender or a food processor I would recommend you use that.

Of course, there was a time when Provençal fish soup existed but electric blenders did not. The form in those days was to forcefully push the contents of the pan through a very coarse strainer and then pass it through a finer one, so if you are blender-'lite' you could revert back to this method. Good luck!

To make the rouille, put the potato in a small pan and just cover with fish stock. Add the garlic, pepper and saffron. Boil for 20 minutes until soft. Cool the mixture slightly, add the egg yolk, then put into a blender and purée. With the motor running, pour in the olive oil in a fine stream until you have a thick mayonnaise-type sauce.

PAN-FRIED LAMB'S KIDNEYS ON TOAST [Ⓟ]

serves: 1   preparation time: 10 minutes   cooking time: 25 minutes

For many years, the only kidneys I cared for were my own. I had eaten lamb's kidneys many times, normally on some 'mixed grill' type of dish where they were surrounded by other more attractive animal bits, such as bacon, steak, sausage, etc. I used to find them slightly bitter and rather dry, but this dish changed all that. Here they are served with glorious tangy gravy, sweet onions and – best of all – sodden toast underneath. Lamb's kidneys are relatively cheap and quick to cook, so I urge you to give them a chance.

Always buy kidneys fresh and cook them within a day. Ask your butcher to remove the fat surrounding them and, if you don't like the messy stuff, instruct him to cut them in half and remove the little gristle found on one side.

a little oil
6 button onions, peeled
1 dessertspoon bacon lardons
4 button mushrooms, quartered
2 lamb's kidneys (or a pair), prepared as above
a splash of red wine vinegar
100ml gravy made from granules
½ tablespoon chopped tarragon
½ tablespoon chopped parsley
a slice of crusty white bread

In a small frying pan, colour and cook the button onions in a little oil – they should end up caramelized all over and soft. Remove and leave to one side. Add a bit more oil to the same pan and fry the lardons and mushrooms for 5 minutes – again, a little colour will develop the overall flavour. Put the bacon and mushrooms with the onions.

Pour a little oil into the pan and, when it is hot, add the kidneys, cut-side down, and fry for about 3 minutes either side – a good roasted colour is the aim, but don't overcook them or they will be terribly dry. Put the kidneys with the onions, bacon and mushrooms.

By now the pan will be really hot and have the residue of the bacon, onions, mushrooms and kidneys in it. Add a splash of vinegar – literally ¼–½ teaspoon. This will lift off those tasty bits from the pan and also give the sauce a pleasing sharpness. The vinegar will sizzle and disappear immediately, so quickly bung in the gravy and add back the kidneys, onions, bacon and mushrooms. Throw in the herbs and hit 'go' on the toaster.

Place the toast in a shallow bowl or plate and spoon the contents of the pan over the top.

SEARED SQUID WITH CHORIZO

serves: 4 as a starter   preparation time: 15 minutes   cooking time: 12 minutes

This is one of the most popular dishes I have ever put on a menu. It is actually a collaborative piece of work between my number two in the kitchen, Chris Marriot, and myself. I very much wanted to pair squid and chorizo sausage and needed the extra bits to tie up the dish. While neither of us is Catalan, it does have a very Spanish feel to it.

Squid may seem like one of those ingredients best left to a restaurant kitchen, but I would beg to differ. As long as you ask your fishmonger to prepare it, there really is nothing more to do than a quick pan-fry. What you are after is the main body of the squid completely clean, so ask for squid 'tubes' and say you want the tentacles too.

for the chickpea purée
1 x 400g tin of chickpeas
2 teaspoons ground cumin
a pinch of chilli flakes
2 cloves of garlic, peeled and crushed
300ml really good extra-virgin olive oil
salt

2 tablespoons Greek yoghurt
1 dessertspoon chopped coriander
500g prepared and cleaned squid, including the tentacles
250g chorizo sausage
12 cherry tomatoes, halved or quartered
juice of ½ lemon
100g soft green leaves, such as pea shoots, rocket or watercress

Begin with the chickpea purée. It's worth doubling the quantities I've given above to make extra, because it's great eaten cold as a dip with pitta for lunch. Drain the chickpeas and put them in a food processor with the cumin, chilli flakes and one of the cloves of garlic. Turn on the processor and, with the engine running, slowly pour in half the olive oil. Switch off the machine and have a taste – it will probably need a touch of salt, which you can add now. Keep this at room temperature if using straight away or store, covered, in the fridge.

Next, mix the Greek yoghurt with the chopped coriander and store in the fridge.

Now cut the squid tubes into rings about 5mm thick. Slice up the chorizo into thickish long, diagonal slices. Heat a large frying pan and add a splash of the remaining olive oil. Fry the chorizo until it colours slightly, then remove it to a bowl. You will have a little chorizo-coloured oil, which you can keep and mix in towards the end. Increase the heat in the pan and throw in the squid. The best tip I can give you is to cook it hot and fast. If squid cooks too slowly or at a low temperature, it will become very rubbery. Flash-fry the squid for about 3–4 minutes maximum, in which time it will firm up and colour slightly. At this point throw in the cooked chorizo, tomatoes and the remaining crushed clove of garlic. Toss everything together and finally add any remaining olive oil and the lemon juice.

To serve, put a dollop of chickpea purée on each plate and evenly spoon around the seared squid and chorizo mixture. Be generous with the oil in the pan – it's a flavourful mix of chorizo and olive oil. Add a spoonful of coriander yoghurt to each plate and serve with some green leaves.

THE TOP TEN MOST WASTED FOODS

JUST AS WE BEGAN FILMING ECONOMY GASTRONOMY, I WAS HANDED AN EYE-OPENING LIST COMPILED BY THE WASTE AND RESOURCES ACTION PROGRAMME (WRAP) OUTLINING THE COUNTRY'S MOST WASTED FOOD ITEMS.

1. **Bread.** No one should waste any bread at all. For a start, old bread makes excellent toast. When past toast-bearing age, bread should be put in a bag in the freezer and then used in treacle tarts or for breadcrumbs to cover a chicken breast.

2. **Potatoes.** Not surprised to see the spud on the list. The problem is that we tend to buy large bags of them instead of the amount we actually need. Try buying them loose as you require them if you can. By the way, it's worth mentioning that lots of people chuck out their potatoes when they see them going a little green. They fear this green is poisonous. They're right, actually – the green bit is not for eating, but if removed with a knife the rest of the potato will be absolutely fine.

3. **Apples.** Everyone buys apples because they are good for you. Quite a lot of us eat them too, yet clearly there are lots who don't. Tired, wrinkly apples make a very good crumble filling – need I say more?

4. **Bananas.** Ah, this is a moot point in our house. We always buy a bunch of bananas and for a couple of days they are enjoyed by all. But as soon as the first signs of browning set in, the banana consumption stops. Then, before the browning bananas have been eaten, another bunch appears and yellow banana consumption begins once more. I have been allocated, apparently, the task of brown banana use-up cookery. Clearly, a few of you need my recipe for Banana Sponge with Toffee Sauce on p.301!

5. **Yoghurts.** Yoghurts are really popular with young and old, and they also have a generous sell-by deadline, so I'm surprised to see them on the list. Apart from blackcurrant yoghurt, that is – it always seems to be left until last in a multi-pack.

6. **Cakes.** Cakes . . . bloody cakes . . . who's throwing away cake? Are you mad? We lurrrve de cake.

7. **Lettuce.** Yep, not a bit surprised to see old Larry the lettuce creep in at number seven. People do insist on buying that pre-washed, nutritionally-lite, prepared stuff. It then goes brown and they chuck it out. Hence there's a waste problem. Buy your lettuce whole, trim off what you need, wrap the rest in a damp cloth and store it in cling film; then it will stay fresh to the last leaf. *Voilà* – no waste problem.

8. **Tomatoes.** Turn to the Bedrock section on p.84 for an enlightening series of recipes utilizing tomatoes in all states of decay. I shall say no more.

9. **Cabbages.** Another dead cert. Crispy, crunchy cabbage is lovely; the limp stuff goes in the bin. Not any more it doesn't. When you next have a tired-looking half-cabbage in your fridge, take it out and shred it up very finely. Fry some sliced onion and garlic with some thyme, add some shredded bacon and fry till brown. Then chuck in the cabbage, pour in half a glass of white wine and a tablespoon or two of cream. Simmer and serve.

10. **Rice.** A world staple. Surely we should feel bad about wasting such a vital food source that many people need so desperately? It actually makes the whole list seem spectacularly selfish and wasteful. Don't contribute to this list.

FRIENDS FOR SUPPER

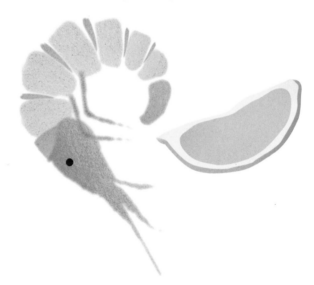

STARTERS:

MEXICAN CEVICHE

TURKEY AND CHICKPEA PATTIES

SIMPLE SUSHI

SPICY CHICKEN BHUNA SALAD
(MUSTARD VINAIGRETTE)

CARAMELIZED ONION
AND CHESHIRE CHEESE TART

SALMON RILLETTES

MAINS:

SPICY SEED-RUBBED BBQ BEEF

GRILLED LAMB'S LIVER
WITH PEAS AND BACON

LIGHT-AS-A-FEATHER
SEAFOOD PANCAKES

BUTTERNUT TAGINE

CHICKEN SURPRISE

SALMON EN CROÛTE

ENTERTAINING CAN BE ANYTHING FROM A LOT OF FUN TO A BIT OF A NIGHTMARE. MANY FACTORS CAN PLAY THEIR PART IN THE SUCCESS OF YOUR EVENING, LIKE HOW WELL YOU KNOW THE PEOPLE, HOW MUCH ENERGY YOU HAVE AND, MOST IMPORTANTLY, WHETHER YOU'RE READY.

Being relaxed is the key to you, the cook, having a good time, which is all Paul and I really care about. The aim is to get you through the night having enjoyed yourself, with a reasonably easy life and ideally spending some quality time with your guests. If you can combine that with putting a feast on the table, whilst not blowing the budget, then we're quids in.

Most people find having folks over a bit stressful and, depending who you have coming over, those stress levels can vary a bit. The solution sounds boring but in truth is what makes it fun: planning. Scrabbling costs time and money, so doing as much in advance as you can (a lot, if you plan) is a really wise down-payment on a fun night. Choosing dishes or recipes you actually have time to cook – preferably while enjoying the experience – is always a plus (and I'd recommend checking through any recipes at least the night before for that immortal first line: 'Marinate/soak overnight . . !).

Supposedly with the economic downturn we're all eating in more, and having friends round for supper. Somehow in my mind this is different from the dinner parties my parents threw in the seventies: I'd come down in the morning to find a cigar stubbed out in the remains of a meringue – and sense I'd missed out on a lot of fun. Because fun is what it's all about. Fun can come from the people (relaxed), the food (impressed yummy noises are a good sign) or just an overall up-for-a-good-night feeling (wine helps).

But what you choose to cook for your best friend as opposed to the boss covers a huge spectrum: my sister Floss (one of the only two people who are not scared of cooking for me, the other being our eldest sister Binky) once served us three courses of pies: a slice of a veggie pastry pie (bought), followed by fish pie, with good old lemon meringue to round off. Top night.

Lots of recipes in this book outside of this chapter would suit being made for company (including the whole of Paul's Gastropubonomy), but sometimes the occasion calls for a little something extra. More than any other chapter in this book, there's a really wide reach of recipes here to try and meet the range of occasions when you're having people over.

And though they're not the cheapest recipes in this book (compared to, say, the Something Out of Nothing chapter), they're all good value for money and, most importantly, come with in-built 'talking points'.

MEXICAN CEVICHE

serves: 6   preparation time: 15 minutes   cooking time: 10 minutes

My, this is easy and tastes like sunshine. I go nuts for Mexico and this tasty little combo makes for a lunch or starter that I could happily eat every day – even better with a bit of warmth on your skin. With an excellent ratio of effort to pleasure, really the only work is in getting good enough fish.

Best to buy the fish on the day you are going to use it and check with your fishmonger that it's the freshest there. Sometimes they have newer stuff out the back, and you need it to be spanking fresh.

If you're prepping this ahead of time, don't put the lime on the fish until about 10 minutes before you serve it. Even though there's no heat involved, technically the lime juice 'cooks' the fish, so no get-out for raw fish wimps here.

Tabasco is a land-locked state in Mexico, so you'd be unwise to eat fish there. However, you might want to put a bottle on the table as I certainly like to shake a few drops of fire on to mine.

400g firm fish fillets (like haddock,
snapper, halibut), skinned and pin-boned
3 limes
3 red chillies, 2 diced small, 1 finely sliced
2 spring onions, sliced
1 pepper (red, yellow or green), cut into 1cm chunks
½ cucumber, peeled, halved lengthways,
deseeded and cut into half moons
1 big handful of coriander, roughly chopped
1 avocado, peeled, destoned and finely sliced
salt and pepper

Put six glasses into the freezer – small wine, cocktail, tumblers, it's up to you – just nothing too huge.

Dice the fish fillets into centimetre cubes and put in a bowl. Squeeze on the juice of one lime to cure it and mix in the two small diced chillies. Stir it all up well and leave aside for 10 minutes.

In a separate bowl, mix together the spring onions, pepper, cucumber, coriander, avocado and the sliced chilli. Squeeze over the juice of another lime and season well with salt and a good crack of pepper.

Mix everything together well and serve in your iced glasses with a fat wedge of lime each.

TURKEY AND CHICKPEA PATTIES

^P

serves: 4 as a starter   preparation time: 25 minutes   cooking time: 15 minutes

You may be tempted to think that, when entertaining at home, chefs produce endless platters of foie gras, truffles, oysters and venison . . . Well, not this one! Turkey and chickpea patties are one of my favourite dishes to cook for friends as a starter or even a light main course.

When my children saw these for the first time they suddenly recalled my lectures about 'always telling the truth' and swiftly informed me that I was actually cooking turkey *burgers*, so I could forget all the pattie nonsense. They are right, of course. Only snobbery has stopped me giving this invention its rightful place in the chain that is burger evolution.

By the way, if you can't easily get hold of plantain, then sweet potato works just as well. These turkey patties (aka burgers) would also go very well in a sesame seed bun with lettuce, red onion and mayo!

150g tinned chickpeas, drained

190g minced turkey (ask your butcher to mince the breast meat for you)

2 cloves of garlic, peeled and finely chopped

1 teaspoon finely chopped mint

1 dessertspoon chopped parsley

a pinch of chilli flakes

1 dessertspoon sweet chilli sauce

1 tablespoon very finely chopped fresh ginger

sea salt

2 tablespoons olive oil

1 large plantain or sweet potato

for the salsa

½ red onion, peeled and very finely chopped

1 ripe plum tomato, very finely chopped

1 tablespoon Greek yoghurt

the juice of 1 lime

1 ripe avocado, peeled and diced

Whizz the chickpeas in a food processor until they are almost as fine as breadcrumbs, then put them in a large bowl with the minced turkey and mix together using your hands. Now add the garlic, mint, parsley, chilli flakes, sweet chilli sauce and ginger, and again work these flavours in using your hands. Season with a pinch of salt if you fancy it, then divide the mixture into four.

To shape the patties you need a plain-edged pastry cutter – the one I use is about 12cm across. Push a dollop of the mixture into the cutter and, using the back of a spoon, smooth it down to form a small burger. You can, of course, do this shaping by hand – just make sure you combine the mixture tightly so there are no air pockets within. The patties can be left in the fridge for a few hours.

To make the salsa, place the very finely chopped red onion and tomato in a mixing bowl. Add the yoghurt, lime juice and avocado and mix everything together. If you wish to store this, pack it tightly into a bowl and cover the surface with cling film to stop it discolouring.

When you are ready to serve, heat a frying pan and add a tablespoon of the olive oil. Place the patties in the pan and let them sizzle away for at least 4 minutes undisturbed. Then gently lift them and check the undersides, which should be golden brown and very slightly crispy. If they are, flip them over and do the same on the other side. When they are ready, remove them from the pan and keep warm. Meanwhile, peel the plantain or sweet potato and cut into four long slices about 3mm thick. Pan-fry these in the remaining olive oil until brown and slightly blistered on both sides – this should take about 7 minutes. Place a patty on a plate, lay a long slice of plantain across it and top with a dollop of salsa. Lovely with a dressed rocket salad and some sweet chilli sauce.

SIMPLE SUSHI

makes: 30–35 pieces of sushi as a starter for 6, or great as canapés
preparation time: 45 minutes

It may just be a myth, but supposedly for the first whole year of becoming a sushi chef, all you do is cook rice. If this is true (and it's brought me amusement and amazement for so many years that I kind of don't want to know if it's not) it's scary for many reasons. Is there really that much to know about rice? And how can anyone care that much?

Getting at least the basics of this great art form is pretty simple – even for someone who's not drawn to precision like me – and the result is so very proud-making. Totally impressive and, as long as you leave yourself enough time, the process can be a really enjoyable one.

Freshly made sushi is a world nicer than old and cold in plastic trays and if you're wondering why I chose to include this recipe, the clue is in the title – Economy Gastronomy. They're cheap, fun and a bit flash.

For those that feel their sushi needs to be fishy, this is delish with thin slivers of mackerel in place of the sesame aubergines.

You need a small bamboo mat for sushi rolling, as well as dried seaweed sheets (nori). The rice you can get in most supermarkets and some of them do the other bits too; otherwise nip into your local Asian shop or order online.

350g sushi rice
a packet of nori (dried seaweed sheets)

for the rice dressing
90ml rice wine vinegar
4 tablespoons caster sugar
1 tablespoon salt

for the fillings
1 aubergine
5 tablespoons sesame oil
salt and pepper
1 tablespoon sesame seeds
1½ tablespoons runny honey

OR
2 x 120–150g mackerel fillets
1 teaspoon dark soy sauce like tamari
PLUS
½ ripe avocado, sliced into long thin shards
1 carrot, peeled and cut into long thin matchsticks
2 spring onions, cut into long thin slices
a handful of coriander sprigs
1 lime

to serve
a jar or packet of pickled ginger
wasabi (making it up from powder to paste is much better than ready in a tube)
soy sauce

To prepare the rice
Cook the rice according to the pack instructions. Knock up the rice dressing by mixing together the rice wine vinegar, sugar and salt, then stir until everything has dissolved.

Tip the cooked rice on to a tray and spread it out. Pour the dressing over the hot rice and, using the side of a wooden spoon or spatula, make valleys in the rice for maximum absorption and leave to cool to room temperature. Once cooled, transfer to a bowl and drape over a tea towel.

To make the veggie filling
If making the aubergine filling, trim the ends, then cut a quarter slice off lengthways. Sit this, flat-side on your board, and make another similar cut to take off another quarter. You are now halfway to blocking it off, so make the remaining two slices to cut off the rest of the skin, so you are left with five pieces of aubergine.

Cut the central block into slices lengthways, about a centimetre thick, then cut all of the pieces into centimetre-wide long sticks – you'll need about 15 good ones for the sushi, so any left over are for snacking.

Put a frying pan on a high heat and pour in half the sesame oil. When the oil is smoking hot, lay in half the sticks. Don't play with them, but as you see them browning on the bottom, turn them over. After about 5 to 7 minutes, they should be nice and golden brown on all sides. Give them a bit of a season.

Once you have a colour you're happy with, tip out any excess oil and keep it for cooking the next batch of aubergine. Sprinkle on the sesame seeds and put a lid on to stop them jumping out. Just a minute later, spoon in half the honey, give the aubergines a roll and coat gently, making sure you don't break them as they are very soft by now. As soon as you have no liquid left in the pan, very gently transfer them out on to a plate, pouring any residual honey on top. Give the pan a quick wash and repeat with the other half of the aubergine, using any reserved oil and the rest of the sesame oil. Before you add the honey, remember to drain off any excess oil again – this time, chuck it away.

To make the fishy filling
Cut the central strip of bones out with a knife (too fiddly to use tweezers), slice the mackerel fillets into long thin strips (you'll need about 10 in total), put them in the bowl and coat them in the soy.

To build your sushi
Have a bowl of water nearby and lay the rolling mat on the table with the smooth side up. Put a sheet of nori (shiny-side down) on the mat. Wet your hands in the water (this stops the rice sticking to your hands), then take about a cup of rice (roughly 175–200g) and spread it evenly over the two-thirds of the nori that is closest to you. Use your dampened fingertips to compress it a bit.

Now, lay two of your aubergine sticks or mackerel strips about a third of the way up the rice, so they span the width from side to side. In careful, close-packed lines, lay on the other ingredients one by one. Finish with a couple of coriander sprigs with the leaves pointing out at either side and a squeeze of lime. For the fishy ones, I think a thin brush of wasabi at the top of the rice gives it an extra bit of wallop, but it's deeply optional.

Use your fingertips to gently wet the exposed top third of the nori. Since the Japanese know best, I have lifted this from the back of my nori packet:

'Hold line of ingredients across rice firmly in place with fingertips. Using thumb, push up and turn bamboo mat edge nearest you up and over filling, pressing firmly to enclose filling and lifting bamboo mat while rolling to keep free from enclosing in sushi roll. Gently, but firmly, press bamboo mat around roll to shape. (The art of making maki-sushi is to get filling ingredients line-up in centre of roll.) Unroll mat.'

Everybody OK with that, then? Lots of fun, amazingly satisfying and not that hard, once you've got the hang of it. Cut into the first one to see how you did, and taste it for balance: you should be able to discern sticky rice, crunchy veg, zippy onion and coriander and the sharpness of the lime to contrast with the sweetness. Make any adjustments to your ratios, and mentally work through any necessary changes to your rolling technique too, then go again. The second one isn't nearly so scary, and by the time you do your fifth and last one, you'll be a real pro.

To finish the sushi
Once you've got a row of firm logs, put them on your chopping board, seam-side down, and choose a sharp, preferably thin knife (wetting your knife gives a neater, cleaner cut). Don't go and ruin all that hard work by tearing them with a dull knife at this stage.

Slice the pieces a couple of centimetres thick. I figure they're about the right height and size if you get seven out of each roll. Serve with a pile of pickled ginger, wasabi and a little individual dish of soy on the side, not to mention a huge amount of pride.

SPICY CHICKEN BHUNA SALAD ℗

serves: 4   preparation time: 25 minutes, plus marinating time   cooking time: 15 minutes

When you see the word 'bhuna' on an Indian menu it generally indicates that the dish has been dry-fried. Before this the meat is often marinated. The recipe below does have a fair few ingredients, but with a little planning it really doesn't take all that much effort. The vinaigrette should be at the ready in your fridge at all times and the marinade can be assembled at least a day in advance (though not with the chicken in).

4 skinless chicken breasts, cut into dice
(about 8 pieces per breast)
1 courgette
1 fresh small coconut
1 x mustard vinaigrette (see recipe below)
vegetable oil
1 teaspoon garam masala
10 mint leaves, chopped
½ red onion, peeled and sliced into very fine rings
2 little gem lettuces, separated into leaves
8 cherry tomatoes, cut in half
a few sprigs of coriander
4 cooked poppadoms

for the marinade
6 tablespoons natural yoghurt
juice of 1 lemon
2 cloves of garlic, peeled and finely crushed
½ teaspoon turmeric
1 tablespoon paprika
1 teaspoon ground cardamom
½ teaspoon salt
1 teaspoon ground chilli
1 teaspoon ground cumin

Mix all the marinade ingredients together in a bowl. Then add the diced chicken breasts and coat thoroughly with the marinade. Ideally they should have at least an hour in the marinade, so store them in the fridge.

Meanwhile, prepare all the bits for the salad, starting with the courgette. These can be sliced very finely and left raw, or pan-fried, or cooked on a ribbed grill pan. Whichever way you choose, they should have a slight crunch. Next crack the coconut in half by wrapping it in a cloth and giving it a sharp smack with a hammer. Remove the hard outer husk and then, using a potato peeler, take long strips from the flesh. Toast these under a hot grill until they are just beginning to brown, turning every minute or so.

Make the mustard vinaigrette now (see below).

Just before serving, remove the chicken from the marinade and pan-fry it in batches in a little vegetable oil. Make sure the pan is hot and not overloaded with chicken – that way you will end up with nicely coloured pieces of chicken. As each batch cooks, finish it with a pinch of garam masala and a little chopped mint.

Arrange all the remaining salad bits in a large bowl, add the courgette, coconut, chicken and vinaigrette, then finish by breaking up the poppadoms and scattering them over the top for a bit of crunch.

MUSTARD VINAIGRETTE

3 tablespoons vegetable oil
¾ tablespoon cider or white wine vinegar
1 dessertspoon caster sugar

1 dessertspoon English mustard
salt and pepper

Place all the ingredients in a jam jar, put the lid on and shake well to create a tangy dressing which goes well with many salads. Adjust the amount of sugar and vinegar to suit your palate.

CARAMELIZED ONION AND CHESHIRE CHEESE TART

serves: 12 as a starter, or 6 as a main   preparation time: 1 hour   cooking time: 1 hour

This is a tart rather than a quiche because it's really all about the onions, with very little of the binding egg custard that defines a quiche. Impossible to go wrong with cheese and onion – it makes a much better filling than salt and vinegar.

Cooking the onions for such a long time makes them very soft and sweet, which is why Cheshire is the perfect match, with its slightly sharp taste and firm, crumbly texture.

for the pastry
300g plain flour
150g butter, cold
2 egg yolks
salt and pepper
a splash of milk

for the filling
60g butter
2kg onions, red, white or a combo, peeled and finely sliced

4 cloves of garlic, peeled and roughly chopped
a handful of thyme on the branch, well-washed and tied together with string
salt and pepper
3 eggs (split one of these and use the white for the egg wash on the pastry)
1 tablespoon milk
250ml double cream
2 tablespoons English mustard
250g Cheshire cheese

To make the pastry, put the flour into a food processor, cut the butter into knobs and drop these individually down the chute as it's spinning until all incorporated. Now drop in the egg yolks, one after the other, and a second later turn it off. Give it a season whilst still in the food processor (it should now have a pale, clumpy, sandy texture), then tip it out, add a splash of milk and wrap it tightly in cling film and put in the freezer for half an hour.

Get a wide heavy-bottomed pan on to a high heat and melt the butter. Tip the onions in and put a lid on – if your pan isn't big enough, do half and wait for them to collapse a bit before adding the rest. Add the garlic and give it a good stir, making sure that nothing is burning at the bottom, then turn the heat down a bit, but keep it medium-high. Toss in the thyme bundle and poke it down into the onions, then put the lid back on.

After 15 minutes, take the lid off and turn the heat down to low. If you've got any brown bits on the bottom of your pan, add a splash of water and scrape them off with a wooden spoon. Give it a good season and cook for a further 35–45 minutes, stirring occasionally. They're done when they are beginning to stick to the bottom of the pan and smell like French onion soup.

Take your crumbly pastry out of the freezer and coarsely grate it directly into a 28cm tart case (3.5cm deep). Use your fingertips to press evenly on the base and up the sides, and save a nugget in case you need to make some repairs later. Put the pastry case back in the freezer for 15 minutes.

Preheat the oven to 180°C/160°C fan/gas mark 4. Blind bake the pastry case by lining it with greaseproof and filling it with baking beans. Pop it into your oven for 10 minutes, then lift out the paper and the beans. Make an egg wash, using the white of one egg, saving the yolk for later, then brush this over the pastry case. If you see any cracks, fill them with a bit of your emergency pastry and put it back in the oven for a further 10 minutes. Keep an eye on it at this stage as all ovens are different and pastry is slightly temperamental – you're looking for an all-over golden brown. Then take it out and drop the oven temp to 160°C/140°C fan/ gas mark 3. Gently do any final emergency repairs – you need her to be water-tight.

Beat the remaining 2 eggs plus the yolk with the milk in a big bowl, then whisk in the cream, mustard and seasoning. Take the thyme out of the onions and crumble in the cheese, keeping a bit for the top. Pour the cream and egg mixture into the onions and stir well. Tip it all into your tart case and spread it out so that it comes up to the edge of the pastry all the way round. Scatter the remaining cheese on top, then stick it in the oven for 40 minutes. Leave to rest for at least 10 minutes before serving with a simple green salad.

SALMON RILLETTES ^P

serves: 4 as a starter/snack   preparation time: 10 minutes   cooking time: 10–15 minutes

This is as glamorous as leftovers can get. The next time you have any trimmings and offcuts left over after prepping fresh salmon this dish is an ideal way to use them up. The smoked salmon is not absolutely necessary, but I do think it makes this something special. I make these at Christmas to serve on toast as canapés before lunch. Posh five-star snacking? I know! But hey, you're worth it.

200g fresh salmon
1 tablespoon crème fraîche or Greek yoghurt
juice of ½ lemon
60g unsalted butter, diced and softened
1 dessertspoon chopped fresh dill
2 teaspoons creamed horseradish from a jar
50g smoked salmon
black pepper
hot brown toast, to serve

Preheat the oven to 180°C/160°C fan/gas mark 4.

Place the fresh salmon in a small ovenproof baking dish and wet it with a dessertspoon of water. Cover the dish with foil and cook for 10–15 minutes. (Obviously the timing depends on how big a piece of salmon you have: lots of little bits will take much less time than a large chunk. The idea is to undercook the salmon slightly, as this way you end up with really moist rillettes.) Remove the fish from the dish and allow it to cool.

When the salmon is cool, flake it into a bowl. Now add the crème fraîche or Greek yoghurt, lemon juice, butter, dill and horseradish – but don't mix it together yet. Shred the smoked salmon into strips and add these to the bowl. Finally add a twist of black pepper, then gently fold and mix everything together, taking care not to break it down to a mush. When everything is thoroughly combined, put in a serving dish and chill in the fridge for at least an hour. Serve with hot brown toast.

SPICY SEED-RUBBED BBQ BEEF

serves: 6–8   preparation time: 10 minutes   cooking time: 30–40 minutes

It's never quite made sense to me that as a nation we love our barbies, taking the time to spark them up at the slightest hint of sunshine and then, for the most part, we throw very mediocre meat on them.

Watching this majestic lump sizzle over coals with the sun above you creates one of those pure 'I love cooking' moments. Don't worry if the seeds on the outside go quite dark, black even, these bits just taste divine at the end.

When it comes to choosing your hunk of beef, rump is the cheapest option, rib-eye works well, as does sirloin but it's more expensive. Quick heads-up: if you marinate the meat overnight, you'll get a good few yards more pleasure out of it.

for the marinade
4 cloves of garlic, peeled and finely chopped
2 tablespoons black peppercorns
1 tablespoon coriander seeds
2 teaspoons fennel seeds
1½ tablespoons dried chilli flakes
1½ teaspoons cumin seeds
1 tablespoon salt
2 tablespoons extra-virgin olive oil

1.2kg quality hunk of beef, at least 6–8cm high,
with any excessive bits of fat trimmed off

In a pestle and mortar or in a spice grinder, mix together everything for the marinade except the oil. Pound and grind alternately, making sure you crush the seeds and crack the peppercorns. It takes about 4 minutes of decent work, and I tend to use the end of a rolling pin rather than the pestle as I think it does the job faster. Stir in just enough olive oil to make a paste.

Rub and smear the paste all over the meat and leave for as long as you can – in the fridge overnight (but take it out way ahead of time so it's not fridge-cold when you cook it) or at room temperature if you've only got a few hours.

Once the coals on the barbecue are white hot, push them round to the outside and sit the meat on the rack in the middle – too much direct flame will bring on excessive blackening – and shut the lid or put something metal over it to capture the heat. A bowl made from foil by moulding it over a mixing bowl works really well.

Don't move the meat around, but turn it after about 8–10 minutes. Repeat for the same amount of time on each of the 4 sides so that it cooks for just over half an hour (obviously these times vary depending on the temperature coming off the coals). To test if the meat is done, stick a skewer or thin knife into the centre of it and gingerly touch it to your top lip. Don't take it off until you feel a distinct warmth, but it shouldn't be anywhere near properly hot.

Give it a good 10 minutes' rest, loosely covered with foil, before slicing with a sharp knife. The seeds will have burnt a bit, but that just makes for added crunch and intensity of flavour to contrast with the beautiful, wobbling flesh inside.

GRILLED LAMB'S LIVER ⓟ
WITH PEAS AND BACON

serves: 4 preparation time: 15 minutes cooking time: 25 minutes

I have a hunch that while you may be the type who makes a beeline for the offal on a restaurant menu, you think it's not the sort of thing you could actually cook yourself. Well, think again! Get your butcher to do all the mucky prep and then give it a go – it really isn't that difficult.

Liver is a fabulous meat. Very nutritious, it just needs to be cooked with a little care. Not all livers are the same, of course. Pig's liver is that dry rubbery stuff we were all fed at school, putting us on a collision course with liver aversion. Pig's liver is very cheap, but frankly it isn't the best. Calves' liver, on the other hand, is the best and, if you can afford it, I wouldn't stop you using it. However, lamb's liver, which we are using here, is both very reasonably priced and tastes great. A decent-sized lamb's liver should comfortably satisfy four people, especially as we are serving it with extra bacon.

Ask your butcher to remove the membrane that covers the liver, then, if you are particularly squeamish, to slice it into eight long, even slices. Now all you need to do is cook it! I am suggesting you use a ribbed griddle pan, but if you don't have one you should (a) sauté the liver in a normal pan and (b) put 'ribbed griddle pan' on your birthday present wish list.

vegetable oil (or 20g butter)
24 whole button onions, peeled
800g lamb's liver, cut into 8 long slices
600ml hot chicken stock
25g flour and 25g softened butter, mixed to a paste
300g peas or petits pois
10 mint leaves, finely chopped
½ head of little gem lettuce, cut very finely across
4 rashers of smoked streaky bacon
4 servings of your finest mashed potato

Heat the oil or butter over a medium heat in a small frying pan and allow the button onions to colour while they cook. They will need to be tossed around occasionally to ensure that they are evenly coloured. Leave them cooling in the pan to one side, because we will be back with them shortly . . .

The liver will need to be lightly oiled on both sides before going into the ribbed griddle pan for no more than 2–3 minutes each side on a high heat. In this time it will cook to the point of medium, which is ideal; it will also take on rather pleasing grill lines from the pan. Take the liver out of the pan and keep it warm by covering with some foil while you finish the rest of the dish.

Put your pan of button onions back on a medium heat and pour in the chicken stock. Allow it to boil and then gradually whisk in the flour and butter paste until the sauce begins to thicken. (Letting the sauce bubble for a couple of minutes gets rid of any uncooked flour flavour and helps it thicken.) Just so you know, this paste is called *beurre manié* in the cooking world and its purpose is to thicken stocks or soups very slightly.

As the thickening stock starts to simmer, throw in the peas and the mint, closely followed by the lettuce. Toss everything around in the pan to allow the peas to get hot, the mint to impart its flavour and the lettuce to whimper and soften slightly. Check for seasoning and it's game on.

While the sauce simmers, throw four rashers of bacon into the griddle pan and cook for 3–4 minutes. To serve, put a dollop of mash on to each plate, spoon over some of the pea mixture and top with the liver and bacon.

LIGHT-AS-A-FEATHER
SEAFOOD PANCAKES

serves: 4   preparation time: 1 hour   cooking time: 50 minutes–1 hour

Many of us still get excited by pancakes – a reminder of childhood, they have the buzz of Event Food. However, nothing could be cheaper and easier, not to mention more fun, than knocking up a batter and flipping away.

And while we're challenging some preconceived time fallacies, debearding this amount of mussels takes about 4 minutes – time you have on your hands anyway as the batter is resting. Just wouldn't want to put you off.

for the batter
180g plain flour
salt and pepper
2 small eggs, beaten
450ml milk
60g butter, for frying

for the filling
600g spuds
salt and pepper
1kg mussels
1 white onion, peeled and finely diced
1 clove of garlic, peeled and finely diced
1 heaped tablespoon butter,
plus ½ tablespoon, softened
a large glass of white wine

a couple of bay leaves
2 eggs
200g diced, skinless boned white fish
(haddock, pollock or plaice)
170g small cooked prawns, shelled
(like prawn-cocktail ones)
a few scrapes of nutmeg
2 tablespoons dill, chopped
a small chunk of Parmesan, finely grated

for the sauce
2 handfuls of frozen peas
70g butter, very soft
a squeeze of lemon juice
salt and pepper
a handful of flat-leaf parsley, picked,
washed and finely chopped

For the batter
Sift the flour and a big pinch of salt into a bowl and make a well in the middle. Pour in the 2 beaten eggs. With a wooden spoon, start to pull in some flour from outside. Then switch to a whisk and gradually add the milk, pulling in more flour until all is incorporated. Season well and set aside for half an hour with a tea towel draped over it.

For the filling
Peel the spuds and halve them, cover with cold water and a hefty pinch of salt. Simmer with a lid on until properly soft but not mushy, then, most crucially, drain thoroughly in a colander before mashing.

Now you have time to debeard your mussels. Grab hold of the bit of stringy stuff sticking out and draw it down towards the pointier end of the mussel before giving it a little tug so it comes out. While you're doing this, keep the mussels you've debearded under running cold water. Chuck the beards away, along with any mussels that are open.

In a pan big enough to hold all the mussels, gently fry the onion and garlic in a little butter on a low to medium heat with a lid on, making sure they soften rather than colour. Stir occasionally for roughly 10 minutes. Add the mussels to the pan and roll them around. Pour in the white wine, add the bay leaves and pop a lid on to steam for 5 minutes, giving them a shake halfway through.

Once your mussels are cooked and open, use a slotted spoon to fish them out on to a tray (leaving behind as much onion as possible). Leave the pan on the heat and reduce the liquor down to a third before you turn it off. Put the mussels aside to cool then pick them out of their shells. Mix them into your spud mash.

Preheat the oven to 180°C/160°C fan/gas mark 4.

To cook the pancakes

Choose a thin pan, preferably non-stick for ease and roughly 25cm in diameter. Get it medium hot, then chuck in a knob of butter and as it fizzles, swirl it all around and up the sides a bit.

Ladle in just enough of the batter to give you a thin layer as you quickly tip it around the pan. After a minute or two, when you can see the edges going brown and turning up, flip it over (be brave) and cook it for another minute or two before turning it on to a plate (you're allowed to have the first one as a cook's snack with lemon and sugar as chances are the first one will be a bit thick).

From there on, just keep melting a new knob of butter and making and stacking pancakes until you've run out of batter. You should get nine pancakes out of this (and I'm assuming you'll have eaten one), which gives you enough for one each and a bit over for seconds.

Separate the eggs, putting the whites in a medium-sized bowl for whisking in a minute. Move your mash to a big metal bowl and stir the yolks into it along with the fish, prawns, some nutmeg, dill, salt and pepper.

Whisk the egg whites until the firm peak stage and fold them into the spud mix in three lots. The first you do quite vigorously, the second much more lightly in arcing motions and the final lot with the strokes of an angel. This is all about the fluffy.

Choose an ovenproof dish big enough to hold all the rolled up pancakes, and butter it.

To serve

Lay out your pancakes two at a time with the light side up and divide a quarter of the filling mix between each two. Put a sausage shape of filling in the centre of each one, roll and sit tight in the dish. Repeat for all the others. Lightly stroke soft butter along the top of each pancake, sprinkle on the Parmesan, season well and put them in the preheated oven for 20–25 minutes.

About 5 minutes before the pancakes come out, bring your mussel liquor up to a simmer for a couple of minutes and then chuck in your frozen peas. Turn the heat off and whisk in your very soft butter in small knobs. Taste and add a squeeze of lemon and seasoning, then finish with finely chopped parsley. Serve with a wedge of lemon and eat straight away, otherwise the fluffy filling will fall.

BUTTERNUT TAGINE ⓟ

serves: 4   preparation time: 30 minutes   cooking time: 40 minutes

If I had to pick one recipe to cook for Allegra, above all the others in this book, this would be it, simply because whenever I go round to her house she always has something similar bubbling away on the stove. To call it a 'tagine' is possibly using a touch of poetic licence, as the word actually refers to dishes cooked in an earthenware vessel of the same name much used in North African cuisine. However, I feel justified in my description, since the end results are pretty much the same.

I have kept things completely vegetarian because the dish has so much flavour, texture and variety it really doesn't need the addition of meat or fish. However, if you are the type who feels the need, then I would suggest chicken or lamb.

200ml olive oil

1.3kg butternut squash, peeled, deseeded and roughly cut into 3cm dice

8 cloves of garlic, peeled and chopped

1 red onion, peeled and diced

1 yellow pepper, deseeded and cut into 3cm dice

1 red pepper, deseeded and cut into 3cm dice

2 x 400g tins of chopped tomatoes

100g stoned dates (medjool are my favourites)

20 green olives, destoned

1 x 400g tin of chickpeas

for the spice mix

½ tablespoon fennel seeds

2 pinches of chilli flakes

½ tablespoon cumin seeds

1 teaspoon coriander seeds

2.5cm piece of cinnamon stick

1 teaspoon ground ginger

½ tablespoon paprika

The first step is to roast and grind the spices. The quantities I've given here work for me, but it's a personal thing, so if you want to play with amounts go ahead. Place a large frying pan on the stove and chuck all the spices in. Allow them to heat up and start toasting very slightly. Remove the spices from the heat, allow them to cool and then grind to a powder using a spice grinder or a pestle and mortar. Any spices you don't use will store well in a jam jar in the cupboard. Mark it 'Tagine' and you're quids in next time.

Now the spices are done you're ready to start the tagine. Heat a good glug of olive oil in a frying pan, dust the diced butternut with a third of the spice mix and fry in manageable batches until browned all over – it does not need to be cooked through at this stage. (Although not vital to the finished dish, browning the butternut gives a much more complex, interesting flavour to the tagine.) Set the spiced butternut aside.

Next, heat a casserole pot on the stove, add a tablespoon of olive oil and gently fry the garlic and red onion. Give them a couple of minutes before adding the peppers. Now add the butternut and another third of the spice mix. Add the tomatoes and bring to a simmer. Cook for about 15 minutes before adding the dates, olives and chickpeas. If it looks too dry, add up to 5 tablespoons of water at this point. Gently simmer until the butternut is just cooked and the dates are starting to break up. Check the seasoning and add a little salt and some more spice mix if required. The tagine can be cooled and reheated whenever required.

This dish is best served with couscous and I would offer flatbreads and a dish of yoghurt with chopped mint.

CHICKEN SURPRISE Ⓐ

serves: 6   preparation time: 25–30 minutes   cooking time: about 1 hour

The surprise being, of course, that you have no idea what's in it – apart from the clue in the origami . . . I'm less of a breast than a leg type (which you'd never guess from looking at me), so this way of steam-roasting them so they don't go dry is my favourite way of cooking chicken breasts.

This hits all my buttons for having friends over. Very easy, bit of a spectacle, you can make them up ahead of time and there's no need for any accompanying veg – it's all in the bird. It's also a great dinner for kids – use less chilli for theirs though.

You need one of those long rolls of foil for this, not the short stubby ones.

180g shiitake mushrooms

3 tablespoons toasted sesame oil

3 to 5 red chillies, thinly sliced

60g ginger, trimmed, thinly sliced and cut into matchsticks

3 cloves of garlic, peeled and roughly chopped

800g fresh egg noodles

100g roasted cashews

3 carrots, peeled and cut into 1cm diagonal chunks

1 head of Chinese cabbage

3 tablespoons sweet chilli sauce

2 tablespoons dark soy sauce like tamari

6 free-range chicken breasts, skin off

100ml oyster sauce

6 spring onions, or 3 fat ones, halved lengthways

4 limes

salt

1 large or 2 small heads of bok choy, sliced through the root into 6 pieces

Wash the mushrooms and tug the stalks from the caps (we're only using the caps in this recipe, but keep the stalks to use in a stock). Pour the toasted sesame oil into a frying pan over a medium heat. Once hot, add the chilli, ginger and garlic and fry for a few minutes until golden, then add the shiitake caps and fry for a further 5 minutes on a low heat.

Put the egg noodles into a big bowl and break them up with your hands. Pour the contents of your frying pan on to them, along with the cashews and the carrot slices. Remove the outer dozen leaves from the Chinese cabbage and set aside. Thinly slice the remaining core and add to the noodles, with the sweet chilli and soy, then use your hands to coat the noodles all over.

Preheat the oven to 220°C/200°C fan/gas mark 7. Put the chicken breasts into a big bowl and pour on the oyster sauce. Roll these all around with your hand so they too get a good even coating. Trim the ends off the spring onions and have the limes at the ready.

Lay out 6 x 45cm square pieces of foil. Divide your noodle mixture into the middle of each one. The mushrooms, carrots and cashews tend to fall to the bottom, so make sure each parcel gets its fair share. Sit a Chinese cabbage leaf on the noodles, concave-side up, going from left to right, then lay the breast on it. Give it a squeeze of lime juice (use two of the limes for this) and a touch of salt and lay another Chinese cabbage leaf on top. Top this off with a piece of bok choy and a spring onion. Bring the sides of the foil together, then fold these loosely over the chicken.

Don't stress about this next bit – it's deceptively easy. Form one end into a fanned out tail and the other into a bird's head, and don't forget the beak. Make sure it's quite well pinched together at the base of the tail and the neck to seal it. Now whip up the rest of the brood.

Arrange them three to a tray and if you have two ovens, use both of them, otherwise do them one above the other and swap them halfway through. Bake for about 45 minutes. Put the chooks straight on your guests' plates with a wedge of lime and let them break into the birds at the table (being careful of the steam).

SALMON EN CROÛTE [Ⓟ]

serves: 6   preparation time: 30 minutes (including egg, rice and mushroom cooking)
cooking time: 40 minutes

In the world of fine dining, one soon comes to realize that anything with a French name can have an extra fiver slapped on the price and no one will complain. Therefore, in the interests of Economy Gastronomy, I shall rename this recipe . . . Salmon Wrapped in Puff Pastry. There, it's cheaper already.

This is a classic restaurant dish. Unfortunately, it is too often done as an individual serving, by which I mean that a single portion of salmon is wrapped in puff pastry, imbalancing the pastry to salmon ratio to the detriment of the salmon.

When you visit the fishmonger ask him for half a side of fresh salmon. I would be fussy if I were you and ask for the head end. Basically this means he will take a 5kg salmon and remove one side or fillet of it. He will then cut it in half and give you the thick end. Now ask him to remove the skin. Result: you will be the proud owner of half a whole fillet of fish, which will give at least six really generous portions. If you are feeding only four people, fear not – it will reheat well tomorrow and is actually very good cold with mayonnaise and a salad.

125g long-grain rice, cooked and cooled

3 eggs, hard-boiled and roughly chopped

500g ready-made puff pastry

2 tablespoons chopped flat-leaf parsley

1 teaspoon curry powder

10 button mushrooms, finely sliced and cooked quickly in a little butter, then allowed to cool

800g skinless salmon fillet, pin-boned

1 egg, beaten

1 tablespoon milk

a pinch of caster sugar

for the sauce

1 glass of white wine

200g butter, cut into small dice

1 tablespoon chopped chives

Boil your rice and eggs in separate pans then drain and put to one side to cool. Peel and roughly chop the eggs when cool enough to handle. Cut off a third of the slab of pastry. On a lightly floured surface roll the two pieces out until you have two oblongs, both about 4mm thick. Aim for the larger one to be 30cm long and 22cm wide; the other 30cm long and 17cm wide. Put these into the fridge either rolled up or on two trays to rest for about 15 minutes for the gluten in the flour to relax. Meanwhile, put the rice in a bowl and mix in the chopped parsley, curry powder, cooked mushrooms and chopped eggs. Have a taste – I expect it will need a little salt and pepper too.

Lay a 35cm x 20cm piece of greaseproof paper on a large baking tray. Put the smaller oblong of pastry on the paper and position the salmon on it centrally. On top of the salmon pack an even layer of the rice mixture, giving the rice a few encouraging squeezes so it won't tumble off.

Brush all the way around the edge of the pastry with the beaten egg. Now lay the bigger sheet of pastry over the salmon and rice. Make sure there is an equal overhang of pastry on all sides. Using your fingers, push the top half of pastry against the base and seal it all round.

Add the milk and sugar to the remaining beaten egg and brush the pastry all over – this will help it take on a rich golden-brown colour. Now put your Salmon en Croûte – for that is what it is – in the fridge. Yep, it needs another bloody rest! It can sit there happily for about 10 hours if necessary, but 30 minutes will do.

About an hour prior to serving, preheat the oven to 190°C/170°C fan/gas mark 5. Slide in the salmon and bake for 20 minutes, then lower the temperature to 160°C/140°C fan/gas mark 3 and bake for another 20 minutes, by which time the pastry will be a rich golden brown.

Meanwhile, pour the wine into a small saucepan and bring to a simmer. Gradually drop in the butter. Stir and, as it begins to melt, blend with a stick blender. Finish the sauce with chives, and serve this alongside the salmon with new potatoes and spinach.

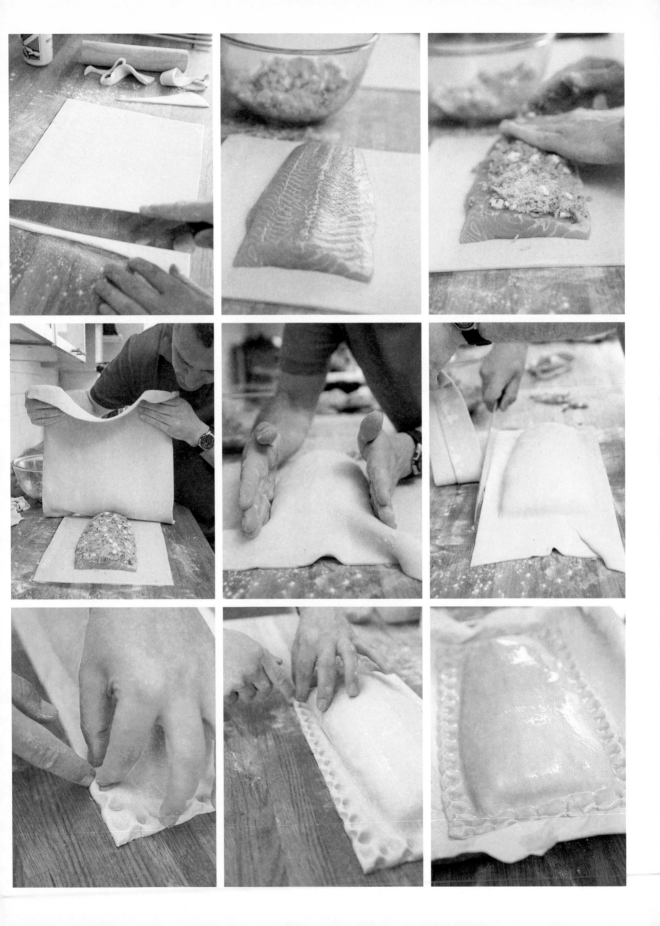

GLUT AND SEASONALITY

BEING A PROFESSIONAL COOK, AS WELL AS BEING A (VERY AMATEUR) VEGETABLE GROWER, HAS GIVEN ME A HUGE RESPECT FOR THE SEASONAL APPROACH TO COOKING. RATHER THAN VIEWING SEASONAL AVAILABILITY AS A BIND, I NOW REGARD IT AS A BONUS. RATHER THAN BEMOANING INGREDIENTS THAT ARE UNAVAILABLE, I POSITIVELY LOOK FORWARD TO THINGS THAT ARE COMING INTO SEASON: EARLY POTATOES, RUNNER BEANS, ASPARAGUS, STRAWBERRIES – I COULD GO ON AND ON – ALL HAVE THEIR MOMENT ON MY CULINARY RADAR.

Seasonal cooking saves money – it's a fact. New potatoes are in the supermarkets all year round, but come May-time the prices drop. This is simply because that's the time when they are most abundant in this country, and so it is with much of the produce we enjoy.

As you sit down to plan your week's eating prior to a shopping expedition, have a thought for what's in season. I would suggest that a pavlova served in November will cost you twice as much as if you served it in July, so the extra moments pondering will eventually save you a fortune.

Of course, each fruit and vegetable has its moment of abundance, and remembering the dates can be a little tricky. However, lots of cookery writers have kindly included seasonal charts in their books, and if you don't own one of those, you can always type the words 'seasonal food' into your search engine of choice, and I guarantee you'll be bombarded by helpful hints.

I have taken all this to the next stage by setting up a system whereby the calendar on my computer automatically emails me just as something is coming into season. For example, each and every year on 10 April I receive an email which simply says 'asparagus'. Upon receipt I can charge down to the market and be first in the queue as the lorry from Norfolk delivers the world's finest example of *asparagus officinalis*. If this approach strikes you as being a little over the top and a touch compulsive, then I am probably married to you! All I can say is that it works for me – I never miss a day's asparagus consumption and the same goes for sprouts, blackcurrants and sweetcorn.

Once you have embraced the seasonal approach, you must prepare to face one of the cook's greatest challenges – dealing with gluts of seasonal vegetables. To the cook, the word 'glut' signifies a large amount of a particular fruit or vegetable which can leave one reeling in bewilderment. For example, you may invite a vegetable-growing friend over to lunch one Sunday in June. You probably hope that your friend will bring with them a decent bottle of wine (which you can bury in the wine rack whilst serving something cheaper – Economy Gastronomy at work!). But as you open the front door you realize that wine buying was far from your friend's mind, and instead they've presented you with 7 kilograms of homegrown rhubarb. This is a glut.

To the cook, a glut is a challenge to be embraced. If it were rhubarb, I would suggest making and freezing two or three batches of crumble filling, perhaps adding a little stem ginger and grated orange zest. Next, you could make a chutney with another kilo of rhubarb – rhubarb chutney not only goes very well with strong cheeses such as Stilton or Cheddar but also surprisingly well with grilled fresh mackerel. You could also make a jam; some fruit purée to serve with ice-cream; and if there's any left, why not roast it dry with sugar and blend it in a smoothie?

When your friend invites you to their house, exact revenge by turning up without wine but with six jars of rhubarb chutney instead!

Of course, gluts are actually a really good thing. Visit your local market late in the day at the right time of year and I guarantee you will be able to pick up boxes of overripe tomatoes on the cheap. These are perfect for making tomato sauce, from which you can create pasta sauces, soups, stews and casseroles all year round. The same goes for oranges, cauliflowers, onions . . .

Gluts are not just to be found at markets or in shops, though. Gluts can turn up while walking to the station or taking the kids to the park. Stinging nettles (soups and risottos), blackberries (crumbles and jams), and elderflower (cordial drinks and summer jellies), are all to be found in my corner of West London, and so much more can be found if you know where to look.

Once you have dealt with your glut of any particular fruit or vegetable, you will be left feeling warm and smug. You'll end up writing special labels for jam jars of home-made delicacies, and start to become very secretive about the precise location of your seasonal bounty in case someone nabs it next year before you do!

Food-swapping with friends – less controversial than wife-swapping – is a brilliant way of distributing home-made jams, jellies and chutneys (I should join the Women's Institute!). The secret is to be prepared – pounce when you come across a glut, and get cooking. It will improve your repertoire and save you money.

Paul.

PUDDINGS AND TREATS

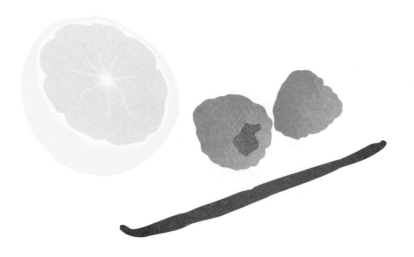

TREACLE TART

CAROL'S BRAN MUFFINS

BANANA SPONGE WITH TOFFEE SAUCE

RHUBARB AND CUSTARD POTS

CHOCOLATE BROWNIE BISCUITS

ANYTIME COOKIES
(FRESH FROM THE FREEZER)

LEMON CREAM
WITH A BERRY COMPOTE

SAD FRUIT MADE HAPPY

EVERYONE NEEDS A SUGAR HIT NOW AND THEN. THIS CHAPTER IS BRIM-FULL OF EASY PUDDINGS AND TREATS WHICH WILL PROVIDE A MOMENT OF PLEASURE AT THE MOMENT OF NEED!

I feel a bit sorry for the poor old pud. Over the years it has taken a bit of flak from the healthy do-gooders to the point where now, to most, it appears to be a 'once a week' treat. The pudding course has also taken quite a hit from the ready-meal department. I have often sat and enjoyed some delicious home-cooked food at friends' houses only for them then to wheel in some awful 'moussey' shop-bought dessert. Why is that? We seem far less concerned over our ownership of the choc-chip cheesecake than we do over the 24-hour slow-cooked lamb that preceded it.

Well, the fight back starts here! The following pages contain some fabulous sweet stuff which will cost you next to nothing in money or effort. The next time you serve a meal to friends, try out one of these puddings and I guarantee you your efforts will not go unnoted.

As for treats ... biscuits, cakes, cookies and sweets all rate as treats in my house. They are often used to coerce my children into doing homework or tidying their rooms. Bribery, they claim. Incentive, we say. Either way, life would be extremely dull without moments of pure indulgence. Let's face it, no one needs a second slice of treacle tart (or indeed the first one) or a stack of chocolate cookies, but once made it would be wrong to let it go to waste ...

TREACLE TART

serves: 8   preparation time: 30 minutes, plus chilling times   cooking time: 1¼ hours

Treacle tart . . . bread and butter pudding . . . treacle tart . . . bread and butter pudding . . . OK, I can't decide which one wins the much coveted title of Paul Merrett's favourite English pudding – it's very close. As a young chef I spent a few years working for Gary Rhodes, who in those days was busy reviving classic British dishes. We cooked both treacle tart and bread and butter pudding regularly. If there was any left over the team were allowed to have their fill – now that's what I call a job perk!

Any bread will do for this recipe and if it's the end of the loaf that nobody will touch, then so much the better. Put any forgotten slices in a freezer bag when you have them and make treacle tart whenever you feel the need.

The tart case is always tricky to make the first time, but practice will make perfect. Any leftover pastry dough can be frozen and reused.

for the sweet pastry
250g plain flour, sifted, plus extra for dusting tin
175g butter, plus extra for greasing
75g icing sugar
2 egg yolks
1 tablespoon (15ml) cold water

for the filling
150g old brown or white bread, crusts removed
650g golden syrup
150g butter
1 egg
50ml double cream
zest of 2 lemons
a good pinch of salt

In a bowl, rub the flour and butter together using your fingertips until the mixture resembles breadcrumbs. Now mix in the icing sugar, egg yolks and cold water. Combine everything together to form a dough, but don't overwork it at this stage. The pastry should be left in the fridge, wrapped in cling film, for a couple of hours to rest and firm up.

To bake the tart case you will need a baking tray lined with non-stick greaseproof paper and a flan ring or loose-bottomed tart tin, 23cm in diameter and 2cm deep. Paint the inside of your flan ring with a little melted butter and dust with flour. Preheat the oven to 200°C/180°C fan/gas mark 6.

Once the pastry has rested it can be removed from the cling film and rolled out on a lightly floured surface until it's about 4mm thick. Roll the pastry up on the rolling pin, then carefully unroll it over the flan ring. Push it down inside the ring, making sure the sides are covered too. Any overhanging pastry can be removed with a sharp knife. Now rest the lined flan ring for a further 30 minutes in the fridge.

When you remove the flan ring from the fridge, prick the base with a fork to stop it puffing up in the oven. Crumple some greaseproof paper, then smooth it out flat. Use this to line the base and sides of the flan ring. Fill the centre with baking beans and bake for 30 minutes. If it is not completely cooked after this time, return it to the oven for another 5 minutes or so. Your tart case is now ready for action.

To make the filling, put the bread in a food processor and whizz it up until you have breadcrumbs, then put these to one side. Pour the golden syrup into a pan and add the butter. Heat them together until the syrup is a runny liquid and the butter has melted. Meanwhile, whisk the egg and cream together until well combined and then pour in the syrup and butter mixture. Next stir in the breadcrumbs, lemon zest and salt, mixing everything together well.

Pour the filling into your cooked pastry case (still in its flan ring and sitting on the baking tray lined with paper). The tart will take about 45 minutes to cook through – at which point it should be a rich golden brown. Give it a few more minutes if it is very soft or under-coloured. Allow it to stand for 15 minutes before serving.

In my view treacle tart should be served warm, never hot, and always with obscene amounts of clotted cream.

CAROL'S BRAN MUFFINS

makes: 20–24   preparation time: 15 minutes   cooking time: 30 minutes

This is one of those recipes where a little bit of work goes a long, long way. The joy of this is that you take the 15 minutes necessary to throw together the mix, then it lasts for a fortnight in the fridge and those you love can have freshly baked, warm muffins daily for zero effort.

Fred, a great friend and kitchen consort, has a lovely mum called Carol and he remembers her making a double batch of this recipe every other Sunday. She could bake enough for the kids and then take extras into work at the potato factory. That sort of kindness comes from living on a small island off the coast of Canada – wouldn't it be great if we could bring a bit of practical New World niceness to our modern British ways? Look out for someone handing round home-baked muffins at a workplace near you.

These muffins are quite dense and filling (as bran should be) and make for a proper breakfast, not like the American-style puffy muffins. They don't rise much, so fill the muffin casings to the size you want them.

240g 100% bran cereal, shaped like sticks
100g butter, soft
200g caster sugar
2 bananas, mashed
2 eggs, beaten
1 lemon
450ml milk
300g plain flour
2½ teaspoons baking powder
½ teaspoon fine sea salt
220g raisins/sultanas/or a mix

If you're planning on baking some today, preheat the oven to 190°C/170°C fan/gas mark 5.

Put half of the bran in a bowl and pour 200ml boiling water over it. In a mixing bowl, cream the butter and sugar together, then stir in the bananas and add the eggs one by one.

Squeeze the juice of the lemon into the milk and pour this into the mixing bowl too. Stir well, then add the cooled soggy bran. At this point, the mixture looks very curdled, but don't worry. Sift the flour and baking powder into the bowl, add the salt and stir in the raisins with the rest of the bran.

Scoop what you want to cook today into a lined muffin tray – I use squares of greaseproof rather than muffin cases, but it's up to you. Bake for 30 minutes. Seriously yummy from the oven, broken open with a bit of butter.

Put the rest of the mix in an airtight container and store in the fridge. When you want freshly baked muffins, just scoop out what you need – don't keep stirring it every time you dig in as the mix doesn't seem to like it.

BANANA SPONGE [Ⓟ]
WITH TOFFEE SAUCE

serves: 6–8   preparation time: 15 minutes   cooking time: 1½ hours

Hands up everyone who has a fruit bowl containing a banana which is rapidly turning from yellow to brown. Lots of us, I bet. In my house this was an ongoing problem because I was the only person prepared to eat browning bananas. But all this changed with my amazing frozen-banana discovery. As soon as you notice a banana that is discolouring, put it straight in the freezer. When you revisit the freezer, you will notice that the yellowing skin is now positively mahogany brown all over, but if you defrost the banana the inside will be the creamy ivory colour all of us wish our bananas to be. It's a bloody miracle!

The downside is you may soon need a second freezer for all the bananas, unless you come up with lots of recipes for them. Well, they work fabulously in smoothies – no need for ice when you have frozen fruit. Banana bread is another good one. But my absolute favourite is this steamed sponge. Imagine for a moment warm sponge, baked with lots of fresh banana, laced with cinnamon and served with toffee sauce. . . I should be writing adverts.

175g softened butter
175g self-raising flour, sifted
1 teaspoon ground cinnamon
½ teaspoon mixed spice
175g caster sugar
3 eggs
3 tablespoons milk
4 bananas, fresh or frozen
1 tub of vanilla ice cream
lashings of dulce de leche toffee sauce

If you have a food mixer with a beater attachment you have just struck it lucky. If not you can mix by hand with a wooden spoon, smug in the knowledge that you are burning calories in readiness for a steamed-sponge fest.

Beat the butter, flour, spices, sugar and eggs until they become a smooth, thick batter. Add the milk and mix in well. Chop the bananas into small chunks and mix these in too.

Butter a 1.2 litre plastic or glass pudding basin and fill it three-quarters full with the sponge mix. Cover the top loosely with a piece of buttered tin foil and secure it tightly with string. Put a large pot on the hob and pour in about 5cm of water. When this is boiling, lower the pudding basin in and put a lid on the pot to retain the steam. Let the pudding boil away on a good medium heat. The sponge will take about 1½ hours to cook.

Check back every so often and top up the water from a boiled kettle if necessary. To test the sponge, stick a metal skewer into it and pull it back out – the skewer should be clean.

The sponge can be served immediately or cooled, refrigerated and microwaved when you want to eat it. It's worth mentioning that I have never managed to cool one and get it to the fridge yet. It's always eaten well before that!

To serve, I would recommend having a decent vanilla ice-cream on hand and also a dollop of dulce de leche. This fabulous Argentinian toffee sauce is available in most good food stores . . . I mean it, I really should have been in advertising!

RHUBARB AND CUSTARD POTS

makes: 6–8 ramekins   preparation time: 20 minutes   cooking time: 50 minutes

British rhubarb has two seasons. The forced stuff, usually from Yorkshire and grown in sheds, appears around early spring, but left to its own devices, the natural season is late spring to summer.

Given its status as one of the all-time British classics, this very straightforward reworking of this exalted combo is a real no-brainer to throw together. We tried them hot, warm, room temperature and cold and, for us, cold from the fridge was the winner ... but you can make up your own mind.

500g rhubarb, trimmed and chopped into 2cm pieces
240g golden granulated sugar
500ml milk
2 star anise
1 vanilla pod
6 eggs
a squeeze of lemon juice

Preheat the oven to 160°C/140°C fan/gas mark 3.

Give the rhubarb a rinse and put it into a pan with a lid on a high heat with half the sugar.

In a separate saucepan, heat the milk and star anise. Split the vanilla pod down the middle and use a knife to scrape out the seeds, dropping both pod and seeds into the milk. Slowly bring this up to steaming for maximum infusion. When almost boiling turn the heat off and leave it to one side.

After 5 minutes of your rhubarb simmering away, take the lid off and turn the heat down a bit. Stir regularly for 15–20 minutes until it looks kind of jammy, then turn the heat off and leave to cool.

Gently whisk the eggs with the rest of the sugar by hand – a machine would make too much air and froth. Boil a full kettle. Pour your milk infusion through a sieve into your egg mixture whilst whisking. You want as little froth as possible, as this will be skimmed and chucked.

Back to your rhubarb – give it a squeeze of lemon, a good stir and then taste your mixture. If it is too tart, add a touch more sugar. Spoon a 1cm layer of rhubarb into the bottom of six to eight 130–180ml ramekins (roughly 40g–50g in each). Don't go more than 2cm high (any leftovers are lovely on muesli with yoghurt).

Use either a ladle or a measuring jug to pour the egg mixture gently on top of the rhubarb, up to the top of the ramekins. Sit the ramekins in a high-sided roasting tray with space between each one and put it in the middle of the oven. Fill the roasting tray with water from the kettle up to the lip of the ramekins – two thirds of the way up will do.

Cook for 25–30 minutes, turning the tray around after 15 minutes to cook evenly. Keep an eye on them, you want them to just dome up. When done, take the ramekins out of the water and let them sit for 15 minutes before putting in the fridge to cool completely. To serve, run a thin knife around the edges of the ramekins and flip the rhubarb and custards out on to little plates.

CHOCOLATE BROWNIE BISCUITS ℗

makes: 20   preparation time: 15 minutes   cooking time: 10 minutes

The Americans know their chocolate brownies, so it's fitting that this recipe has truly stateside origins – it was given to me by a New York chef who came to work in my kitchen. What's unusual is that rather than baking the mixture in a tray and then cutting it into slabs, this recipe delivers much lighter biscuits (or cookies, as they are known over there) which have all the characteristics of the classic brownie. I like macadamia or hazelnuts added to mine, but it works with any nuts or indeed none at all, in which case use more chocolate.

A word of warning . . . these are truly irresistible. You will not be able to stop at just eating one. And everybody in the house, even those who seem to have a genetic inability to cook, will suddenly appear at your side, pretending to be very interested in brownie production. They are simply trying to claim first place in the queue. Personally, I would suggest you lock the kitchen door to make sure you get first tasting!

2 eggs
130g caster sugar
½ tablespoon strong coffee
20g butter
200g dark chocolate, broken into pieces
30g plain flour, sifted
¼ teaspoon baking powder
a pinch of salt
50g nuts, halved
50g white chocolate, chopped into small chunks

Preheat the oven to 180°C/160°C fan/gas mark 4.

Whisk together the eggs, sugar and coffee thoroughly. The mixture will eventually lighten in colour and thicken slightly as the eggs trap the air being whisked in. This could take 7–8 minutes with an electric hand whisk, or considerably longer by hand. Put the mixture to one side for a moment.

Melt the butter and chocolate by placing them in a bowl and putting the bowl over a pan of steaming water. Once melted, remove the bowl from the pan and allow the butter and chocolate mixture to cool for 5 minutes before gently stirring it into the whisked eggs.

It's important not to overwork the mixing in of the remaining ingredients or you will knock all the air out of the original egg mix, so use a folding-turning motion to combine them. First, fold in the flour and baking powder and add the pinch of salt. Then fold in the nuts and chocolate chunks.

Line a very shallow baking tray (or two) with non-stick baking paper and drop on evenly spaced heaped dessertspoon-sized dollops of the batter. Bake for 10 minutes until the mixture has risen, the tops have cracked slightly but the centre is still gooey. If you can, allow the biscuits to cool completely on the trays (they break up otherwise) before diving in.

ANYTIME COOKIES Ⓐ
(FRESH FROM THE FREEZER)

makes: 30 cookies   preparation time: 10–15 minutes   cooking time: 8 minutes

Like the muffins on p.298 that are ready to go from the fridge, this cookie recipe follows the same lines – do a little prep when you have a few minutes, then reap the rewards of freshly baked cookies anytime. You make the dough, freeze it as a log and then just cut off discs with a knife as and when the cookie monster shows up. Stud them with whatever you want, from hazelnuts to chocolate to crystallized ginger to nothing at all.

Who knew providing instant fun and joy could be quite so easy.

250g butter, soft
150g golden granulated sugar
a few drops of vanilla extract
1 egg, beaten
220g plain flour
1 teaspoon baking powder
a pinch of salt (if your butter is unsalted)

for the toppers
choc chips
broken up bits of chocolate
nuts
crystallized ginger

If you want to bake the cookies today, preheat the oven to 200°C/180°C fan/gas mark 6.

In a big bowl, mix the butter and sugar until there are no lumps of butter left. Stir in the vanilla and egg. Sift the flour, baking powder and salt, if using, into the bowl and give it a quick, thorough mix.

Lay out a square of cling film, about 30cm x 30cm, and tip the mix into the middle of it. Bring the far edge of the cling film over and towards you, then use the side of a palette knife to press into the base of the cling film to make it into a tight sausage about 7–8cm wide. Tie the ends and chill in the fridge until fairly solid.

Before it sets rock hard, reshape it with your hands so your cookies don't have a flat side, then put in the freezer until needed (the dough will keep for up to six weeks). If that need is now, cut discs (a hot knife makes it easier) about 1cm thick and put them on a baking tray, spaced well apart.

Sit whatever you fancy (or nothing, as they're pretty light and buttery as is) on top of them without pushing – the toppers will sink in as the cookies soften in the oven. Cook for about 8 minutes, until the edges are just going golden.

Leave the cookies to firm up on the tray for just a minute, then lift on to a wire rack to cool. Eat now.

LEMON CREAM
WITH A BERRY COMPOTE
serves: 4   preparation time: 15 minutes, plus chilling time   cooking time: 10 minutes

If you didn't get round to freezing any berries last summer you should have a go at doing so this year. Pick them in season, freeze them and use them all year round. This is the only way to eat berries in December in my opinion. The flown-in rubbish is simply not an option. Lemons, on the other hand, are fairly reliable all year and having this recipe up your sleeve means you are only one pan and twenty minutes away from knocking up a pretty impressive pudding. The berries add to the overall thing, but they are not a necessity. Strawberries, raspberries, blackberries, blackcurrants, redcurrants or gooseberries all work well – together or individually.

for the lemon cream
600ml double cream
250g caster sugar
the juice and zest of 5 lemons

for the berry compote (optional)
400g fresh or defrosted berries
150g caster sugar

To make the lemon cream, put the double cream in a thick-based pan and bring to boiling point. Add the sugar, then reduce the heat and simmer for 3 minutes, stirring. Pour in the lemon juice and zest and, while the cream is simmering, stir for 30 seconds. Turn off the heat and allow to stand and cool for 10 minutes, then pour the lemony cream into glasses and set in the fridge for at least 2 hours.

Meanwhile, place the berries and sugar in a pan and bring to a simmer. Simmer for about 5 minutes, then remove from the heat and cool – job done.

Serve a small pot of the berry compote next to each glass of lemon cream or spoon over the top. Shortbread would round things off nicely.

SAD FRUIT MADE HAPPY

Fruit is attractive and good for you. It also goes off, sometimes at an alarming rate. Apples and bananas are at numbers three and four respectively of the top-ten most thrown away foods in the country. Often we are guilty of writing off these previously perfect symbols of well-being as soon as they exhibit a blemish, and from then on they're history in our eyes.

But there is a magic window where we can give them a last lovely lease of life, whether their destination is a smoothie, juice or compote.

SMOOTHIES

A smoothie should have the following staple ingredients: banana, yoghurt and milk. Ice is optional and add honey if necessary. There's also something called a 'thickie' and the difference is to do with whether it has dairy or not, but I don't think it sounds very nice anyway.

Fruit that works well: mangoes, peaches, berries, nectarines, apricots and pineapple, soft fruit and cooked hard fruit, like rhubarb. On the next page is a recipe idea you can run with.

JUICES

Bread-maker, pilates video, ice-cream machine . . . do you really need a juicer? After engaging and disengaging with them for many years, I think the answer is 'yes'. They are useful, helpful and make delicious and soul-healing drinks. However, if you don't clean it there and then, well, you might as well chuck it out and get a new one.

And as a final thought, if you do have a juicer, you can also use sad veg – our all-time house favourite is beetroot and celery, with a little apple.

- **Fruit that suits juicing:** orchard fruits, citrus, melons.
- **And veg:** beetroot, carrots, celery, spinach, watercress.
- **And herbs:** mint, parsley.
- **And others:** ginger, chilli.

And as for a recipe: in goes unhappy fruit and out comes juice filled with vigour. It's hard to go wrong.

COMPOTES

Weirdly, some of the stone fruits, like plums, peaches, kiwis and nectarines, never seem to ripen (happens more often with those from the supermarket) and by cooking them into a compote before they become wax effigies of themselves, somehow their flavour is outed.

A compote is to jam what a burger is to steak. A steak may be superior, but a burger tastes good and is never more than half an hour away. Sad fruit in pot, bit of sugar (or not), bubble for a bit and hey presto – fruity goop that tastes delicious.

Muesli, toast, ice-cream, porridge, with pud or milkshakes/smoothies. Very good idea.

Fruit that suits 'compote-ing': berries, rhubarb, stone fruit (peaches, greengages, cherries, nectarines, plums), apples, pears. Most of the hard and soft natives and some of the imports. Dodgy ground with citrus, except marmalade of course, which is closer to a jam.

I've given you a recipe for a strawberry and plum compote over the page, just so you get the general idea.

MANGO SMOOTHIE

makes: 2 long glasses   preparation time: 5 minutes

1 dying mango
1 banana, preferably not totally black
3 heaped tablespoons Greek yoghurt
300ml milk
ice, if you like it cold and crunchy

Chuck everything into the blender and give it a good blitz until it starts to go frothy.

STRAWBERRY AND PLUM COMPOTE

makes: roughly 2 x jam jars (480g)   preparation time: 10–15 minutes   cooking time: 45 minutes

350g unsatisfying plums, halved, but don't bother digging the stones out as it is easier once they've been cooked
2 tablespoons caster sugar

1 tablespoon water
optional: vanilla (pod or extract), star anise
350g strawberries, past their best

Put everything apart from the strawberries into a saucepan with a lid on a medium heat. Hull the strawberries and add these too.

After 15 minutes, take the lid off. Depending on what fruit you're cooking, it may look kind of soupy right now – what happens with a compote is all the water comes out of the fruit and evaporates away whilst the flavour is absorbed. Once your compote has started to thicken up, lower the heat, stir well and make sure it's not catching on the bottom. For this combo, it took about another 30 minutes after the lid came off to hit the right loose, jammy consistency, but obviously that varies enormously with what fruit you're using and how sad it is. The time to turn the heat off is when it's really beginning to stick on the bottom.

Leave to cool whilst you soak two jars and their lids in a bowl of boiling water or run them through the dishwasher on a hot cycle, then lift the jars out and spoon the compote in. Leave to cool and then keep in the fridge for up to a couple of weeks.

GRAPEY SPRITZER

makes: 2 glasses   preparation time: 5 minutes

This is a ridiculously refreshing boozy one for summer evenings.

2 handfuls (180–200g) of sad grapes
2 tablespoons elderflower cordial
8 ice cubes, plus more for serving

1 glass (150ml) of wine
4 leaves of mint
sparkling water

Blitz all the ingredients, apart from the water, and pour into tall glasses with more ice. Top up with sparkling water. The great Laura Herring at Penguin suggests making this with a shot of gin instead of the wine. We like that.

INDEX

THANKS

From both of us . . .

If people judge a cookbook by the pictures, then we are on safe ground. Many thanks are due to the impressively talented Georgia Glynn Smith and Sue Prescott for the fantastic photography in our book. The deadlines were tight, the days long, but the results speak for themselves.

Thanks are also due to John Hamilton at Penguin. His creative vision for the book was always an inspiration, both in terms of the finished feel of the book and during the photography sessions.

Lindsey Evans at Penguin deserves special thanks for masterminding much of the operation. Her support is immeasurable, plus she quietly made sure we made all our deadlines without raising her voice or swearing – she's obviously not a chef!

From the Penguin side, lovely Laura Herring was a pure joy to work with: expansive in her thinking and always honest and deliberate with her words. Others in the editorial team who have worked ceaselessly to meet the tightest of deadlines are Sarah Hulbert and Bethan O'Connor, so thank you to them. The design team was steered by John – however, it was Sarah Fraser and Airelle Depreux who were responsible for pulling together the clean, clear and appealing look of the book, and we are very grateful for the great job you've done. Thanks to Katya Shipster for rustling up the publicity interest, and Chantal Noel for sorting out the rights. The high production values are down to James Blackman, and it's thanks to Tom Chicken and his team that hopefully this book will always be available in a bookstore near you. And on the internet. And anywhere else anyone's ever bought a book. At the shoots it was Sarah Waller who provided us with all the necessary cutters, crockers and backdrops to make the book feel right; and a massive thanks to Bren Parkins-Knight and Amy Carter for the excellent and useful recipe testing.

As regards the idea of *Economy Gastronomy*, before Penguin there was Outline, Helen Veale and Laura Mansfield's production company, who came up with the whole concept. We feel so darned lucky to have earned our places as the faces for this simple and, frankly, rather necessary way of re-evaluating the way we as a nation choose to spend and cook. None of that would have been possible without the inimitable Helen, a true one-off in the world. You can tell a person by the company they keep, and when she brought on the divine Paul Tasker and masterful Dominic Cyriax, we chefs felt in very safe and caring hands. Other Outline folk who need a mention for their dedication to the cause are Libby and Mark (the directors), Vicky and Emma (in the office) and runner Aran for doing all that bloody driving, including the now legendary last leg home. And to Jo Ball at the BBC – thanks for all your support with this project. The old saying 'It's not what you know, it's who you know' has never felt truer than it does now.

FROM PAUL

At times, writing a book can feel like a very lonely journey. However, on reflection, I realize that I could not have completed that journey without the help of many people. Firstly I would like to thank Allegra. Before *Economy Gastronomy* was born, Allegra and I had never met, yet within hours of meeting we were fronting up a television programme and had signed up to co-author a book! As it turned out, my on-screen buddy could not have been a better choice. Allegra is now both a culinary inspiration and a true mate.

Thanks are also due to Greg Bellamy, my business partner who ably ran operations at The Victoria in Sheen while I charged round the country making a television programme. Your support was crucial, mate. My kitchen team at The Victoria also went far beyond the call of duty to assist my book-writing requirements. Thanks, guys, for all your help. My number two is Chris Marriott, who deserves special thanks for running the kitchen in my absence and for providing me with so much inspiration when it came to deciding on recipes and allowing me to steal more than one of his own culinary creations.

My sister, Ali, helped out as chief washer-upper and coffee maker on my photo shoots, as well as eating everything shortly after the picture was taken! A good dollop of thanks is due to Borra Garson and Emma Hughes at DML for helping me manage a restaurant and write a book at the same time. Finally a big shout out to my family: my wife, MJ, and my kids, Ellie and Richie, who put up with all my tantrums when I was stricken with writer's block, as well as taking on the role of recipe tasters. I love you guys.

FROM ALLEGRA

Though Paul's and my names are on the cover, it's really just representative of the collective effort of some great friends and helpers. So, a big hand out to . . .

First and foremost, Lorraine Martin, who keeps the show on the road. Pa knew.

Fred, whose creativity is without constraint, and whose involvement in any and all of my projects is a total blessing. To do all that while still providing me with the best belly-aching laugh of the book (how to tackle a naked aubergine) makes me feel lucky beyond belief for our twenty-year culinary friendship. The gorgeous Dan Dan, who kept the house straight when it all went a bit wonky. You are unerring in your love and support, and we feel the same way towards you and Benj.

Shout out to my sister Floss (and Sylvester, Alfie, Grace, Ursie and Hal), who helpfully came and took away all the food after another shoot day where we'd cumulatively cooked for 56. And of course there's the blisterhood, too.

Liz next door, who was generous with her oven, ice trays and ingredients – far surpassing the usual neighbourly bowl of sugar – and all with such a wonderful grace and willingness to help. We lucked out having you over the garden wall.

Matt, Gill and Mikey at The Anglesea Arms – cheffy support, culinary inspiration, bar to lean on and a desperate eel emergency at midnight on a Friday – what more could you wish for in a local? Sarah, my mother-in-law, for lending me the quiet place that got me started, as well as providing support in a way that only an older generation can. My new friends at United Agents – Rosemary and Wendy – who are the best thing to have happened to me this year. To John and Perry at Stentons – never could a woman hope to have so much stunning raw meat at the end of her road. Chef's Connection – as ever, appreciation to Stuart and his team for providing us with the literal inspiration for our cooking. For me, it all starts with breathtaking veg.

I've dedicated this book to my wife with good reason: I'm not at all sure I could have done this one without you, babe. x

And no book of mine can be complete without a mention for my Ma and Pa, whose input and influence I felt on every page. Though it's been a while, you're still right there for me.

The last of my personal shout-outs must go to my co-pilot, Mr Merrett. I know you hate cheese (the verbal kind), so I'm not going there, but suffice it to say that working with you has been a mind-opening revelation: who knew that two people who seemed so different (not to mention difficult) could end up having such a proper laugh together? And, though our extended road trip had some necessary highs and lows, the last leg home was, as you say, quite simply the best car journey ever.